D1541937

PREPARING FOR THE
LOSS OF YOUR PET

MYRNA MILANI, D.V.M.

PREPARING for the LOSS OF YOUR PET

SAYING GOODBYE WITH LOVE,

DIGNITY, AND PEACE OF MIND

Prima Publishing

155.937
MIL

© 1998 by Myrna Milani

All rights reserved. No part of this book may be reproduced or transmitted in any form or by any means, electronic or mechanical, including photocopying, recording, or by any information storage or retrieval system, without written permission from Prima Publishing, except for the inclusion of quotations in a review.

PRIMA PUBLISHING and colophon are registered trademarks of Prima Communications, Inc.

All of the characters in this book are based on real persons, but in most cases, names have been omitted or changed to protect the privacy of the people involved. Therefore, any resemblance to actual persons, living or dead, is purely coincidental, unless authorized by the actual persons mentioned.

Library of Congress Cataloging-in-Publication Data
Milani, Myrna M.
    Preparing for the loss of your pet : saying goodbye with love, dignity, and peace of mind / by Myrna Milani.
        p.   cm.
    Includes index.
    ISBN 0-7615-1648-4
    1. Pet owners—Psychology.   2. Pet loss—Psychological aspects.
3. Bereavement—Psychological aspects.   I. Title.
SF411.47.M55   1998
155.9'37—dc21   98-38778
                                                                                    CIP

98 99 00 01 HH 10 9 8 7 6 5 4 3 2 1
Printed in the United States of America

How to Order
Single copies may be ordered from Prima Publishing, P.O. Box 1260BK, Rocklin, CA 95677; telephone (916) 632-4400. Quantity discounts are also available. On your letterhead, include information concerning the intended use of the books and the number of books you wish to purchase.

Visit us online at www.primalife.com

For Ann Firestone, my best friend and professional colleague with whom I've shared the loss of so many wonderful patients and pets over the years and learned so much about love along the way.

CONTENTS

INTRODUCTION

EVERYONE IN the county looked forward to the Rocky Hill Pet Fair, the premier social event of the year. While some attendants vied to claim trophies for the most unusual, best-dressed, funniest, most beautiful, or best behaved pets, others participated in a variety of games with their furred, feathered, or scaled best friends. Many people, though, just came to see all the animals and their people, and to celebrate the wonderful relationships between them.

However, eavesdropping at the perimeter of the festivities often yielded some surprises about those human–animal relationships.

"Look, there's Lily with Sebastian!" one woman exclaims to her two companions, gesturing toward a thirty-something woman with a black Lab. "Don't the two of them look wonderful together?"

"A perfect pair, if I ever saw one," replies the first companion. "But God forbid that anything ever happens to that dog. Lily will go completely to pieces."

"You gotta be kidding!" exclaims the second. "He's only a dog!"

A short distance away, elderly Earl Myers, whose cat had just claimed first prize in the Oldest Pet contest, croons to his pet affectionately, "What do those young folks know about getting old, hey Dusty? You and I are going to live forever, no matter what the vet said about that tumor of yours." Earl's sentiment brings tears to his daughter Kelly's eyes.

On the periphery of the ring in which children show their pets, a man holds his breath as his six-year-old daughter marches importantly around the ring with Bear, the family St. Bernard, while the audience applauds appreciatively.

"There, you see. He behaved perfectly," he comments to his wife with a relieved sigh. "Still, I'm glad the judge was a woman. Bear doesn't seem to like any men but me lately."

"Bear doesn't seem to like a lot of people lately," his wife corrects him. "I really think we should find a new home for him before something terrible happens."

"I'd agree if it weren't for Tara," her spouse replies as the little girl comes running toward them. "She'd never forgive us if we got rid of her dog."

Suddenly an announcement blares over the public address system, shattering the pastoral setting.

"Escaped pot-bellied pig from ring three! Escaped pot-bellied pig from ring three!"

No sooner does the amplified voice fade than another cry pierces the once peaceful afternoon and causes all of the assembled pet lovers' hearts to leap into their throats.

"Jilly, Jilly, come back! No, no! Don't run into the highway!"

OF ALL the different aspects of the human–animal bond, none evokes such a wide range of responses as pet loss. At one end of the spectrum, avid pet lovers like Lily find the idea of losing their pets so terrifying that they don't even want to consider it. At the other end, we find people like Lily's skeptical friend who doesn't comprehend the nature of her relationship with her pet at all, although he cares deeply about her and wants to support her through any traumatic event.

"You must admit that the idea of sinking into depression because you lose an *animal* does stretch the limits of credibility," declares the skeptic.

Sadly, this erroneous belief plagues pet lovers as well as those who are unfamiliar with this phenomenon. However, as we'll see in the pages ahead, the nature of the human–animal bond affects both the physiology and the behavior of human and animal in an infinite number of ways. When death or loss by some other means severs that bond, the owner *will* feel this, even if he or she cannot clearly explain these feelings to others. To deny the validity of those feelings because we don't think others will understand them is to deny ourselves the healing process necessary to make peace with the loss. To deny those feelings in others because we personally don't happen to feel that way about that particular animal—or any animal—ranks on a par with denying the existence of the reds and greens they can see simply because we're colorblind.

If you find it difficult to understand such strong emotional attachment to pets, this book will sensitize you to the many different ways pet loss occurs and how owners respond. My hope is that you can learn to offer meaningful support to animal-loving friends and family members even if you can't fully comprehend the loss yourself. If you harbor no doubts that the loss of a pet by any means will leave a void in your life, I hope you will see how *Preparing for the Loss of Your Pet* reflects my total conviction—based on working with pets and owners for more than twenty-five years—that nothing terrifies us more and causes us more avoidable grief than our fears of the unknown.

"Surely nothing can be worse than losing a pet to death," Lily states adamantly.

Not true. Unfortunately, many people erroneously view those who give up pets as heartless clods who treat animals as throwaways. When questioned by nonjudgmental interviewers in nonthreatening surroundings, however, people who give up their pets often confess heart-wrenching stories of hiding beloved pets from landlords, taking in strays they couldn't afford to keep, or trying to solve pet-related problems under overwhelming circumstances. In almost all cases, those who give up their pets speak of agonizing long and hard over the choice, often for many months. When pressured by "animal lovers" to explain all that led up to this difficult decision in a few sentences, though, like those asked to explain why they chose to euthanize their pets, these owners may feel so overwhelmed by emotion that they can summon no adequate reply.

Similarly, pet owners whose animals disappear often face a grieving process that rivals and even exceeds that experienced by those who lose a pet to death. No matter what we may want to tell ourselves, a lack of training or other owner negligence almost invariably contributes to pet disappearance. Not only does that awareness give others the right to look askance at us when we lose our pets in this manner, but it also sets us up for a double dose of guilt.

Those familiar with my work know that the more severe the problem, the more I champion a proactive preparedness and prevention approach. However, to accomplish that, we need to face all of our fears about pet loss up front. Coward that I am about losing any of my own pets, I maintain that we should do this under the best possible circumstances: when our pets are still with us, and we can take some time to make any changes that will make our parting easier.

To that end, this book begins with a sometimes graphic discussion of what happens when animals die naturally or as a result of euthanasia. In chapter two we delve into what happens to pets we lose to causes other than death: What happens to pets we give up? Where do pets go when they run away? How long should we look for them? As in all other chapters, tips about preventing these problems as well as discussions of the special challenges they present will help alleviate any fears you may harbor about losing your own pet under similar circumstances. Next we'll explore the physical, behavioral, and bond problems that may snatch a pet from us suddenly, and those that may drag on for months or even years before the relationship ends.

The next five chapters look at the different ways we respond to the loss of a pet, beginning with guilt and the denial-anger-bargaining-depression-acceptance sequence documented in human loss literature. Many parallels exist between human and animal loss, but a few differences exist, too. The very nature of the human–animal bond guarantees that we'll intuitively react to the loss on a most intimate and primitive level. Unless we recognize the role that both our more feminine nurturing and our more masculine logical selves play in our relationships with our pets, we may feel embarrassed or even guilty about acknowledging how the loss affects us.

As a society, we automatically want to shelter children and adults with special needs. Unfortunately, though, this may lead us to run rough-shod over their unique concerns when pet loss occurs. Ironically, we often view the youngest children as the most vulnerable, when in reality teenagers and even young adults may find the loss of a pet much more difficult to accept. The very nature of the bond once again guarantees that the physically, mentally, and/or emotionally disadvantaged almost certainly will notice the loss of a pet, albeit in ways we may not begin to comprehend. We owe it to these people and their pets to recognize their unique relationships and do everything possible to meet their needs as well as those of the animal.

Preparing for the Loss of Your Pet closes with an overview of three approaches to death or other types of pet loss that owners will find particularly helpful as they seek to overcome their fears. At-home hospice care can enable dying pets and their owners to say goodbye in familiar surroundings. Writing advance directives or a "living will" for your pet lets you determine your values regarding what constitutes a quality life for you and your pet, and then test these values in some common life-threatening situations for your pet. A technique called imaging can permit those of you who can't bear the thought of *anything* horrible happening to your pet to face that fear, little by little and on your own terms, and to formulate a plan of action that, at best, could save your pet's life and, at worst, will help you face the loss without guilt.

I use primarily dog and cat examples because the bulk of the data available pertains to these most common companion animal species. However, no doubt exists in my mind that those who form relationships with *any* animal may experience these same phenomena and benefit from the information provided.

While I worked on this book, several people asked me if I intended to talk about whether animals go to heaven and whether they become angels if they do. When I told them I intended to talk about some of the most frightening aspects of pet loss, some of them said that sounded more like hell to them. Considering these comments and our reluctance to even imagine in advance what the loss of our pets might mean to us, I recalled a biblical passage that sums up my feelings on the matter. This passage from the New Testament (Hebrews 13:2) reflects a sentiment that recurs in many theologies worldwide: "Be not forgetful to entertain strangers; for thereby some have entertained angels unaware."

In the pages ahead I invite you to entertain the strange and often frightening idea of losing your pet, and to explore your possible responses to that event. What you learn as you do so will, I hope, bring you peace no matter how and when your relationship with your pet ends.

CHAPTER ONE

THE FINAL JOURNEY

Natural Death and Euthanasia

The fear of death is more to be feared than death itself.

—Publilius Syrus

Maxim 511

CHICO DIED as he had lived, his fourteen-year-old Chihuahua features frozen into one last vicious snarl for all eternity. Anita Jandrow stood with her eleven-year-old twins, Jason and Katie, gazing down at the furry gargoyle stretched out on the stainless steel table. Jason's stony expression reflected no emotion at all. Katie looked like she could throw up at any minute. Just as Anita reached out to give the little dog's head one farewell pat, his body suddenly twitched.

"Oh, my God, he's still alive!" Katie shrieked and bolted from the room.

"That's only a reflex," the veterinarian, Dr. Cramer, murmured soothingly to Anita and Jason. "Trust me, he's gone."

1

Still stunned by what she'd just seen, Anita barely heard Dr. Cramer ask, "What do you want done with Chico's body?"

In that instant it dawned on Anita that it was not some wild impulse that had suddenly convinced her workaholic husband, Paul, to go on a wilderness camping trip for the first time in his life. No, this solid family man and founder of the area's largest, most successful company had run away because he knew his dog was going to die.

In answer to Dr. Cramer's most practical question, Anita could only sigh and confess, "He's my husband's dog. I haven't a clue."

IN THIS chapter we commence our exploration of the different ways we lose pets and react to that loss, beginning with a close look at death itself. In 1789, Benjamin Franklin wrote to a friend that nothing in this world is certain but death and taxes. And while our pets may escape the scourge of taxes, they all inevitably die. Nonetheless, just as many of us resist contemplating our own deaths, we'd just as soon avoid this aspect of pet ownership, too.

"Like Paul!" Anita puffs up with indignation. "What a coward to run off camping instead of taking care of Chico himself!"

While Anita might be right, let's consider her judgment in the context of her own relationship with the family cat, Adagio. How does she feel about his dying?

"What do you mean 'How do I feel about his dying?' He's only two years old, for Pete's sake!"

Both Anita's and her husband's orientations are understandable, but neither addresses two of the most critical aspects of all human–animal relationships:

1. Given the shorter life spans of many companion animals, many owners will outlive at least some of their pets.

2. The nature of the human–animal bond dictates that the death of a pet, by any means, will affect the owner, no matter when and how it happens.

Given those two realities and the awareness that fear of the unknown often leads us to make decisions we later regret, it makes sense to learn as much as we can about the nature of pet death. To that end, let's first consider what death means in terms of the animal's physical body.

PHYSICAL SIGNS OF DEATH

Even though most of us would rather not think about death, we also believe that we'll somehow know it when we see it. Moreover, we often assume automatically that others share our views. However, the more sophisticated medical technology becomes, the more resistant to definition death becomes, too.

"I don't understand." Confusion furrows Anita's brow. "Isn't dead, well, dead?"

Not necessarily. Let's compare how the typical pet owner and the experts view death to see where they might agree and disagree.

THE OWNER'S VIEW

In spite of the fact that most of us insist that we'll recognize death when we see it, we tend to greet it with shock rather than any sense of recognition when it does arrive. Owners asked to describe the aspects of a pet's death that most upset them typically mention the animal's:

- Vocalization
- Gasping
- Urination and/or defecation
- Wide-open, staring eyes

What physiological changes account for these often highly unnerving responses? Dying cats, for example, may emit a peculiar howl unlike any other and, unfortunately, no satisfactory explanation exists for its cause. Other animals may whimper, sigh, chirp softly, or snort. The gasping, sometimes inappropriately called "agonal breathing," erroneously implying that the breaths were taken in agony, occurs as a postmortem reflex when the respiratory and circulatory systems no longer function at a level capable of sustaining life.

Other death-related physical changes result because it takes energy to contract muscles and without that energy the muscles naturally relax. Relaxation of the circular muscles that normally prevent the passage of urine and stool from the bladder and rectum may lead to spontaneous urination and/or defecation at the time of death. Similarly, because it requires muscle contraction to close the eyelids, they remain open. The pupils of the eyes become fully dilated, or wide open, following death because it requires muscle contraction to close these structures, too. When we combine these two changes with the postmortem drying and dullness of the normally clear and moist outer covering of the eye, the cornea, we get that characteristic fixed stare.

"What about Chico's spooky jerking when he died?" Katie pipes up, wanting a solid explanation for that troublesome event.

Involuntary muscle activity explains that and other spontaneous body movements, such as pets stretching their legs out at the moment of death. A fair number of animals also may move their tails, a reflex dog owners often interpret as a farewell wag; cat owners may see it as evidence of their pet's anger or distress. When this happens, the dog owners' projected views definitely serve them much better than those of their feline-owning counterparts.

When we think about death as portrayed by the media, we often think of rigor mortis, the stiffening of the body following death—hence all those fictional characters who refer to dead bodies as "stiffs." However, when rigor mortis occurs and how long it persists depends on the temperature of the animal's body as well as that of its surroundings. Consequently, owners may or may not encounter this phenomenon when their pets die.

THE EXPERTS' VIEW

Even though it seems quite logical to Anita to define "dead" as "dead" because she can't imagine anything more obvious, few contemporary experts share that view. During Franklin's time and into the early 1800s, family members, clergy, or local government officials pronounced humans dead based on whatever criteria seemed to work for them (such as holding a mirror or lighted candle under the deceased's nose to check for air flow). Pet owners did much the same thing.

However, this convention began to fall from favor in the middle of the eighteenth century when a French physician named Jean Jacques Winslow spearheaded a movement to make physicians the ultimate authority when it came to separating living humans from dead ones. Although you might imagine Winslow's motives to be based on his knowledge of physiology, personal experience rather than reverence for science more likely drove him: Twice during his childhood Winslow awoke in a coffin destined for burial, a fate that befell about 2 percent of the "deceased" prior to the use of embalming (which then killed that 2 percent as well as preserving the truly dead).

The medical profession's right to determine death remained unchallenged until the 1960s. Then, as organ transplants emerged as a valid solution to many human medical problems, physicians asked for a legal definition of death so that they wouldn't inadvertently remove an organ from a living body. This request shocked many members of both the general public and the medical profession, and led to a survey of medical-school graduates, the results of which proved to be even more shocking: *None* of the physicians interviewed remembered ever being taught how to diagnose death.

As bizarre as this sounds, two personal experiences during my stint in veterinary medical practice in the 1970s clearly illustrate that physicians' inability to recognize death doesn't just apply to humans. In one case, a physician's dog was hit by a car. He pronounced her dead and placed her in a box outdoors, believing his young son would want to say goodbye to the animal before the father buried her. When the child arrived home that evening and went to the box, the "dead" dog wagged her tail weakly and licked the

> *In spite of the fact that most of us insist that we'll recognize death when we see it, we tend to greet it with shock rather than any sense of recognition when it does arrive.*

child's hand. Later the physician expressed wonder that traumatized animals could go into shock and look dead, "just like a person."

In the second case, a physician left a panicked message on my answering machine saying his Labrador had just killed his terrier. Because I knew both dogs, I found this difficult to believe and returned the call immediately. By then, however, the owner had found the terrier staggering around the yard "looking dazed," most likely the victim of a seizure that drew the other dog's attention, rather than the victim of a murderous canine assault.

The realization that physicians couldn't define death created quite a stir, and scientists, theologians, philosophers, and lawyers have struggled to resolve this dilemma ever since. So far, everyone agrees that *something* irreversible happens at death, but few can agree on what. Among the possibilities under consideration, death can be defined as the irreversible cessation of:

1. All body cell, tissue, and organ function.
2. The flow of air and blood.
3. Heart and lung function.
4. Spontaneous heart and lung function.
5. Spontaneous whole brain function.
6. Complete higher-brain center function.
7. All but minimal functioning of the higher brain centers.
8. The embodied capacity for consciousness.

Each one of these definitions of death possesses advantages and disadvantages, and each reflects our beliefs in science and medical technology. For example, few of us consider an obviously decomposing body that still possesses one or two functioning body cells to be alive, as we must if we adhere to the first definition. The third definition, which uses heart and lung function to define death, gave way to the fourth when it turned out that cardiopulmonary resuscitation (CPR) could reverse this so-called "chest death." Similarly, the fourth definition, which describes death as the loss of *spontaneous* heart and lung function, fell prey to medical science, too, when pacemakers and respirators enabled people who did not have this ability to remain living.

Within the animal arena, most of us agree that a pet's lack of a heartbeat or breathing doesn't bode well, but these symptoms don't necessarily signal an irreversible change for many owners, either. In such cases, CPR and/or other timely medical intervention can save an animal's (as well as a person's) life.

This lack of an absolute physiological definition of death led the experts to next focus on the brain's role in human life and death. After all, the heart can function without the brain, but we need a functioning brain stem to breathe. Not only that, most of us consider the brain to be the center of life. After all, it's the source of our thoughts and emotions, those particular qualities that make us alive. However, brain death raises its own problems. A hopelessly comatose individual can breathe, maintain body temperature and blood pressure, track light, and respond to pain. Thanks to modern technology, individuals in this state can now "live" for years.

As much as the arguments about the nature of human death now focus more and more on the last three definitions, none of these offers much hope for pet owners seeking an official definition of animal death.

"Why not?" Anita wants to know as she and the twins relax with Adagio after their traumatic interlude with Chico and Dr. Cramer. "Like you said, most of us consider life the embodiment of all those unique qualities and behaviors that make our pets special to us. When Adagio drags my socks to the door to greet me, isn't that evidence of his higher brain function as well as of his consciousness?"

As valid as Anita's remarks may sound to most pet owners, the scientific, theological, philosophical, and legal community remains mired in an often bitter debate: Many doubt whether animals can experience any thoughts or emotions *at all*, let alone those on the elevated plane to which most of us assign our pets' behavior and interactions with us and other people. Further complicating matters, veterinary medical technology now enables us to sustain animals in some of the same gray areas between life and death in which some humans dwell. Consequently, it behooves us to work through all of our ideas about these higher definitions of death, too, so we can make our peace with any death-related decisions we must make for our pets.

ANIMAL MINDS AND SPIRITS

When asked how she'll know when Adagio has died, Anita reaffirms her original position: "I don't know how I'll know, but I *will!*"

Admittedly some of Anita's passionate certainty arises from the fact that she wants to believe she'll know death when she sees it because she finds the alternative too ghastly to consider. On the other hand, like many pet owners, she believes that Adagio also thinks for himself and feels emotions. Furthermore, she believes that he possesses his own unique spirit or soul, and her definition of animal death takes this into account, too.

At this point about half of the animal-owning population would nod its collective head in agreement, and the other half would snort something like, "Give me a break!" Moreover, members of each group would feel so secure in their respective beliefs that they'd feel no need to defend themselves. Those who believe their pets possess higher mental and spiritual qualities can't imagine how anyone the least bit familiar with animals could believe otherwise. Those who dismiss the idea of animals thinking and experiencing emotions, let alone possessing souls, claim their views as proven scientific fact.

In reality, both orientations possess elements of truth and fantasy. A growing collection of studies of animal thinking indicates that animals do think and experience emotions, but probably not in the same way we do. Thus if Anita projects her own thoughts and emotions on Adagio, she runs the risk of denying him his unique feline needs. At the same time, other studies have demonstrated how animals function as little more than animated robots. However, the core beliefs that underlie the design of these experiments and the interpretation of their results may belong more in the realm of scientific tradition and politics than any quest for truth.

For owners facing the death of a pet, though, both orientations offer advantages and disadvantages during a difficult time. Although those who believe that their pet possesses a spirit may find comfort in knowing that this part of the animal will always remain with them, this belief may undermine their ultimate acceptance of the animal's death. Those who perceive their relationship with their pets as completely tied up in the animal's physical presence may feel utterly lost and abandoned when that animal dies.

"But what do *you* think?" asks Katie almost defiantly, seeking to nail down some concrete facts like any normal preteen. "Do *you* believe that animals have spirits?"

As uncomfortable as Katie's question may make me feel personally, she raises a critical point. It really doesn't matter whether others believe that animals possess any higher brain or spiritual capacities. When a pet dies, all that really matters is what we believe ourselves.

As far as my own beliefs go, let me hedge a bit by first noting that if you read a lot of animal-related fiction and nonfiction as I do, you quickly realize that the loss of a beloved pet elicits a deep emotional response. Part of this may result from the fact that most of us first experience the loss of a loved one in the form of a family pet. Thus, Rover's or Fluffy's death provides us with our first glimpse into that valley of shadows from which none returns, and this event prepares us for the eventual loss of human loved ones, too.

However, a significant number of these novels, short stories, and articles treat the animal's death as more than a mirror upon which people project their fears of death and vicariously work these out to their satisfaction. Additionally, most of these written accounts assign a spiritual element to the deceased animal. I can understand this because, in addition to wanting to know what will happen to me and my human loved ones at the moment of death and beyond, I'd like to know what will happen to all my cherished nonhuman loved ones, too.

Although my strict Christian upbringing that maintains that animals have no souls keeps me ever alert for celestial lightning bolts when admitting this, I can recall one medical case that convinced me that death doesn't so much consist of an irreversible cessation of something, as the experts claim, but rather of an irreversible *departure* of something currently beyond human comprehension.

This revelation occurred when parvovirus first hit the canine population in my area years ago, and those of us in the veterinary community could do nothing beyond offering these animals as much medical and emotional support as possible, then hoping for the best. By the time scientists isolated the viral villain and developed a vaccine, we saw many dogs, and especially young pups, die from this sudden and devastating disease. At first I remembered each and every animal that died during that wretched period. Over time, though, most of these memories faded until the death of only one pup remains vivid twenty years later.

The pup in question, a Doberman, had two strikes against him before the virus scored a direct hit. His parasite-infested, scrawny body attested to a short life spent under conditions that would make surviving to adulthood a challenge even without the presence of a life-threatening disease. With such a disease, he didn't stand a chance.

Still, we tried to help him, daily administering intravenous fluids, antibiotics, and anything else the veterinary rumor mill said might help. For a few days, he hung in there against the overwhelming odds with such extraordinary grace for one so young that I found myself falling in love with him and hoping for a miraculous recovery.

On his last day I sat on the floor in front of his open cage with his head in my lap as my technician set up yet another round of IVs behind me. (We took turns getting the medications ready so we'd both get a chance to hold the animals.) I put my hand on the pup's head to pet him, we locked eyes, and then it happened.

Poof!

It was as if someone or something had blown out a candle, a rush of air that drew a vacuum and instantly took the pup's breath as well as some of my own with it. I was in the process of telling myself I must have imagined it when my technician, who still stood with her back to the pup and me, suddenly cried, "What was that? Did you feel it?"

> *In addition to wanting to know what will happen to me and my human loved ones at the moment of death and beyond, I'd like to know what will happen to all my cherished nonhuman loved ones, too.*

Now I suppose that a sonic boom from a plane far overhead may have created a change in atmospheric pressure that we both sensed at the exact same moment. However, since that time, I've encountered people from all walks of life who have experienced a similar event. One hunter who felt it the instant his bullet penetrated the heart of a doe put down his gun and never hunted again. Others who face animal death routinely, such as veterinarians and those who work in animal shelters, often view these experiences as the source of an even greater reverence for life and its continuity in the face of death.

Do such tales support the existence of animal spirits? Perhaps. But they certainly do underscore the power of the human–animal bond.

BONDED FOR LIFE

Long before the term gained recognition, the human–animal bond struck me as the most intriguing and profound aspect of animal ownership. It seemed so reasonable that humans and animals could and would affect each other both physically and behaviorally. However, even though more and more studies of the many facets of the bond slowly make their way into scientific literature, most in the media still view the bond as a warm fuzzy concept invented by sentimental animal lovers who project their own feelings onto their pets.

"What's wrong with that?" Jason demands somewhat irritably. "Don't you like stories about pets who save their owners' lives or make sick people in nursing homes feel better?"

I do find such reports heartwarming, but to me such animals don't display extraordinary skills, but rather those qualities within the capacity of almost any pet. We know, for example, that most of the true animal heroes turn out to be normal, happy-go-lucky household pets. And while pets do indeed brighten the lives of those in nursing homes, animals also may beneficially affect their owners' blood pressure, heart rate, pulse, and cholesterol and triglyceride levels, not to mention their sense of mental and emotional well-being. Moreover, other studies indicate that we similarly affect our pets, too.

However, just because humans and animals can and do affect each other's physical and mental health, this in no way guarantees that we'll always affect each other *beneficially*. All romantic notions of the bond aside, any bonded pair also consists of separate human and animal beings, each with his or her own particular needs. This raises the possibility that owners and pets may become involved in push–pull struggles where the owner wants one thing and the animal wants another, with the resultant discord subconsciously altering the other's physiology and behavior in the process. This possibility, in turn, raised the question in my mind: What happens when owners want an animal to live but the animal wants to die?

Experience and anecdotal evidence suggests that it depends on the person and the animal as much as, if not more than, it depends on our medical technology. The notion of a "will to live" crops up in veterinary medicine as often as it does in human medicine, most commonly when technology fails and clinicians seek to explain why.

"I'm so sorry, Mr. Jandrow," Dr. Cramer said to Paul two days before Paul suddenly decided to take his wilderness vacation. "I've done everything possible, but Chico seems to have lost the will to live."

Suppose Chico experienced his final medical crisis a week earlier with his beloved Paul rather than with the ambivalent Anita and children at his side. Would Paul's presence and his relationship with his dog have made a difference? We can never know, but I do recall one case that offers some tantalizing clues regarding the effects of the human–animal bond on a terminally ill or injured animal.

One night I received a frantic call from two elderly clients whose ancient poodle had just been hit by a car. The somewhat confused seniors had put their equally confused and almost completely blind and deaf arthritic pet out to relieve himself one cold, rainy night. The little black dog became disoriented and wandered into the road, directly into the path of a car whose driver never saw him. When the owners carried the dog into the clinic, they could barely control their emotions.

"You *must* save Dijon!" the couple moaned in unison, clutching each other for support, tears streaming down their faces. "We can't live without him."

Having treated Dijon over the years, I knew they spoke the truth. Their whole life centered on that dog, with their stories of his past escapades gradually replacing those of his present activities as first one, then another system in his body succumbed to the ravages of time. If owner love fueled any animal, it surely fueled Dijon, somehow keeping that leaky old heart pumping, those tired kidneys and liver functioning, and those rickety old bones strong enough to allow the old dog to totter outside twice a day to relieve himself for at least a year longer than medical science would have predicted possible.

And now this, the kind of case that creates the worst nightmare for veterinarians. Dijon's owners had denied the possibility of his death from the day they got him as a pup. Lately, they'd deliberately sidestepped any attempts family, friends, or I made to discuss what they would do—for themselves and for Dijon—when that inevitable day came. Ironically, I'd become an unwitting accomplice in this charade, pulling medical tricks out of my bag to buy the dog more time. Because of that, I now wanted Dijon to live for myself as well as for his owners, no matter how much his old body screamed for relief.

I don't remember how many hours I worked on that dog, trying to stabilize him enough to begin repairing the damage. Eventually, though, I had to face reality: Dijon wasn't going to make it. Nonetheless, I sat down beside the exam table, held his paw, and told him over and over again that he *had* to make it because his owners loved him so much. I could vividly imagine them thinking the same thing and, in my exhausted mind, our feelings became a fragile thread that kept that dog connected to us and to life itself.

A few hours later a nearly bursting bladder urged me to leave the dog just for a minute or two, but I resisted. What if only my presence were keeping that dog alive? My scientific training and my own discomfort argued against that: Dijon's living or dying depended solely on his response to the medical treatment I gave him. Period.

Nonetheless, I voted for a compromise, racing down the hallway to the employee's lounge, and leaving the door open while I used the facilities so I could continue beaming my best thoughts toward my patient. The instant I left the treatment room, though, I felt that fragile thread break. I told myself I didn't, but I knew it did. An amazing coincidence?

When the Doberman pup died of parvo, I also felt something beyond the irreversible cessation of life. But with Dijon I felt that even more strongly, and I attribute this to both the greater magnitude and the duration of the bond that I'd formed with him and his owners. When he died, I felt as if a definite connection between the two of us had been severed, stretched too far for his weakened conditioned to sustain when I left him.

As I ran back to the treatment room, I recall thinking that maybe that love link had somehow snapped back into his body and invigorated him as love had so many times in the past.

It hadn't. I immediately called his owners. They picked up the phone on the first ring. Before I could utter a word, they said in unison, "We know he just died, Doctor. We felt it. Thank for you trying."

After studying the bond for more than twenty-five years, I know that it exists and that it can exert a profound effect on animal and human alike. Nothing reveals its strengths—and weaknesses—like the specter of death.

"We'll always wonder if we should have asked you to put Dijon to sleep," the old poodle's owners commented when they came to retrieve his body the next day.

And I'll always wonder if I should have asked them to do so.

However, if our thoughts and emotions about our pets and death can send us into a tailspin when our animals naturally succumb to a terminal illness or injury, that's nothing compared to what the idea of euthanasia can do to us.

THE BIG SLEEP

Not surprisingly, scientists, theologians, lawyers, and philosophers argue about the definition of euthanasia, too. Most dictionaries define it as a "good death," translating the Greek *eu* as "good" and *thanatos* as "death." However, traditional scientific and medical terminology uses that same *eu* to mean "normal," so that eupnea and euthyroid refer to normal breathing and normal thyroid gland activity. Within this context, euthanasia becomes a normal death. Once again, though, a great deal of disagreement surrounds what constitutes a normal death, let alone a good one, thanks to all the advances in medical technology. Currently the experts differentiate between two kinds of euthanasia: *passive* and *active.*

Passive euthanasia refers to stopping or withholding life-sustaining treatment, whereas active euthanasia indicates the use of a specific substance to terminate life. Although Paul didn't think of it that way, he practiced passive euthanasia when he opted not to consider a kidney transplant for Chico. Admittedly the 300-mile drive to the nearest veterinary teaching facility as well as the expense of the operation played a role in his decision, but the idea of exposing the people-hating old dog to all that discomfort bothered him a great deal more. Instead, he opted to make Chico as comfortable as he could at home for as long as possible, an approach we'll discuss in more detail in chapter ten.

Most of us know about active euthanasia and, even though the American Veterinary Medical Association recognizes several humane ways to perform it, most owners of companion animals generally only recognize one: the use of injectable drugs. Euphemisms for euthanasia using an injectable drug include "putting the animal down" or "putting the animal to sleep." The former comes from the farm animal realm, where the euthanasia of standing animals more commonly occurs; as death ensues, the animal sinks down to the ground. The connection between euthanasia and putting a pet to sleep arises from what first happens to smaller animals, such as cats and dogs, which appear to fall asleep before dying.

Like natural death, the euthanasia of an animal possesses physical, behavioral, and bonding elements that may enhance or undermine the process. Knowing about these issues may make it easier for owners facing this event.

In many ways, the first euthanasia-related act often strikes owners as the most difficult: signing a release.

"I know exactly what you mean!" Anita exclaims. "I felt 100 percent sure I was doing the right thing for Chico until Dr. Cramer's receptionist asked me to sign that paper. Then I felt like I was signing Chico's death warrant!"

What does the release say? In order to comply with state rabies laws, euthanasia forms typically ask you to vouch that the animal in question hasn't bitten anyone in the last ten days. Many of these forms also ask you to describe why you want the animal euthanized, a question that may cause unprepared owners a great deal of distress. For some owners, the reason seems so obvious that they can't imagine why anyone would ask them to describe it at such an emotional time. Others experience difficulty expressing their feelings under the best of conditions, and can't bring themselves to discuss the subject at all. Still another group may come to the decision after weighing so many factors that it would take hours to explain them all. And, finally, some owners think that their reasons are no one else's business. We'll discuss the validity of these human responses in more detail later in subsequent chapters. For now, simply keep in mind that you will be asked to sign some kind of legal statement if you request euthanasia for your pet.

Next, you must decide where you want your pet euthanized—in your home or at the veterinary clinic—who you want to do it, and if you want to be present or not. Ideally, your answers should reflect a desire to make this as stress-free as possible for your pet first, and yourself second. Some animals react much more defensively toward strangers in strange surroundings than in their own homes; other pets respond just the opposite. Adagio trembles at the sight of Dr. Cramer at the clinic, but immediately nudges the veterinarian for a scratch on the head when he visits the Jandrows' home. Whether you should remain with your pet during the procedure depends on your pet's behavior and your relationship. But, before we discuss that, let's take a moment to discuss the physical changes that occur during euthanasia.

THE MECHANICS OF EUTHANASIA

The drugs used to euthanize animals often mimic the actions of very strong anesthetics, which precipitate a sequence that consists of four distinct physiological stages:

1. Sedation.
2. Excitement.
3. Surgical anesthesia.
4. Death.

Divorced from all its emotional, behavioral, and bonding considerations, euthanasia with an injectable substance is a relatively simple process. Dr. Cramer threads a flexible catheter (tiny tube) into the prominent vein on Chico's front leg while a technician holds the dog. He then flushes the catheter with a saline solution to ensure that it functions properly.

"Why doesn't he just inject the drug right into the vein and get it over with?" Anita asks herself during Chico's final moments. Many owners witnessing this procedure for the first time wonder the same thing.

Sometimes veterinarians will do this if the animal has good veins and a good temperament, and if they feel confident about their technique. If doubts exist, though, most will use a catheter, which ensures that all the solution will go into the bloodstream, rather than risk puncturing the vein during the procedure.

"What difference does it make if some leaks out? Can't the veterinarian just give the animal more?" Katie's curiosity helps her subordinate her fears about this touchy subject.

Veterinarians do everything in their power to keep all of the euthanasia solution in the vein for two reasons. First, like many intravenous drugs, euthanasia solutions that get outside the vein may cause discomfort. Second, the failure to inject the right amount of drug at the proper rate could cause the animal to linger in the excitement stage rather than progress rapidly through it into surgical anesthesia and death. Although animals (and humans) that experience a prolonged excitement stage don't appear to suffer any harmful effects, observing them in this phase can prove extremely upsetting to human witnesses, especially owners seeking serene memories of their pet's final moments. Because of this, some veterinarians may also inject a sedative first to ensure that the animal won't remain in the excitement stage during euthanasia.

Ideally, euthanasia proceeds rapidly and uneventfully. However, just as in natural death, euthanized animals may gasp, vocalize, urinate, and defecate, and some owners react more negatively to these changes than others. And just as it takes some animals longer to die naturally than others, it may take longer for a euthanasia solution to affect animals with compromised circulatory function (such as that which arises from heart problems) or other medical conditions. Similarly, an animal's negative behavior also may affect its euthanasia.

EUTHANASIA AND THE
PROBLEM-BEHAVIOR PET

Although owners of unmanageable or aggressive animals often hope for miracles that will make euthanasia a tranquil experience for their pets, expecting an animal who always hated trips to the veterinary clinic to suddenly behave defies logic. Unfortunately, logic often escapes owners who find themselves in this position, and they may take any one of several approaches that make matters worse for their pets at this difficult time.

Some, like Paul, may abandon the pet completely. Not all owners disappear into the wilderness, but some do just drop off the animal at the veterinary clinic with nary a word about Snoopy's tendency to bite when held or Fluffy's killer response to anyone who tries to take her out of her carrier. This in no way means you must stay with your pet during euthanasia if doing so upsets you, but you owe it to the animal and the veterinary staff to brief them on everything about your pet that might affect its euthanasia.

Other owners who feel frightened or embarrassed by their pet's bad temperament may delay euthanizing the animal. Over the years, Paul ignored numerous suggestions about ways to improve Chico's disposition. Although he accepted the notion of Dr. Cramer vaccinating a snarling, snapping Chico held in a technician's death grip, he couldn't bear the thought that he and his dog would spend their final moments together like that. Rather than face this, he chose denial, telling himself that Chico would die comfortably in his sleep. Instead, the dog's physical problems only grew worse, further undermining his already bad behavior.

A variation on this theme occurs when embarrassed owners take their problem-behavior pets to a different veterinarian for euthanasia. Some do this hoping that the new veterinarian will relate to the animal in a way that doesn't precipitate the negative behavior exhibited in the past, or that the veterinarian will possess some miraculous way of dealing with the pet's misbehavior. Actually, as much as this may seem like wishful thinking on the owner's part, some logic may underlie this rationale. Some dogs who routinely act up with male veterinarians will readily allow female practitioners to work on them. Other times, odors or other environmental factors in a particular clinic may elicit negative behaviors that don't arise in other settings. Still, given the threat an aggressive pet poses to the owner as well as the veterinary staff, 'fessing up on Rex's touchiness or Snowball's out-and-out killer nature up front will make things much easier for human and animal alike.

A fourth group of owners opts to bite the bullet and face the fact that it may require heroic efforts to restrain the animal, who may go berserk.

"I admit that's what I did," Anita confesses. "When I realized Chico was suffering, and that I had to make the decision, I called Dr. Cramer's office and said I wanted the dog put down. They asked me if I'd like to give him an oral or injectable sedative at home to make the trip and procedure easier on him, but once I made up my mind, I wanted to take him right in and get it over with as soon as possible. In retrospect, though, I wish I'd done what they suggested. It would have been so much better for everyone."

> *Some animals react much more defensively toward strangers in strange surroundings than in their own homes; other pets respond just the opposite.*

Perhaps, but sedating fractious pets at home only works if the owner can get the sedative into the animal. Many terminally ill animals won't eat, and even the weakest animal can bite the hand trying to shove a pill down its throat. Such a bite can negate euthanasia because rabies laws require that the animal be quarantined for ten days. Although some veterinarians will dispense sedatives in an injectable form, many owners feel even more leery about sticking needles into their pets, and less-than-tractable animals don't appreciate this much, either. Even if administering the medication in this manner doesn't bother the owner or the animal, some veterinarians may hesitate to dispense drugs in injectable form for any reason.

The desire to get it all over with as soon as possible once they've made up their minds doesn't only apply to owners of animals with problem behavior like Chico. In fact, such owner reactions more commonly spring from the nature of the human–animal bond than from an animal's bad temperament.

EUTHANASIA AND THE HUMAN–ANIMAL BOND

I don't ever recall any owner, even owners of the most miserable pets, wishing their animals anything but an optimal euthanasia. Pet owners want this final event to progress smoothly and quickly. However, no such agreement exists regarding their own role in this process. Although Paul found the idea of attending Chico's death so horrifying that he left town, Anita felt exactly the opposite.

"Much as the little monster hated me from the day Paul and I had our first date years ago, I couldn't just leave him at Dr. Cramer's," she explained without any hesitation. "I felt I *had* to stay with him right to the end."

"I went because I didn't want Mom to go through that alone," Jason volunteers, obviously relishing his role as the man of the house in his father's absence.

"I was grossed out by the whole thing and only went because Mom made me," says Katie.

However, even though all of the Jandrows felt strongly about their unique roles in relationship to Chico, all of them failed to consider how these bonds might affect the dog. The presence of Chico's beloved owner, who was the only person the dog trusted, could have made the Chihuahua's final moments much less traumatic. On the other hand, having one hated person (Anita), one disinterested one (Jason), and one repulsed one (Katie) in on the process with Dr. Cramer and his technician probably served to compound the dog's fears immensely.

Does this mean that Paul should have stayed with his pet even if he didn't want to? Not at all. Looking at it strictly from the animal's perspective, the presence of a fearful and distraught owner doesn't help the animal much at all.

"Why not?" Anita wants to know. "I thought you said that having Paul there would have helped calm Chico."

True, but only if Paul *wanted* to be there. If he did, he'd consciously and subconsciously communicate this to his pet in countless reassuring ways. On the other hand, if he feared either the process or his ability to cope with the loss of his pet, he'd communicate those fears to Chico as well. In the latter case, rather than calming his pet during those final moments, his presence would have simply added to the dog's anxiety.

Most veterinarians will allow you to stay with your pet during euthanasia. However, some may suggest that you wait in another room during the actual process, then invite you to spend as much time as you wish with the body afterward. Veterinarians typically suggest this for one of three reasons:

1. They doubt themselves.
2. They doubt the animal.
3. They doubt the owner.

Many veterinarians rank euthanasia as the most difficult task they perform because of its intense emotional demands. If they don't feel comfortable with it, they may want to eliminate the owner from the process for their own convenience. Other times, veterinarians may request the owner's absence because they either know from past experience or suspect from their own knowledge of animal behavior that the pet will respond more positively if the owner isn't there. Veterinarians may suggest that highly emotional owners not attend the procedure because of any negative effects their presence may have on the pet.

If your veterinarian makes this suggestion, evaluate it in terms of how your absence might benefit your pet. If you still feel strongly about being present, insist on it. Once most owners learn how their own emotions can negatively affect their pet during the procedure, they make a special effort to relate to the animal in only the most positive and reassuring manner right up to the very end.

Having put the animal first in this discussion, let me close by reversing my stance long enough to note that, regardless of what's best for the animal from a behavioral point of view, and regardless what anyone tells you, when it comes to euthanasia you *must* do what *you* believe is the right thing to do. If you wait too long or do it too soon, if you stay in the room when you don't want to or don't stay when you do, or if you allow a veterinarian you don't trust to do it, you certainly will find it harder to accept your pet's death. Because of this, it makes sense to learn as much as possible about animal death and our responses to it beforehand, so that we can feel sure of our beliefs when the time comes.

FINAL RESTING PLACES

If most people give little thought to their pet's death, they give even less to what to do with the remains—until they're faced with the problem. However, some people maintain a state of denial right up to the end. Dr. Cramer had to tuck Chico's body into a far corner of his freezer to await direction from Paul on its disposal. It never came, and everyone forgot about the dog until a technician defrosted the freezer eight months later. Veterinarians and grief counselors tell tales of owners who fill their own freezers with deceased animal bodies. Some owners purchase freezers specifically for this purpose; others tuck canaries, hamsters, and cats among the frozen vegetables and meats.

Most of us, however, seek a more conventional solution. If you live in a remote area like I do, you can bury your pet on your own property. Then it becomes a question of finding the right spot. Some folks prefer to group all pet graves together, whereas others select a favorite spot where the animal liked to nap or play. Markers run the gamut from nothing at all to piles of rocks (to keep scavengers from disturbing the body) to homemade signs to professionally engraved stones.

In more populated areas, local ordinances may prohibit you from burying your pet on your own property. If so, you usually have two other burial options. First, the town may provide a common grave for animals that usually consists of a large hole periodically covered with soil. In areas with such facilities, veterinarians may place each animal in a separate, heavy plastic cadaver bag and transport the animal's remains for the owner. The second option, a privately owned pet cemetery, may offer a wide range of services spanning the spectrum from interring the animal in a simple wooden box to a full-blown funeral with a casket, flowers, tombstone, and perpetual care of the grave site.

> I t makes sense to learn as much as possible about animal death and our responses to it beforehand, so that we can feel sure of our beliefs when the time comes.

Some owners prefer to cremate their pet's remains instead. Some do this because they don't like the idea of a common grave or the thought that animal scavengers may dig up their pet's remains. Others want their pet's ashes to dispose of as they choose. Most veterinary clinics possess or have access to the facilities to do this. Of course, some perform this service with greater care than others. Because it takes such an intense amount of heat to reduce an animal's body to ash, cremation can become an expensive proposition. It's even more expensive if you want your pet's ashes returned to you to keep in an urn or scatter in some special place. You will pay more, and sometimes a great deal more, in this case because the crematorium must be thoroughly cleaned before your pet's body is placed in it, and it costs the facility more to maintain the system at a high enough temperature long enough to reduce the body to ashes.

It definitely pays to discuss your expectations before the fact with those responsible for cremating your pet. More than one owner has opened a canister theoretically containing their pet's remains expecting to see fine ash, only to discover bone fragments and teeth, and even partially melted license or name tags—some of them obviously not from their own pet. The more you know about the service available in your particular area, the less likely it is that the cost or results will surprise you.

Much less commonly owners may seek to preserve the animal's body in a more permanent, realistic form. Although humans have used taxidermy to stuff and mount wild animals for years, the idea of doing this with the family pet causes many to blanch. On the other hand, I've heard from taxidermists that it's not that rare an occurrence, either.

More rarely, owners may opt for freeze-drying or mummification, both highly specialized techniques offered by only a few companies. Freeze-drying supposedly maintains the animal in a more lifelike condition than taxidermy. Owners who opt for mummification, which preserves the body with special oils, spices, and fabric wrapping, typically desire this type of treatment for their own remains, too.

The pet memorial classified ads in most dog and cat magazines, along with ads scattered throughout such publications, will give you a good idea of the variety of death-related products and services available, as well as where to get additional information about any options that appeal to you. Here again, the more you learn about your options before you need them, the less likely you'll do something you later regret.

Admittedly, thinking about what to do with your pet's remains may seem as unnatural, and even ghoulish, as thinking about what will happen to their bodies when they die. However, as we'll see in the next chapter, the loss of a pet due to causes other than death may prove every bit as difficult for owners to accept.

CHAPTER TWO

SOMEWHERE
over the RAINBOW

Pet Loss from Causes Other Than Death

*It is the desperateness of losing which picks
the flowers of memory and binds the bouquet.*

—COLETTE
Mes Apprentissages

DAN RYAN and Becky Wheeler had planned
their cross-country vacation for months.

"We're going to spend the whole summer exploring
the country," Dan boasted to his neighbors as he stroked
his and Becky's mixed-breed pooch, Homer. "Homer
the condo pup is finally going to get to see some of the
world."

Two weeks later, as the couple took in the panoramic
view from a remote rest stop on a scenic highway thread-
ing through the Great Smokey Mountains, Homer
bolted after a rabbit that had hopped practically up to his
nose before pivoting in surprise and bounding off into
the dense undergrowth. Before either of his owners

could react, the dog disappeared, heedless of their frantic calls. After spending a whole month trying to find their beloved pet, Dan and Becky cut their vacation short and returned home.

"I still have nightmares about it," Becky explained to their friends a few months later at a neighborhood party. "We still talk about Homer every day. What if he got lost or hurt in the woods? What if someone found him and mistreated him? What if . . . ."

But before Becky could finish listing all the dreadful things that might have befallen their lost pet, a young woman in the group uttered a strangled sob and fled the room.

"What's wrong with Laurel?" asked Dan, startled by their new neighbor's reaction.

Their hostess shook her head sadly.

"She gave her cat Presley away right before she moved here and isn't sure she did the right thing."

ONE POEM about pet death describes pets crossing over a rainbow bridge into more heavenly surroundings. For owners who lose their pets to causes other than death, however, this rainbow bridge offers little consolation. Whether an owner gives up a pet or it disappears, the owners never experience the sense of closure that surrounds the death of a pet. In spite of the emotional trauma of a pet's demise, the very nature of death inexorably nudges us toward acceptance.

Pet loss from causes other than death, however, more often than not leaves us in limbo. We're full of doubts and unanswered questions, with no end in sight. As long as we think the animal may be alive somewhere, it's difficult to make peace with the loss.

Before we delve into the different ways owners respond to these types of pet loss, we need to know more about them. We can divide pet losses from causes other than death into two major categories:

1. Those that occur against the owner's will.

2. Those that occur with the owner's cooperation.

Understanding what each involves can help us avoid the first type and find other ways to help us cope with the second.

LOSSES BEYOND THE OWNER'S CONTROL

Admittedly, one owner may disagree with another's definition of what constitutes pet loss beyond the owner's control. However, let's assume that forces beyond the owner's control come into play in three situations:

1. The pet becomes lost.

2. The pet is stolen.

3. The pet is legally awarded to someone else in court.

When we add the feelings of personal impotence engendered by these losses to those of uncertainty and a lack of finality, we can appreciate how owners who find themselves in these situations may quickly succumb to their imaginations. Add the fact that all three of these forms of loss involve at least *some* owner complicity—though it may not necessarily be conscious—and we can see why Becky and Dan might take losing Homer as a fate worse than death.

THE LOST PET

In talking with owners of lost pets, I've found that the loss occurs due to a lack of one or more of the following:

- Some form of reliable physical restraint
- Proper training
- Proper identification
- An organized attempt to locate the pet
- A solid owner–pet bond

How do these deficits come into play when pets get lost? Although most owners view their pets' disappearance as an abnormal phenomenon, most animals become lost pursuing perfectly predictable animal activities. What could be more normal than an unleashed, unsupervised dog chasing a rabbit, or a cat fleeing through a suburban housing development to get away from another cat, a dog, or some other perceived threat? Only some form of reliable restraint can prevent this from happening.

"But why didn't Homer come when we called him?" asks Becky. "He always came at home."

Granted, many dogs and even some cats routinely come when called in familiar environments and under familiar circumstances. However, more often these animals come because they want to come, rather than because their owners actually trained them to do so. The proof of training doesn't lie in the number of times the animal responds to the command, but whether it responds when it would rather do something else. Unless owners deliberately place their pets in controlled, but pet-enticing or threatening conditions where they can test whether the unleashed animal will come on command every time, they have no way of knowing how the animal will respond in such a situation.

Although most owners view their pet's disappearance as an abnormal phenomenon, most animals become lost pursuing perfectly predictable animal activities.

If your pet bolts, does it have readily accessible identification? Collars with tags, tattoos, and microchips serve as the most common pet identifiers. Most new dog owners immediately go out and buy their pet a collar, and then adorn it with at least a license and rabies tag, and possibly another tag providing the animal's name, the owner's phone number, and other pertinent data. On the other hand, cat owners may not give collars a thought at all or dismiss them as potentially dangerous.

"Absolutely!" Laurel agrees emphatically. "I heard of a cat who strangled itself when its collar got caught on a branch."

A lot of us have heard this story. Unfortunately, we lack the necessary facts to know if we all heard about the same instance or if this actually occurs fairly often. Even if it does happen regularly, we must ask how those numbers compare to the number of lost cats euthanized in shelters for want of proper identification.

Ideally, pets with tattoos or microchips wear collars that tell people that this identification exists as well as how to locate the animal's owner. Theoretically, tattooing the animal or implanting a microchip—both simple procedures—resolves the identification problems that arise when lost pets lose their collars or don't wear them. But this only holds true if the person who finds your pet knows to look for a tattoo or chip and how to use the information to track down the owner.

A tattoo will serve Homer well if he allows a stranger to roll him onto his back to see it on his tummy, and if that person knows who to contact to convert the tattooed data into a viable owner contact. Similarly, a microchip ID may serve the collarless pet that gets lost in an area with an animal shelter equipped with a scanner and residents aware of this service. On the other hand, when Homer disappears into the wilds of the Smokey Mountains, where an occasional camper or only a handful of residents might encounter him, a distinctive collar and tag with his owner's address and phone number will serve him much better. A distinctive, brightly colored collar may serve as the sole link between a lost pet and its owners if the animal won't allow strangers to get close enough to read any other form of identification.

A clear, up-to-date photo provides another excellent form of identification that many owners overlook. Perhaps fearing what others might say, some of us feel self-conscious about taking our pet's picture, let alone carrying it in our wallets. Or, like many parents, we may take a lot of pictures when we first get the new pup or kitten, but then forget to update these over time. When the pet gets lost, we realize that photo of the squashed-nosed, big-eared, big-eyed baby looks nothing like the adult animal at all. When we try to describe to others how the lost pet looks now, our emotions about the animal and its loss scramble our thoughts.

"Homer's a mixed breed, weighs about twenty-five to thirty-five pounds. We think he has some spaniel in him, but maybe it's poodle because his coat is kind of curly." Becky starts her description confidently, but then she falters. "His coat is kind of brown and grayish black. Or would you say he's more brown than black, Dan? And which one of his feet has that gray smudge? Is it his right front or left? I can't remember."

The more Becky and Dan try to remember and can't, the more distraught they become, and the more their description of Homer deteriorates. How much simpler for all involved if they could just open their wallets and take out a recent snapshot of their lost pet!

Other times, owners fail to conduct a systematic search for their lost pets. In his *Owner's Guide to Better Behavior in Dogs & Cats* (American Veterinary Publications, 1986), behaviorist William Campbell outlines an excellent plan that includes determining the time and wind direction when the animal disappeared (because most animals follow their noses into the wind). Pets who disappear from home often head off in the same direction family members do or in the direction the pet most frequently travels with the owner. Notify the local police, ambulance, and taxi services, in addition to any animal shelters and veterinary clinics, leaving a friend's name and phone number as well as your own in case someone wants to reach you while you're out searching for your pet.

In addition to using photos and posters that provide a picture of the animal and critical information, Campbell suggests that owners of lost pets pay particular attention to three areas:

1. Places where food is available.

2. Places where children routinely congregate.

3. Houses or areas with other dogs or cats.

Many lost pets automatically zero in on food sources because they lack the necessary skills or experience to hunt live prey like their wild ancestors. Many also enjoy the relatively nonthreatening companionship and activities offered by children and other animals.

This brings us to the last and most troubling characteristic that sometimes applies to lost pets: the lack of a solid pet–owner bond. If the owner views the pet as more of a liability than an asset, he or she won't try to locate the pet as long or as persistently as owners who adore their animals. For example, someone may have received the pet as an unsolicited gift, bought the pet for their children, or acquired a dog for "protection" or a cat to catch mice. Although some of these owners may become attached to the animal over time, others may find that fulfilling their pets' physical and behavioral needs takes more energy than they want to give. When the pet disappears, these owners may come up with all kinds of reasons to mount only the most limited search, or they may not look for the animal at all.

Solid bonds also lead owners to seek meaningful information about their pets' normal behavior. Devoted owners of lost pets of certain species such as cats, some birds, and pocket pets like hamsters and gerbils may jump to one or both of two erroneous conclusions:

1. Unlike dogs, many of these creatures can take care of themselves, even in the wild.

2. It's useless to look for such a pet because you'll never find it.

Obviously, enough lost and abandoned cats have survived to the point that the feral cat population has become problematic in some areas, proving they don't all need human companionship to survive. (Feral cats are domestic cats gone wild.) However, many cats and other pets live quite sheltered lives and flounder helplessly when they suddenly find themselves out of their owners' care. Because of this, most will seek to stay fairly close to home or near places that carry familiar scents. If they can't find their exact owners, many pets are more likely to seek out other people than they are wild animals, even those of their own kind. Because of this it makes sense to systematically search for *any* lost pet.

"That's all well and good," admits Dan, thinking of his own efforts to find his dog. "But what if someone steals your pet?"

Stolen Treasures

When pets disappear, theft often springs first into the minds of worried owners. When it does, owners of dogs and cats routinely envision mad scientists cruising the streets in search of subjects for nefarious experiments. Although in days gone by such unscrupulous behavior did occur, it doesn't happen nearly as often as some owners of lost pets imagine. First, medical research has become so sophisticated and expensive, using "street animals" of unknown origin for experiments doesn't make much sense anymore.

"What do you mean?" Dan huffs indignantly. "Homer was no street dog! He had the best of care!"

True as that may be, researchers can't possibly know this, and they can't afford the time and effort involved in proving an animal's background to the degree necessary for most experiments. Moreover, these scientists would need to quarantine any stolen animal during this process so it wouldn't affect any resident animals if it happened to carry a contagious disease. This, in turn, would make an already expensive proposition more so.

Second, for scientific as well as ethical reasons, our society is trying to move away from experiments that use animals. With time, researchers will turn to more and more new methods that replace animal experiments. Additionally, more of us willingly assume any risks involved in using products not tested on animals, even if it means paying a higher price for those products, and this makes it economically feasible for more manufacturers to consider taking this route.

On the other hand, we also know that the interest in purebred animals has spawned a thriving industry where demand exceeds supply as well as some people's ability to pay the going price. Sufficient numbers of people find the idea of owning a purebred pet so irresistible that we can see why an unscrupulous person who notices such an animal wandering about the neighborhood, sitting in an unlocked car, or lounging unattended in the owner's yard might see this as a golden opportunity to make a quick buck. The friendly pet goes to the beckoning stranger with the meatball, the stranger spirits the animal away, and then offers it for sale at "a great price because I lost her papers" in some town a hundred miles away. Because many people don't realize that only those papers, not the animal's looks, differentiate a mixed breed from a purebred, they think they got a real bargain when they paid only $100 for a Doberman or a Siamese cat.

Most local law enforcement agencies lack both the time and the resources to differentiate lost from stolen pets, or to track pet thieves. Animal control officers may possess the authority to do so, but handling the far greater numbers of abandoned and genuinely lost pets often leaves them with little time or resources to respond to what may only amount to an owner's suspicion of theft. Some animal lovers may view this as gross negligence on the part of the law enforcement community, but, as we'll see in the next section, when the law does become involved with them and their pets, many owners wish it hadn't.

PET LOSS FROM LEGAL ACTION

Ten years ago, the idea of losing a pet as the result of legal action would have raised images of breeders reclaiming animals that owners refused to pay for, or the local authorities impounding abused pets. In such cases, the owners typically don't share a strong bond with the animals in question. Nowadays, however, custody of the family pet may become an issue when couples separate or divorce, and especially when both enjoy what they consider a quality relationship with the pet.

> *The human–animal bond is a biological and psychological entity upon which we and our pets rely for our physical and mental well-being.*

"At first I almost laughed when you said that," Becky admits cautiously. "But then I thought about how I'd feel if Dan and I ever split up and we still had Homer. I know I'd want to keep Homer because I'd need him more than ever to help me make it through the split."

"Yeah," Dan agrees, shaking his head in wonderment. "And I know I'd want him, too, for exactly the same reasons."

The human–animal bond as a biological and psychological entity upon which we and our pets rely for our physical and mental well-being will recur throughout this book. Whether we possess concrete proof of its existence, anyone who loves a pet can imagine what the loss of that pet would mean. The idea of facing a stressful situation like divorce without that pet seems impossible. This realization, in turn, causes some couples to fight to gain custody of the family pet more viciously than they fight to gain custody of their children.

"Be serious!" Dan and Becky exclaim in unison.

"I think I can understand that," counters the couple's friend Laurel. "When my ex and I split up, I got both the kids and Presley the cat. While I loved them all, the kids needed even more of my time and attention during that period of adjustment, whereas the cat was there, just purring and loving us all as usual. Where the kids always seemed to be taking from me, the cat was giving, and that helped a lot."

Given these benefits, we can see why some third party may need to decide who gets Pluto or Felix when owners disagree. Furthermore, we can appreciate how making sound judgments in this regard requires an understanding of the human–animal bond. Because such knowledge doesn't comprise a routine part of legal education, this means that couples who can't resolve pet-custody issues on their own may need to educate their lawyers so that they may properly educate the judge who acts on the case. Otherwise what the couple might consider an issue of the gravest importance may receive capricious handling at best.

Along those same lines, it also makes sense for couples to put aside their differences long enough to address any custody issues equitably for the animal's sake, too. Like children, animals often react more strongly to the *how* of custody battles than the *who*. Pets who are shuttled back and forth between owners who once were in love but now hate each other pick up many conscious and subconscious conflicting human messages—with their much greater perceptual abilities—far more readily than a child might. All those negative owner responses to the former partner could leave the pet's gut churning, too.

Losing a pet by one of the means described in this chapter so far would certainly be awful. However, many owners who find themselves in these situations take solace in the fact that they can attribute at least some aspect of the loss, no matter how minor, to forces beyond their control. But when we deliberately give up an animal, we lose whatever small comfort this belief might offer, too. "Tell me about it," Laurel murmurs softly as she looks at the picture of Presley she keeps in her wallet.

CHOOSING TO GIVE UP YOUR PET

Like most owners in this position, giving up Presley left Laurel most troubled by two aspects of the event: why she gave up her pet and to whom she gave him. When asked why they gave up a particular animal, owners provide a collection of answers as varied as the owners and animals themselves. However, closer scrutiny reveals that owners who choose to give up pets tend to fall into one of two groups:

1. Those who knew from the beginning that they would eventually give up the pet.
2. Those who got the pet with the idea of keeping it, but then it didn't work out for some reason.

The reasons owners give up their pets definitely affect how they respond to the loss. Let's look at the two groups in more detail.

TEMPORARY PET OWNERSHIP

To most people, the idea of owning a pet that you know you must eventually give up seems ludicrous. On the other hand, the ability to give up a pet plays a critical role in the relationship between two groups of owners and their animals: breeders and foster pet owners.

Typically, breeders strive to raise and show the best purebred animals. When offspring arrive, most breeders keep the ones they want to show and add to their breeding programs, and sell the rest. In a line of purebreds with a healthy gene pool where the majority of the young in a particular litter may not measure up to show standards, this can mean parting with a fair number of animals with which the breeder has interacted during the most appealing part of the animals' lives.

Compare these professionals to two groups of unknowledgeable pet owners. In the first group are folks who get pets and don't neuter them for one reason or another. The animals become pregnant and the owners must find homes for any offspring—not always an easy task. The second group consists of those who adopt an animal to enjoy at their vacation residence, then give up or abandon it (and any of its offspring) when they return to their regular homes in the fall.

Light-years away from those folks, we find people who serve as foster parents for pets. They are often affiliated with one of three different kinds of organizations:

- Service-animal groups
- Animal shelters
- Rescue groups

Because training and placing service animals, such as guide dogs for the blind, requires so much effort, those who are involved in this work want to train only the most physically sound and mentally stable animals. To ensure this, some organizations place young animals with willing volunteers who then raise them to meet these high standards. When the time comes for the pet to begin its formal training, the foster parent returns the pet and may never see it again.

Other times those who train service animals will adopt older pets from shelters or accept them from private owners. Before commencing any formal training, the trainer may place the animal with a knowledgeable foster parent for a certain period to see if any medical or behavioral problems crop up in that environment.

Animal shelters primarily use foster parents to raise orphaned animals. This may require a great deal of time that busy shelter workers simply don't have. Ideally, those who raise orphans do so with enough knowledge of that type of pet to ensure the orphan's normal physical and behavioral development. More commonly, though, foster care may focus primarily on getting the animal to eat on its own. Once that happens, the foster parent returns it to the shelter, where someone may or may not adopt it.

The majority of rescue groups concentrate all of their efforts on one particular breed, although some may focus on a species such as pot-bellied pigs or iguanas. Unlike those who foster shelter animals, people involved in rescue work see far more adult than young animals. And because many of the animals that are given up have problems, people who foster rescued pets may become involved in evaluating these animals for their existing problems, as well as treating the animals for any new problems they discover.

Pets Who Don't Work Out

By far, pets who don't work out comprise the largest group of animals who are given up. Pets usually don't work out for one of five reasons:

1. Owner's medical condition.

2. Owner's lifestyle.

3. Animal's medical condition.

4. Animal's behavior.

5. Lack of human–animal bond.

Although more than a few perfectly healthy owners cite medical problems as the reason they must give up a pet, legitimate medical reasons do exist. Admittedly, most allergic animal lovers know well in advance that a pet most likely will cause sneezing, wheezing, or other allergic symptoms, and they prepare for this possibility. They may select species or breeds less likely to trigger such reactions, or they may establish a pet-free room (usually a bedroom) where allergy sufferers can retreat when necessary. Although desensitizing people with pet allergies may offer some relief, this costly, time-consuming treatment leaves much to be desired. However, a vaccine currently under development to protect those with allergies to cats shows great promise and may signal a new era in treating allergies to other animals, too.

Some people may develop problems that affect their immune response, leaving them more vulnerable to infection. Because human medical education views animals primarily as disease carriers and teaches little or nothing about the benefits of animal companionship, physicians may advise owners who develop such immune deficiencies to get rid of their pets. However, sometimes asking another person to perform any high-risk task (such as cleaning out the litter box) or routine the owner lacks the strength to do (such as exercising the pet) permits those with many medical problems to enjoy the benefits of their pets' companionship without the health hazards.

A variation on this theme involves caregivers, social workers, family members, and friends who urge devoted pet owners in need of some sort of assisted living arrangement to give up their pets so they can move into such a facility. Sadly, this advice overlooks the beneficial role those pets may play in their owners' lives.

Fortunately, more options now exist for animal lovers with special housing needs. Some enlightened facilities now offer accommodations for pets as well as their owners. Others maintain their own cadre of resident pets to make life more enjoyable for the animal lovers who live there. A third group of facilities schedule regular visits of well-behaved pets from the community and/or invite family members to bring the loved one's pet when they visit.

Another reason people give up their pets is because they're just too busy to care for them properly. Some owners also mention a lack of financial, emotional, or physical wherewithal necessary to make their dream pet a lasting reality. This problem occurs so often that I wrote two books, *DogSmart* and *CatSmart* (Contemporary Books, 1997 and 1998), for the express purpose of helping prospective owners work out lifestyle and other issues *before* they get a pet.

Even so, situations sometimes arise in which a once-optimum owner lifestyle gives way to one that undermines the animal's welfare as well as the human–animal relationship. When this occurs, pet owners may opt to give up the pet to someone who they hope can provide the animal with the kind of environment it needs or who will find someone who can.

> By far, pets who don't work out comprise the largest group of animals that are given up.

"That's what happened to me," Laurel explains candidly. "After the divorce, things really went down the tubes. I couldn't afford to keep the house, and every rental I could afford that would accept kids wouldn't allow pets, or vice versa. Time was running out and I finally chose the place we're in now because the kids can go to their old school. But they miss Presley as much as I do, so I'm not sure I did the right thing. . . ."

If our society lags considerably in recognizing the role that animal companionship plays in the lives of those with medical problems, it lags even further behind when it comes to appreciating their value for "normal" folks as they face the changes associated with everyday life. Moving into a new home, divorcing, losing a job or beginning a new one all generate stress, even under the best of circumstances. Moreover, many people move as a result of changes in relationships or employment, thereby adding even more stress to their lives. Even though giving up your pet may seem like the most logical thing to do at such times, sometimes doing so may only make adjusting to the change even more difficult.

"In retrospect, I should have thought things through more carefully, as well as accepted how much Presley meant to me and the kids," Laurel admits as she watches her youngest try to lure a stray cat from under a neighbor's porch. "At the time, my sister told me I was nuts for letting a pet influence where the kids and I would live. Now I think I was nuts for listening to her. In a way, it would have been so much easier to give him up if he'd had some problem."

Probably not. Specific medical, behavioral, or bond problems add so many different ingredients to the pet loss stew that we'll devote the next two chapters to the topic. Suffice it to say that although some owners may find it easier to give up a problem pet than a healthy one, an equal number find it much more difficult. However, one more general quality of the bond does come into play when we lose or give up pets, and it merits mention here.

THE SEARCH GOES ON— BUT FOR HOW LONG?

As I've said before, I equate the bond with love, and I'm convinced that anyone who interacts with an animal forms *some* kind of bond with it. However, with age and experience, I also realize that we each define love in our own unique way, and that just because we love a pet, that love in no way guarantees that animal's good health and behavior or that we'll enjoy a perfect relationship with it.

As animals play a more and more important role in our physical and emotional well-being and become members of our families, it seems reasonable to apply the same "until death do us part" standard to our relationships with our pets that we apply to human relationships. But as we so often discover in our relationships with other people, duration doesn't provide a true measure of the quality of a relationship with an animal, either.

"I agree completely," Dan chimes in. "We only had Homer for a year, but we were a lot closer to him than my folks are to the old dog they've owned for more than ten. When we told them we spent a whole month looking for Homer, they couldn't believe it. They said they'd give up looking for their dog after a week."

How long should we keep looking for a lost pet? As we'll see in chapters five through nine, it depends on your relationship with your pet.

For example, even though Dan sees his and Becky's extended quest to find Homer as evidence that they love their pet more than Dan's parents love theirs, Dan's response might comprise more of a value judgment than a statement of fact. Dan and Becky might feel driven to search high and low for Homer because they find the idea of losing *any* family member impossible to accept, and this fear, rather than any great love for their dog, may serve as their primary motivation. Because Dan's parents have faced the loss of other loved ones over the years, the loss of their pet may not elicit similar feelings.

And although Dan may see his and Becky's intense feelings for Homer as proof of a great love that could only grow through the years, his parents' more mellow ten-year relationship with their own dog may convince the older folks that they'll know exactly how to locate their pet if she gets lost, and how long to look for her before giving up.

"I can't really explain it," Dan's mother says apologetically. "I just know I'll know if that dog needs me."

From this we can see that, even though we point to factors such as the weather or limited time as reasons to abort a search, more likely we search long enough to fulfill some definition that we tried to find the lost animal. I deliberately refer to *some* definition that we tried because, although all owners think they'll know exactly how long to keep looking, this isn't always the case. More commonly, our definition of what constitutes looking "long enough" evolves during the process of looking rather than as the result of any conscious plan.

Sometimes the loss overwhelms us so much that we don't want to look at all. Other times, we feel so certain that the old cat has gone off into the woods to die, that searching for him seems not so much foolish as somehow inappropriate or even disloyal. However, other family members may not share that view and they may organize a search that we feel obligated to participate in lest we upset them.

If we don't know how long to look, but want to put some limits on the search, we may seek out expert opinions. If these strike us as reasonable, given what we know about ourselves and the lost pet, we may accept them. Or we may double them to be on the safe side, or select a specific date, such as the animal's birthday, to mark the end of the search.

As arbitrary as all this may sound, it serves a beneficial purpose. If we quit too soon, we'll feel we abandoned rather than lost the animal. Not only will this make it impossible for us to accept the loss (more on this in chapter five), but these feelings may affect our relationship with every pet in our lives from then on. Paradoxically, the same holds true at the opposite end of the spectrum: If we don't give up the search at a reasonable point, that too will block acceptance of the loss and undermine our relationship with any subsequent pet.

With any relationship with a pet, owners inevitably face situations for which no right answer exists. Having watched owners grapple with troubling questions about their pets over the years, I've come to the conclusion that the worst choice is not, as so many fear, making the wrong decision. The worst choice is being afraid to make any decision at all. This is especially true in the case of letting go of a lost or given-up pet.

"I understand all that. I really do," Becky insists. "But how can I let go when I don't know what happened to Homer?"

"Believe me, knowing doesn't have anything to do with it," counters Laurel. "I know exactly what happened to Presley and it doesn't help one bit."

Because our imaginations often shift into high gear when we think about what might have happened to a pet whom we lost or gave up, let's take a closer look at this critical part of the equation.

WHAT HAPPENS TO LOST OR GIVEN-UP PETS?

Thinking back on the disappearance of several very special pets over my lifetime, my first instinct is to present the answer to this question in as positive a light as possible. Keep in mind, however, that such bias, no matter how well-meaning, does little to address the underlying fears that plague us when our pets disappear or get taken in by strangers. After much thought, I've decided that perhaps a brutally frank answer will better serve those who face or will face this kind of pet loss.

In a nutshell, a lost or relinquished animal will either live or die.

"So who makes it and who doesn't?" Dan fires back.

Unfortunately, that's very difficult to say. Pets who are or become ill or injured after separation from their owners tend to fare worse than physically sound animals. On the other hand, a limping dog or cat may elicit more sympathy and help from a stranger than an apparently healthy pet.

Statistically, an older dog or cat with problems who winds up in a shelter is more likely to die there; conversely, though, that older animal may possess the knowledge and experience to survive on its own a lot longer than a pup or kitten. Lost or abandoned pups and kittens often get adopted almost immediately from a shelter or rescue group, but those same young animals may last only a day or two outside on their own.

I put the idea of pets either making it or not up front because some owners immediately imagine the worst has befallen their pet, even though just the opposite might hold true. Once owners allow their emotions to dominate their thoughts, they tend to react emotionally rather than in a thoughtful manner that might better help them locate a lost pet or ensure that a pet they must give up goes to a good home.

"I can understand not getting all emotional when a pet gets lost and you need to mount a systematic search for it," Laurel concedes. "But how can you ensure that a pet you lost or gave up goes to a good home?"

To answer this question, let's take a look at the different places where a lost or given-up pet may wind up:

- Police or public works facilities
- Veterinary clinics
- Shelters
- Rescue groups
- A friend's home
- A stranger's home

THE DEAD, SERIOUSLY ILL, OR INJURED PET

Animals found dead along roadsides or on public grounds may be picked up by the area's law enforcement or public works employees for disposal. Whether these officials will make any attempt to locate the owner depends on two factors: the presence of some sort of meaningful identification on the animal and the time necessary to track down the owner.

Many pets wear local licenses, which may provide little meaningful information to anyone unfamiliar with that area. For example, the official license tag in my small town lists only the town name, an ID number, and an expiration date; it makes no mention of the state at all. Consequently, if my dogs became lost out-of-state or even in a different part of this state, their license tags would offer no clue regarding where they live.

Other times, the quality of the pet's identification tag may deteriorate until it becomes unreadable. Becky and Dan bought Homer a wonderful ID tag when they first got him, but they failed to notice how all his cavorting had scratched and obliterated the information on it after a while. Under these circumstances, and given all the average public servants' other chores, road crews probably won't spend much time trying to locate the owner of a dead animal.

Whether local officials will scan a dead animal for a microchip depends on the condition of the animal's body and whether they possess ready access to scanning equipment. On the other hand, most officials will notify owners if they pick up a body (or a live animal) that matches a photo and clearly written description sent to them by the owner.

Police or local animal control officers will take seriously ill or injured animals to a veterinarian for care. If the veterinarian believes that the animal suffers from terminal illness or injury, he or she may euthanize the animal rather than attempt to treat it. How much treatment the veterinarian will provide depends on that person's personal philosophy and/or any agreements with the local town or shelter. Some veterinarians may focus primarily on stabilizing and making the animal comfortable pending the location of the owner; some towns or animal shelters that retain veterinarians to treat ill or injured strays may only pay for minimal service. Other times, the veterinarian's personality and/or shelter policy may lead him or her to do everything possible to sustain the animal's life. The latter policy is certainly comforting to some owners, but remember that those who locate their pets will be expected to pay for this treatment. In the case of a purebred animal, the veterinarian may contact a rescue group, which may make the choice to treat it or not.

When friends or strangers find an ill or injured animal they, too, may decide whether to seek treatment for it. Although veterinarians normally expect those who present the animal to assume financial responsibility for its care, friends may tell the veterinarian to do everything possible because they don't want the owner to think they'd let the pet die, or because they assume that the owner will happily pay for any treatment.

Strangers who assume the responsibility for a lost animal rather than calling animal control also may make these same assumptions *and* expect the owner to feel grateful enough for this extra caring service to offer an additional reward. Those assumptions may, however, be false.

"I know what you mean," Dan says, nodding his head in agreement. "Some friends' old dog wandered off and got hit by a car while they were at work. The driver rushed the dog to the vet's and by the time the owners located the dog, the bill was over a thousand dollars and included treatment they never would have put the old guy through had they been there. It was really tough for them because they didn't want to appear ungrateful, but it wasn't what they would have done."

In chapter ten we'll discuss ways to avoid this particularly troubling scenario. For now, simply note that the amount of medical treatment a seriously ill or injured animal receives can vary greatly.

THE HEALTHY LOST PET

Our hearts may go out to the shy or terrified animal, but a lost, well-socialized, happy animal tends to generate the most positive human response.

"I don't understand," Laurel counters. "Wouldn't people want to help a frightened animal more?"

Certainly, but the animal's fear may not allow us to do so. Imagine pulling into a rest area on your way to some scheduled event and spying a timid cat or dog slinking through the undergrowth. Now imagine that same scene, but this time that lost animal readily approaches you and wags its tail or rubs its head on your ankles. Which pet could you help the most easily, given your own limits?

The same holds true when strays wind up in veterinary clinics, shelters, or with rescue groups. Some of these organizations claim a no-kill policy (that is, they don't euthanize animals under any circumstances), but most will perform euthanasia in certain cases—such as when an animal's problem jeopardizes their entire animal population or poses a risk to the facility's staff. For most shelters, the sad reality is that the number of adult animals coming through their doors exceeds the number of people willing to adopt these pets. This means that even physically healthy animals may be euthanized. Although some shelters may make this determination based strictly on the numbers—designating an animal not claimed or placed within a certain time as "unadoptable"—other shelters may keep animals with friendly personalities around much longer, even making them mascots or adopting them themselves.

> *Our hearts may go out to the shy or terrified animal, but a lost, well-socialized, happy animal tends to generate the most positive human response.*

Sadly, owners of animals with medical problems may use the animal's problems as a reason not to involve their pet in any kind of training program to build its confidence and social skills. These animals then wind up with two strikes against them should they become lost or should problems arise that necessitate finding a new home for the pet.

SPECIAL CONSIDERATIONS
WHEN GIVING UP A PET

Unlike those who lose their pets, those who give them up exercise a certain amount of control over what happens to the animal; however, those who give their pets up to shelters or rescue groups exert the least control. By turning the animal over to a shelter or rescue group, the owner essentially gives the organization the right to do what it can or sees fit to do with the animal. Again, in the case of medical or behavioral problems, that may mean putting the animal down; and, in fact, some rescue groups won't even accept pets with a history of aggressive behavior. The best organizations will evaluate each animal and treat any treatable problems before placing it in a new home. However, they will charge the person who gives up the animal as well as the new owner to cover the cost of this service.

Although few owners who give up their pets to shelters or rescue groups want to know that the animal was euthanized, many would like to know if their pet goes to a good home. However, they seldom will find this out unless the agency passes on the former owner's name and the new owner chooses to contact that person. New owners may choose not to contact the previous owner because they want their new pet to bond with them; they may also harbor negative images of anyone who would give up a pet.

Some owners who give up their pets also speak of going through a period when every golden retriever or Persian cat reminds them of the one they gave up. Not surprisingly, such feelings may routinely plague those who give up their pets to local organizations, with some finding comfort and others anguish in these encounters. Those who relinquish their pets to purebred rescue groups that place animals all over the country may find either comfort or despair in the knowledge that they may never see their pets again. On the other hand, the owner who gives up a pet locally realistically can give up looking for that animal outside that area, but those who relinquish their pets to rescue groups may seek evidence of their former pets everywhere they go.

Making the effort to place an animal in a private home, either with friends or strangers, gives the owner the most control over the situation. But again, doubts may arise.

"I gave Presley to the aunt of a woman I work with," Laurel says. "I like my coworker and she's really into cats, but I only met her aunt once. She seemed nice enough too, but . . . ."

Again, we'll discuss the nature of those "buts" and how they may affect our response to the loss of a pet in more detail throughout the book. Relative to placing an animal in a new home, though, one point stands out: The more time and effort owners put into the process of finding the right home for their pets, the more chance that animal will succeed in that new environment and that the original owner will accept the loss with few or no regrets.

PREVENTION IN A NUTSHELL

So far we've discussed some of the ways we may lose pets to causes other than death. Although each cause presents us with its own special considerations, we can summarize the critical points as follows:

1. Relate to and train your pet in a manner that will endear it to others. Although this may make it a more

vulnerable target for thieves, such thefts are far less common than strays that are ignored or euthanized because others can't approach and handle them.

2. Identify your pet in a readily accessible manner. Don't rely solely on invisible or hard-to-read identification such as microchips or tattoos; instead, couple these with a distinctive collar. Keep a recent photo of your pet in your wallet as well as at home; select one that clearly shows the animal's physical features.

3. Undertake a systematic search for your lost pet. Think about this now so you'll know what to do should this unhappy event occur.

4. Only get a pet because you really want one. This fosters a bond with your pet that will help sustain you during the time of loss.

5. If you want a shelter or rescue group to find the best home for your pet, expect to pay for this service.

6. The more you become personally involved in the placement of your pet, the fewer doubts you will harbor about that animal's new home.

By keeping these basic principles in mind, you can meet your pet's and your own best interests should that animal become lost or should you need to give it up.

Now that we know the nature of the various endpoints at which human–animal relationships may arrive by happenstance or by choice, let's turn our attention to the kinds of events that commonly precede the loss, beginning with problems that appear to assault us and our pets without warning.

CHAPTER THREE

A BOLT OUT
of the BLUE

Pet Loss As a Result of Acute Problems

Small showers last long, but summer storms are short.
—WILLIAM SHAKESPEARE
Richard II

LATER, TRISH Schroeder remembered her dog Caleb's accident in brutally vivid detail, as if it had happened in slow motion: opening the door for the Girl Scout who was selling cookies, Caleb streaking through the doorway and into the street, the car hitting him, his body spinning through the air, his front legs hitting the asphalt and then collapsing beneath the weight of the impact.

What came after that dissolved into a blur, from which emerged the image of Caleb's veterinarian.

"I'm so sorry, Ms. Schroeder," Trish clearly remembered the veterinarian saying. "There was nothing we could do."

When Trish's co-worker, Jeff DiMateo, listens to her story the next day, he can barely control his emotions.

"You were so lucky!" he wanted to blurt out. "My cat lived after her accident and I had to choose whether to treat her or put her down!"

IN MEDICINE, the term *acute* refers to situations that arise quickly and follow a relatively short and severe course. When most of us think of losing a pet under such circumstances, we envision accidents or overwhelming infections that suddenly assault the animal's physical body. However, sudden behavioral problems or changes in the human–animal bond also may result in the loss of a pet. Virtually every *unexpected* medical, behavioral, or bond problem that arises has the potential to end that animal's life or end its relationship with that particular owner. I deliberately emphasize the word "unexpected" because, as we shall see, sometimes what owners perceive as a bolt-out-of-the-blue tragedy actually represents the final chapter of a long-running work-in-progress.

Like all other animal-related problems, acute ones affect the animal's physical health, its behavior, and its bond with its owner. The extent to which an acute problem may threaten an animal's life depends on how the condition affects both the owner and the animal itself. An animal may suffer from an acute, untreatable terminal disease, but an owner also may choose to euthanize a pet rather than treat an acute treatable problem.

"Are you saying that problems that don't actually threaten an animal's life in and of themselves could bother owners enough that they put down the pet or give it up?" Jeff asks.

Exactly. For example, when Jeff's cat Lucky leapt onto a set of unsteady shelves in the garage and brought them and their contents down on top of herself, the event forced Jeff not only to consider what Lucky's injuries meant to his pet, but also what her injuries meant to him. To understand how these two factors may come into play, let's apply them to acute problems in each of the three categories—physical, behavioral, and bond. That way, we can pick up clues that will help us to avoid these problems or to cope with them if they arise.

ACUTE PHYSICAL PROBLEMS

We can group acute physical problems that may befall a pet into the following categories:

- Accidental or deliberate trauma
- Accidental or deliberate poisoning
- Allergic reactions
- Obstructions and foreign bodies
- Infections
- Gastric torsion
- Urinary blockages
- Environmental hazards

Accidental or deliberate trauma most commonly includes vehicle injuries, attacks by humans or other animals, burns from fire or chemicals, or traps. Traumatic injuries may affect virtually any and every system in the animal's body. When so much damage occurs that the animal can't compensate for it with or without medical help, it dies. For example, when Caleb darted in front of the car that was going forty miles per hour, his collision with the car's bumper fractured his pelvis and one hind leg. When his body hit the ground, he fractured both front legs and broke his lower jaw. In addition, the force of the impact propelled his abdominal organs forward with sufficient force to rupture major blood vessels as well as his diaphragm and put life-threatening pressure on his heart and lungs.

Deliberate human attacks on pets usually involve kicks or blows with a blunt instrument, gunshot wounds, or drowning, whereas attacks from other animals usually result in puncture and tearing bite wounds to the neck and chest or crushing of the trachea (windpipe). Although some demented souls may deliberately burn an animal, more commonly pets die in house fires unwittingly caused by their owners or others who may not even know of the animal's presence. Most traps will only hold a larger animal by the leg, but it may bleed to death or die of shock or exposure if not rescued soon after becoming caught.

So many substances may deliberately or accidentally poison pets that it would take a whole book to describe them all. In addition to the commonly recognized pesticides, herbicides, and fertilizers, we can add toxic substances found in many households such as cleaning agents and cosmetics, as well as human and animal medications, and even chocolate.

Like humans, animals may suffer from sudden, life-threatening allergic reactions that produce anaphylactic shock, which, if untreated, may lead to sudden collapse, seizures, coma, and death. Causes include certain drugs, vaccines, or foods to which the animal has developed a sensitivity.

Foreign bodies that interfere with a dog's healthy functioning primarily consist of toys, bits of clothing, and other objects the animal accidentally or deliberately swallows. Cats more commonly succumb to the life-threatening effects of swallowed string or yarn. Animals of all species may ingest packaging materials (especially those used to protect food) in sufficient quantities to cause life-threatening obstructions. Additionally, one section of an animal's intestine may telescope into another and effectively block that organ, or a blood clot may lodge in a primary blood vessel, producing a sudden loss of circulation to life-sustaining organs.

Given all the marvelous drugs available today, the idea of an animal succumbing to an infection seems impossible. However, drug-resistant, disease-causing organisms attack animals as well as people. Moreover, we see more and more animals with depressed immune responses, which leave them vulnerable to infections that other animals easily shake off with or without medical help.

Canine anatomy sets up some dogs for gastric torsion, during which the animal's stomach twists. In addition to the negative effects caused by the buildup of gas in the twisted organ, the obstruction of its blood supply leads to shock and collapse. Although cats rarely succumb to gastric torsion, male cats may experience urinary blockages, which, if unrelieved, can lead to the animal's death in a relatively short time.

Finally, any pet may fall victim to the elements. Although extreme heat or cold can threaten any animal's life, less extreme temperatures may pose a risk to the very young or old, or animals with other preexisting problems. Because some people enjoy sharing more demanding physical lifestyles with their pets, animals may fall out of boats and drown, or slip and fall while hiking with their owners.

Each one of these scenarios could snuff out an animal's life in a matter of minutes, hours, or days. However, even if the animal survives the physical crisis, the owner may not survive the relationship crisis that these sudden physical problems may precipitate.

ACUTE PHYSICAL PROBLEMS
THAT CAUSE OWNER STRESS

As hopeless as some physical trauma seems, many animals can and do survive it, thanks to quick thinking on their owners' parts and the advances in veterinary medicine. However, as Jeff will tell you, saving an animal's life doesn't necessarily mean saving its health and well-being.

"Lucky landed on her head when she pulled that shelving down. Although she survived, she lost one eye and smashed her muzzle so badly, the veterinarian said she'd always have breathing problems. I just couldn't deal with that for a lot of reasons."

Among the reasons owners give for euthanizing or giving up injured or seriously ill animals rather than treating them are:

- Disfigurement
- Loss of function
- Cost of treatment
- Required aftercare

For some people, the idea of a one-eyed cat or a three-legged dog bothers them so much that they could never respond in a positive way to such a pet. Other people feel the same way about other problems that may leave their pets physically impaired. In the heat of the moment Trish claimed that she would do anything to keep Caleb alive, but practically all of her interaction with him centered around her physically active life. Would she willingly stop hiking, canoeing, swimming, and biking in favor of spending all those hours taking her dog for sedate walks around the block?

"I honestly didn't think about that," she admits. "At the time, I just wanted him to live because nothing seemed worse than losing him."

Many people cite cost as the reason for not treating an animal with a life-threatening physical condition. Admittedly, circumstances do exist in which the financial burden created by treatment could undermine the relationship. If every spare cent he can scrape together must go into Lucky's treatment, Jeff's constant worry about paying his bills could undermine his once-solid relationship with his pet.

"No, I can't afford to go to the movies with you," Jeff might have to tell his friends. "Lucky's treatment costs so much, I can barely make ends meet."

Such negative feelings also might cause him to resent his injured pet—resulting in a tendency to ignore her rather than hold and pet her the way he did before her accident.

Under these circumstances, both Jeff and his pet would fare better if he had her euthanized or gave her to someone able to care for an injured pet. Some animal lovers may consider it heartless to put down a treatable pet, but withholding emotional support from a seriously ill or injured animal hardly ranks as a caring gesture, either.

> *Some animal lovers may consider it heartless to put down a treatable pet, but withholding emotional support from a seriously ill or injured animal hardly ranks as a caring gesture, either.*

Unfortunately, owners who mention cost as the reason for not treating a pet usually do so because most people will accept this explanation. Most of us know what it feels like to scrimp from paycheck to paycheck, and we can sympathize with those who don't want to take on the additional financial burden of treating a seriously injured or ill pet, even if we disagree with the person's choice. Compare your response to "I really wanted to treat Buster, but I just couldn't afford it" to how you feel when someone says, "I didn't want to put all that money into treating Buster because he's only an animal." Most of us find the second statement so cold-hearted that we'd find it very difficult not to disapprove of Buster's owner. Because most owners know how animal-loving friends and veterinary staff expect them to feel about their pets, they'll use cost to cover up a less acceptable reason, such as a less-than-perfect relationship.

Finally, the amount of aftercare that is required following an acute illness or injury may lead some owners to relinquish their pets. Like most medical practitioners, I quickly discovered that owners faced with a critically ill or injured animal typically prepare themselves for one of two outcomes: that the animal will die or that it will recover completely. And they expect the outcome to occur within a relatively short period of time. However, many acute, life-threatening conditions may take weeks or even months to resolve completely. Others never completely go away, becoming instead chronic problems with their own challenges to the quality and duration of the animal's life, a subject we'll explore in chapter four.

PREVENTING ACUTE LIFE-THREATENING SITUATIONS

What often appears to be a sudden problem almost invariably represents the end of a sequence of events we just didn't notice. Admittedly, Trish couldn't possibly know that the driver of the car that hit Caleb would choose that particular time to come speeding down her street. On the other hand, she did know that Caleb would dash through an open door if given the chance, and wouldn't come back when called.

Owners can avoid much of the risk posed by deliberate and accidental trauma, poisons, or other environmental hazards by following four simple rules:

1. Carefully inspect areas where you plan to let your pet roam *before* you allow it into that area. Be sure to check the human and animal population as well as any other potential hazards.
2. Train your pet to come on command.
3. Accept full responsibility for any problem that befalls your pet while it is unsupervised.
4. Prepare yourself to respond quickly and knowledgeably to any pet-related emergency.

Many apparently sudden medical crises arise when owners miss or ignore early, subtle warning signs. Cat owners may not notice early signs of urinary problems in their pets because they don't know how much their cats normally eat, drink, or urinate; dog owners who turn their pets loose to relieve themselves may not notice the diarrhea until it gets so bad that the animal relieves itself indoors. The more you know about your pet's normal eating, drinking, and elimination habits, as well as your pet's normal temperature, weight, and other physiological characteristics, the more quickly you can detect changes. (Consult my books *DogSmart* and *CatSmart* for a discussion of comprehensive at-home pet examinations you can do in about two minutes.) The more quickly you can detect changes, the more likely you can keep a minor early warning symptom from blowing up into a "sudden" medical crisis.

To avoid a financial crisis in case of emergency, discuss any financial limits with your veterinarian and set up a payment plan that will meet your needs *before* you give the go-ahead for treatment. Similarly, owners facing the treatment of a seriously ill or injured pet should raise the issue of aftercare if the veterinarian doesn't. You might discover that you can't provide your pet with the aftercare it needs. On the other hand, raising the issue beforehand allows you and your veterinarian to discuss options that might never occur to you otherwise.

ACUTE BEHAVIORAL PROBLEMS

It should come as no surprise that the behaviors that most often cost an animal its life typically involve aggression toward people, other animals, and/or vehicles. Although these three problems share some similarities, their unique differences warrant consideration.

PETS WHO BITE PEOPLE

Traditionally, courts have allowed dogs one bite and pretty much granted cats the right to do what they wish. But today's litigious society no longer operates that way. The increased numbers and financial value of claims filed by dog-bite victims have already led providers of homeowner-liability insurance to deny coverage to owners of certain breeds or to add a surcharge to their premiums. However, the claims that have been filed and breeds that have been blackballed don't reveal a complete picture of the canine biters. Many, many more dogs bite than get reported, and most of these dogs aren't pit bulls, Dobermans, or rottweilers. Also, contrary to popular belief, dogs more commonly bite children in their own homes or neighborhoods, not strangers.

Because of a cat's smaller mouth size, cat bites usually affect a smaller area than dog bites do. However, microorganisms more commonly found in some cats' saliva may make some people seriously ill. Consequently, although a cat's size and solitary nature precludes it from bringing down a child or frail senior citizen, cats can do quite a bit of damage with their teeth. Additionally, unlike dogs, cats can inflict serious wounds with their claws, too.

Most cases of pet aggression toward humans stem from the owner's lack of familiarity with that animal's normal behavior coupled with a lack of training that takes this behavior into account. Canine aggression usually arises from a breakdown in the human–canine pack structure that occurs when owners fail to communicate human leadership to their pets. Feline aggression more commonly springs more from a cat's sexual behaviors coupled with its predatory nature. Unknowledgeable people may stroke cats in a manner that causes them to hold with teeth and claws—a sexual response—but then really dig in when the person protests. (Again, see *DogSmart* and *CatSmart* for a complete discussion of these behaviors.)

Despite any clear-cut scientific understanding of biting behavior and how to cure it, two other issues may stymie any retraining program and lead the owner to give up the pet.

First, some owners simply can't tolerate the idea that their pet would bite anyone. Others will make excuses for the dog or cat who only bites strangers, friends, or neighbors—or maybe only the owners themselves. Wherever owners draw the line, when the pet crosses it, the owners feel so betrayed that they know they'll never trust the animal again. This lack of trust between owner and pet practically guarantees that the animal will bite again, which drastically reduces the chance of that person successfully resolving the problem.

Second, aggression aimed at people almost always indicates far deeper problems. Consequently, working on the biting behavior alone won't resolve underlying relationship issues, and the biting probably will recur. On the other hand, resolving those issues requires a great deal of time and commitment to the animal—two qualities busy owners with complex lives may not have.

PETS WHO ATTACK OTHER ANIMALS

We need only to follow the media flap that occurs when officials condemn some free-roaming pet dog to death for chasing deer or livestock to realize that many pet owners raised in urban or suburban areas don't realize that most, if not all, states have laws forbidding this behavior. Instead, these people tearfully tell themselves (and the press) that "Smiley wouldn't hurt a flea," or "He couldn't catch a deer if his life depended on it," or "He'd never seen a sheep before and was just curious."

Maybe Smiley wouldn't intentionally hurt another animal, but a lot of dogs *would*. Veterinarians, farmers, ranchers, and wildlife officials nationwide have seen mangled deer and livestock killed outright or left to die by lovable family pets. When a dog chases after another animal, can we realistically expect a farmer, rancher, or game warden to follow that dog to see if it means to cause harm? Even if we dog lovers would financially support such an endeavor, in my densely wooded area of New England, for example, the dog's target easily could wind up dead before someone caught up with it. Worse, the person might meet the dog trotting back, providing no clue to where any wounded animal might lie needing help or to be put out of its misery.

What's more, even though we may feel that our dogs should run free to do as they please, the law dictates that they cannot kill certain other animals. Consequently, owners who want their pets to run free face two choices: They can train their dogs to stay within the boundaries of their own property, never chase other animals, and always come when called. Or they can accept responsibility for their pet's death if they don't wish to train it and the untrained dog gets caught breaking the law.

"Phew!" exclaims Jeff. "I'm glad I prefer cats over dogs so I don't have to worry about that!"

Jeff can safely say that now, but that might not always hold true. As the number of pet and feral cats continues to grow, so does concern about the numbers of birds and wild creatures that these free-roaming felines consume. Already battles rage about the cat's role in our declining songbird population, and some areas even have feline leash laws. Moreover, the cat's relatively recent domestication (which barely dulled its excellent predatory skills in most cases) makes it a threat worthy of consideration. In other countries, such as Australia and New Zealand, free-roaming cats have decimated certain native wildlife populations and, without proper control, the same could certainly happen in the United States.

In spite of the brutal manner in which pets sometimes attack members of a different species, a certain amount of intraspecies fighting (that is, fighting between members of the same species) occurs, too. Dogs use their scuffles to determine pack order, a basic requirement for peaceful canine coexistence. These confrontations often make us cringe, but dogs engage in this behavior in order to *avoid* a knock-down, drag-out fight to the death.

Unlike social dogs who fight for position, more solitary cats commonly fight over territory. Because of this, free-roaming cats may fight with the same cats day after day, and they may fight more often during the breeding season—despite the fact that a resident cat may be neutered. Owners who can't bear the thought of their cats fighting should keep them indoors and choose any feline playmates for their indoor pets *very* carefully. Cats will fight every bit as vigorously—and maybe more so—to protect a stake in the owner's bedroom as they will to protect their backyard.

> *Cats will fight every bit as vigorously—and maybe more so—to protect a stake in the owner's bedroom as they will to protect their backyard.*

Some owners consider the behavior of animals attacking other animals to be quite natural animal behavior, while others find it intolerable and see it as a legitimate reason to terminate the relationship. Other owners see predatory behavior toward other animals as a prelude to similar behavior toward people. Some very well trained animals who attack other animals don't exhibit the same aggressive tendencies toward people. Unfortunately, most predatory dogs also exhibit behaviors that clearly indicate that they don't recognize their owners as leaders of their human–canine pack. In which case, the dog accustomed to biting other animals probably wouldn't hesitate to bite a person under certain circumstances. Similarly, cat owners may unwittingly involve their pets in predator–prey types of play that precipitate aggressive behavior toward people.

"Well, at least I don't need to worry about my cat attacking cars!" Jeff laughs.

True, but that doesn't let cats off the hook in relation to vehicles entirely.

PETS WHO TANGLE WITH VEHICLES

Dogs who chase cars, and pets of any species who lack vehicle or road savvy may pay a sudden and awful price. Most dogs pursue cars because their free-roaming lifestyle leads them to claim both sides of a stretch of the road as their territory, which they feel duty-bound to protect. Thus the dog will chase any car, truck, or bicycle that enters that stretch. Animals with herding instincts may try to nip at the tires of moving vehicles, while others will run alongside a car, presumably with the idea of leaping on it and immobilizing it as they would their prey.

Needless to say, no matter how well these strategies work on live prey, they fail miserably when it comes to most cars and trucks. Most vehicle-chasers wind up getting hit. Pets who chase bicycles also present their owners with the chilling possibility that the animal could topple a bike, leaving the rider to cope with an animal in a predatory mode in addition to any injuries that person may have sustained in the fall. For owners who lack the time and commitment to train their pets properly, an awareness of the moral, legal, and financial costs of any injury to the animal as a result of its behavior, as well as injury to anyone riding in the vehicle, may lead them to get rid of the animal.

Free-roaming pets who consider vehicles territorial violations quickly get eliminated in the wild, whereas road savvy is rewarded with the opportunity to mature, reproduce, and pass that quality on to offspring. Pet cats, though, often lead a peculiarly schizophrenic life. We often indulge and baby them as kittens and indoor adults. However, when we open the door and let them out, we expect them to fend for themselves. Lacking any guidance in the matter, the cat can only learn by trial and error. If it fails, it gets hit by a car; if it succeeds, it doesn't. Here again, owners who fear this happening to their pets will opt to keep them indoors. If this is not an option, they'll often consider getting rid of the cat.

ACUTE BEHAVIORAL PROBLEMS
THAT CAUSE OWNER STRESS

Clearly, the legal and moral implications of owning a pet whose behavior endangers others may lead an owner to terminate the human–animal relationship following even just one such incident or even a hint of the possibility. However, single episodes of three types of nonaggressive canine and feline behaviors also may earn the family pet a one-way ticket out of the household simply because they are so upsetting to the owner. They are:

- Vocalizing
- Inappropriate elimination
- Destructive chewing, digging, clawing, or scratching

The first day Trish leaves her new pup alone, the dog barks incessantly. When Trish returns home from work, she finds nasty notes from two neighbors and a warning from the local animal control officer, citing her pet's barking as a "public nuisance."

"I know barking is perfectly normal puppy behavior and that there are all kinds of ways to stop it," she admits. "But I just moved into this place and I don't want to upset my neighbors, let alone get in trouble with the law!" Instead, she opts to give the pup back to the couple from whom she adopted him.

Any cat may vocalize, but Siamese and their derivatives do so more commonly than other breeds. Although some owners find this enchanting and even encourage the cat to "talk," others find it highly irritating to the point of filing complaints with police or animal control officers. If the chatty cat's owners lack the wherewithal to resolve the problem in the short time these officials often allow, the owners may give up their pet.

Twenty years ago, dog owners routinely complained about their dogs urinating or defecating indoors in the owner's absence, a complaint you never heard about cats. Today, canine aggression replaces territorial marking as the chief complaint of dog owners, while cat owners rate not using the litter box as the number one feline behavioral problem. Space doesn't permit a full discussion of how these changes came about or what causes the behavior. Suffice it to say that inappropriate elimination may cause owners to terminate the relationship for one or more of the following reasons:

- Their reaction to animal waste
- The location of the waste
- The negative symbolism they attach to the animal's elimination behavior

Some people simply cannot deal with the idea of urine, feces, or any bodily waste anywhere. They turn their pets loose to eliminate in some discreet corner of the yard in which they never venture. The very sight, not to mention the smell, of waste products makes them physically ill, and the idea of such things appearing in their homes so violates their senses that they'll divest themselves of the waste-producer as quickly as possible.

Other owners can tolerate their animals relieving themselves near the back or front doors, but not in the bathroom (where they accidentally may step on it in the middle of the night), and most certainly not on their beds. Because bathrooms, bedrooms, and the owner's bed serve as logical marking places in some circumstances, a pet whose temperament leads it toward this display may find itself out on the street after one episode.

Still other owners can accept stool and urine just about anywhere—as long as they believe it results from a medical problem. However, if they discover that no medical cause for the problem exists, they conclude that the animal urinates or defecates indoors out of spite or some other negative animal emotion. Owners who believe they don't deserve such treatment may opt to get rid of the "ungrateful" pet.

The same holds true for clawing, scratching, and other destructive behaviors: If the owner's sense of esthetics doesn't allow for a pup who digs anywhere in the yard or a cat who claws anything, then a single episode may end the relationship. Other owners may tolerate digging anywhere but in the rose garden and scratching on anything but the Louis XIV loveseat. When the pet violates that sacred space, it's history. Once again, lacking an acceptable medical reason for the pet's negative behavior, uneducated owners may attribute the destruction to negative animal emotions rather than to remediable behavioral causes, thereby closing the door to any solution.

Preventing Acute Behavioral Problems

Prevention and knowledge go together like peanut butter and jelly, and nowhere does this hold truer than in the prevention of behavioral problems. Resolving such problems often takes longer because owners may wildly misunderstand what their pet communicates via the negative behavior and what their own behavior communicates to the animal. Consequently, in order to make lasting changes in an animal's behavior, owners often must make some major changes in their own behavior, too. Because the traditional treatment of animal medical problems has programmed us to see any cure as requiring little more than popping a pill into the pet's mouth two or three times a day, trying to pick up all the necessary background knowledge *and* deal with the problem behavior may seem overwhelming.

However, owners who enjoy learning all they can about their pet's species, breed, and individual behaviors gain an advantage on two fronts. First, just as knowledge of their pet's normal physiology enables them to notice and respond to medical problems sooner, their knowledge of their pet's normal behavior enables them to detect problems in this area more quickly, too. Second, knowledge frees owners from falling into the trap of assuming their pet's behavior means something that it couldn't possibly—such as revenge or spite.

Dogs who belong to owners who recognize the value of a human-centered human–canine pack structure don't display aggression toward people, other animals, or vehicles. Owners who introduce their pups to as many other dogs as possible to ensure that their pets learn the rules of normal canine social interaction early don't have to worry about their dogs getting into fights with other dogs. When their dogs do mix it up with other dogs, they know enough to stay out of it because interfering increases the probability that someone—including the owners—could get seriously hurt.

Knowledgeable cat owners understand the roles their pets' solitary, territorial, sexual, and predatory natures play in how and when the animals display aggression or mark their territory with claws, urine, or feces. Using this knowledge, they then create an environment that frees the cat from these behavioral pressures, such as providing their pets with access to carriers or other snug havens.

Knowledge about your pet certainly increases the likelihood that you will notice behavioral problems sooner and respond to them more appropriately, and that knowledge will help you avoid acute interference with the human–animal bond, too.

ACUTE BOND PROBLEMS

If we think of the bond as representing the quality of love shared by owner and pet, it seems that anything that would sever that connection in an instant must surely fall in the realm of physical or behavioral problems. Most of us can imagine requesting euthanasia for a pet suffering from a painful, terminal physical condition. Similarly, few of us would consider keeping an animal who attacked a loved one and left that person physically and emotionally scarred.

However, while our bonds with our pets inevitably affect the resolution of such acute physical and behavioral problems, problems strictly related to the bond itself usually arise when people get a pet for reasons other than that they truly want that animal for its own sake. Pets commonly fall prey to this form of aborted relationship when owners obtain the animal primarily for:

- Protection
- Companionship
- Sports

- Show
- Image

People who want a pet for protection typically choose dogs, although some owners may purchase or adopt parrots, geese, iguanas, and even cats for this purpose. People who buy young animals with the idea of training them to become aggressive, typically although unwittingly, reinforce the animal's fear rather than its courage. The less confident the young animal, the more readily you can teach it to respond out of fear. Like humans, animals can respond to fear in one of three ways: They can freeze, fight, or run. Obviously, an animal who freezes or flees when frightened won't do a very good job of protecting its owner, whereas one who attacks will at least create the illusion that it can. Needless to say, owners who know that all three behaviors signal fear will keep the "brave" biter and get rid of any "cowardly" freezers or runners as quickly as possible.

At the opposite end of the spectrum we see owners who not only get animals for companionship, but for a very specific kind of companionship. Again, these relationships may occur with pets of any species, but I hear the most complaints from cat and small-dog owners. The fifteen-year-old lumpen Persian dies and the owner gets a three-month-old Abyssinian mischief maker they hate within a matter of days.

"Cats are supposed to sit beside you and purr, not climb the walls and unravel the toilet paper," they complain.

Or they get a dachshund, terrier, or corgi, assuming its smaller size automatically makes it a lapdog. When the dog excavates the entire backyard in an afternoon or takes down a cute little bunny like a trained assassin, these owners want those dogs out of their homes *now!*

Other times owners get their pets another pet for companionship. Owners of single cats who know nothing about their pet's solitary nature routinely go out and get a second cat to keep their first cat company. When one or both of the cats makes it clear that it would rather die than live with another cat, these owners immediately evict the new cat, falsely blaming the animal rather than their own faulty thinking.

Prospective dog and cat owners routinely ask me, "What's the best breed for kids?" In spite of all the cat and dog breed books out there earnestly offering exactly that information, you'll never catch me answering that question.

"Why not?" Trish pipes up. "Everyone knows that golden retrievers love kids."

Unfortunately, like the glittering generalities applied to all breeds, the retriever–kid connection more often springs from hearsay than fact. In reality, and as with every single breed of pet animal, you can find individuals that adore kids and others you wouldn't want anywhere

> *Put a child-neutral pup in an environment with an aggressive child and it may grow up to be a kid-biter, while that same pup raised with a gentle, respectful child could become the darling of the schoolyard.*

near your child. How pups and adults react to children depends on many factors. Put a child-neutral pup in an environment with an aggressive child and it may grow up to be a kid-biter, while that same pup raised with a gentle, respectful child could become the darling of the schoolyard.

The same applies to how animals relate to one other. Although certain breeds of dogs may have earned reputations as predators, whether they develop this kind of behavior depends on their specific breeding and upbringing. Admittedly, a malamute allowed to run free may more readily develop the mind-set of a skilled predator than a Yorkshire terrier in that same environment. On the other hand, a malamute whose suburban owner channels that dog's energy toward obedience training or therapy work may never display any predatory behaviors at all, while a Yorkie who lacks training may attack anything he finds anywhere near his owner's apartment.

Rather than imposing some imaginary function upon the pet and then terminating the relationship when the animal doesn't fulfill his expectations, some owners get pets specifically to perform known species- or breed-related functions. Brittany spaniels or beagle pups who turn tail and run at the sound of the first gunshot may find themselves on their way to a new home before day's end. Cats obtained to rid old farmhouses of mice in exchange for room and board may become *felis non grata* when their owner spies them sharing their crunchies with a resident rodent.

Within the canine realm, we also see more owners participating in human-devised sports designed to mimic a particular breed's historical function. Greyhounds race around courses after scented lures; terriers charge through tiny, human-dug tunnels seeking to locate the "prey" in the shortest amount of time; huskies and malamutes pull sleds or weight-bearing pallets; and every breed imaginable leaps over barriers, climbs ladders, and performs other tests of agility for owners hoping to break one record or another. While most of the owners involved in these sports simply enjoy working with their pets, some adopt a "winning is everything" attitude. Consequently, pups who don't show the right stuff within a relatively short time, or adult animals who commit any one of a number of unforgivable sins during training or competition may find themselves looking for a new home.

This same unfortunate mentality also crops up in the show arena. Some people become so engrossed in breeding animals who conform to an arbitrary human standard that they see their animals as ribbons and trophies rather than living beings. When color, coat length, or ear size takes precedence over everything else, an animal who doesn't meet those standards loses its value in the owner's eyes. Some breeders will destroy at birth kittens and pups who have the "wrong" color or coat texture. Others will give the young animals all kinds of special care in hopes of encouraging the development of those ideals, but then will immediately withdraw any financial or emotional investment when they realize the animal will never measure up.

A variation on this theme plagues wild hybrid cats and dogs and many exotic or rare pets such as amphibians, reptiles, and some birds. Unfortunately, some people obtain these pets because they crave the attention that having an unusual pet will gain them, rather than because they care about that particular animal or its needs. When they discover that, by golly, that wolf hybrid doesn't train nearly as easily as their mom's miniature poodle, or that Bengal (a small wildcat–domestic cat cross) exhibits a much stronger predatory response than their Himalayan, they want out of the relationship—fast! After everyone in the condo complex becomes bored with *oohing* and *aahing* over the resident iguana or boa constrictor, the owner still must meet these animals' often highly specific and demanding dietary and habitat needs. Similarly, the person who buys a gorgeous but feisty parrot simply to bask in the admiration of his friends may quickly lose interest after the helpful intern who stitches up his bird-bite wounds mentions that some parrots live more than a hundred years!

While some owners of "image pets" may bail out as soon as the attention from others ceases to compensate for the time it takes to care for their pets, others may hang on until the pet's first breeding season. Abandonment may occur at this time because many animals, especially wild or semi-wild ones, display quite different behaviors during the breeding season. Male iguanas may ram themselves repeatedly into the sides of their glass enclosures in an attempt to attack their owners. Aside from the danger these animals pose to themselves, watching a self-mutilating animal through blood-smeared glass isn't what most people consider a peak pet-owning experience. Thus, the exotic animal's perfectly normal (though disturbing) behavior may serve to drive the owner's friends away. If so, that person may terminate the pet–owner relationship abruptly.

Unlike owners who give up a pet because it displays a specific behavior they find intolerable, owners concerned with image terminate the relationship because the animal fails to live up to their expectations, which typically involve displaying characteristics beyond the animal's control. Because these owners bought an image rather than a pet, they expect nothing short of perfection. When the animal doesn't measure up, they get rid of it.

"Why won't they treat problems?" Jeff wants to know. "After all, nobody's perfect."

The rush these people get comes from owning the "perfect" pet, whatever their definition of perfect may be. A good protection dog must show killer instincts from the get-go; a good mouser must hit the ground hunting; a good show animal must meet the standard; a good boa, iguana, or macaw must behave perfectly and require minimal care. The mere idea that the animal can't conform to their standard of perfection makes it imperfect in these owners' eyes; thus, they find no reason to treat it.

ACUTE BOND PROBLEMS THAT CAUSE OWNER STRESS

Some owners may opt to get rid of their pets when life alterations suddenly reveal a previously acceptable relationship with a pet as a liability. Practically all of these involve changes in owner lifestyle, including:

- The appearance of a significant other in the single owner's life
- A move to a new home
- loss of owner function

Many times, owners may foster neediness in their pets. These people view the animal's dependence and their devotion to it as proof of their great love. Unless these owners feel totally secure about their approach they, too, may do an about-face when others who might question the wisdom of this orientation come into their lives. Here again, fear or embarrassment may play a more influential role than any doubts the owner might harbor regarding the soundness of such a relationship: The brawny construction worker might not want his new love to know that he cooks for his cat or feeds her from a spoon, even though he sees this as a perfectly acceptable way to interact with a pet. Other times owners discover that they fostered their pet's neediness because they had nothing better to do with their time. When a new acquaintance presents them with other options, they suddenly see the formerly endearing pet behavior as irritating and want to shed its source as quickly as possible.

Understandably, many single owners who find themselves involved in a new human relationship may ban their pets from the bed. Although this may seem like a purely behavioral issue with the owner, an animal who sleeps in the owner's bed may share a completely different kind of bond with that person than the pet who sleeps in its own bed or on the floor. Thus, sudden banishment from the bed may completely disorient the animal. Some pets may urinate or defecate on the owner's or the intruder's belongings, or chew on furnishings or their own skin during the period of exile. One enterprising sheepdog charged into the bedroom the instant his owner opened the door and ripped a large hole in her king-size water bed, effectively dampening the dog's relationship with his owner and her new love—to say nothing of the whole room! Other pets may vomit or develop diarrhea in response to similar perceived assaults on their relationship with their owners. Once again, owners who don't understand the nature of the human–animal bond may give up these animals, labeling them as spiteful and mean for deliberately trying to ruin their owner's happiness.

An impending move to a new home may lead some people to suddenly view a previously accepted and even nurtured relationship as a liability. Owners who turned their pets loose in suburbia because they viewed them as freedom symbols may give the animals up when a new job necessitates a move into the city. Although many of these people insist they gave the animals up because they couldn't find suitable living quarters, more commonly the owners had changed their expectations of animal companionship.

"That's terrible!" Trish exclaims. "What kind of a jerk would do that?"

While some may shed an animal when they move simply because it no longer conforms to their new image of themselves, others see the problem in terms of the third group of lifestyle changes: those that affect owner function. None of us would blame the owner of a high-energy pet for giving it up because that person succumbed to a debilitating illness. In fact, we might even commend that owner for recognizing his or her new limitations and giving the pet to someone who could better meet its needs. We can even accept the owner having the pet euthanized rather than risk it harming itself or someone else who lacked the physical wherewithal to properly oversee its behavior. And most of us accept giving up a pet because the owner can't afford to care for it. Unfortunately, however, few of us extend that understanding into the less concrete but equally problematic realm of emotional function.

Like taking a new job or becoming involved in a new relationship, moving into a new home provides many people with the opportunity to start over. Because our pets often serve as painfully clear mirrors of our most intimate selves, such changes may cause us to suddenly see them and our relationship with them in a new light. If we don't like what we see, the pet becomes a painful reminder of what we are, rather than what we hope to be in the new phase of our lives. This, in turn, leaves us facing the prospect of changing the pet and ourselves while adapting to the new lifestyle. Because owners who wind up in this position most often do so because they lack knowledge about their pets' needs as well as the nature of the human–animal bond, the idea of educating themselves in addition to everything else overwhelms them.

"I said it before and I'll say it again," Trish huffs. "That's terrible."

I don't like it, either. But although emotion rather than knowledge may rule these folks at this time, some sound logic underlies it. Consistency ranks as the number one necessity for making lasting improvements in a pet's physical state or behavior, as well as strengthening the bond. Owners who can't provide this consistency only make existing problems worse. Aside from undermining the owner's relationship with his or her pet, inconsistency makes it less likely that any future owner can resolve the pet's problems, either. And that, of course, brings us to prevention.

PREVENTING ACUTE BOND PROBLEMS

I define well-bonded pets as those who could live with anyone but choose to live with their owners. Compare the pet who loves all people and who all people adore to the one who runs and hides or requires constant attention of one kind or another. Owners who lack self-confidence and knowledge about their pets' needs may deliberately or inadvertently develop relationships with them based on physical and behavioral problems rather than the animal's health. Rather than treating Spot's or Fluffy's treatable medical or behavioral problems, the owners give themselves points for tolerating these "flaws." Aside from the fact that this belief doesn't bode well for the resolution of the animal's problems, such relationships tend only to work within very narrow limits. As soon as the animal's problems or the owner's lifestyle changes, the owner is forced beyond those limits and the relationship crumbles.

Because of this, it makes sense to create relationships with our pets that celebrate our pets' as well as our own strengths, rather than weaknesses. That, in turn, will confer two benefits. First, acute, life-threatening bond problems are less likely to occur and, second, if they do, we'll more likely find ways to resolve them satisfactorily.

> I t makes sense to create relationships with our pets that celebrate our pets' as well as our own strengths, rather than weaknesses.

Acute bond and behavioral problems demand that owners trust themselves. If something about your relationship with your pet bothers you, deal with it, no matter how minor it may seem. Otherwise, it may suddenly rear up and shatter your otherwise lovely relationship like a bolt out of the blue.

Throughout this discussion, we have seen that acute problems always possess the potential to become chronic, just as chronic problems can precipitate an acute crisis. In the next chapter, we'll explore how such long-term physical, behavioral, and bond problems can lead to the loss of a pet.

CHAPTER FOUR

THE LONG GOODBYE

Pet Loss As a Result of Old Age and/or Chronic Problems

For age is opportunity no less
Than youth itself.

—HENRY WADSWORTH LONGFELLOW
Morituri Salutamus

NO ONE who knew the couple could deny that Jim and Jodie Macleod's eight-year-old cat, Jasmine, owed her life to her owners.

"Can you imagine treating a cat for cancer?" people murmured when the Macleods undertook that very task three years earlier.

During that time, Jasmine underwent numerous tests and weathered both major and minor medical crises. The last crisis, though, proved one more than her owners could bear, and they opted to euthanize her.

Just down the street, the Pellerin family awoke that same morning to find their fifteen-year-old beagle Daren dead in his bed. When both the Macleods and the

Pellerins learned that another neighbor, Tia Raynor, had just given up Fu, her two-year-old shar-pei, because she couldn't deal with his chronic skin problems anymore, they couldn't believe it.

"How could anyone give up a pet just because it needed a bath once a week?" Jim asked Mrs. Pellerin, shaking his head in disgust.

CONTINUING OUR overview of the reasons human–animal relationships end, we now turn our attention to chronic or long-term problems. Owners who lose pets as a result of a sudden crisis often say they wish they'd had more warning so they could have prepared themselves for the loss. However, conditions that occur over a period of weeks, months, or years take their toll, too. When Jim and Jodie first noticed Jasmine's intermittent diarrhea, they dismissed it, saying, "She's always scrounging around the kitchen floor and probably ate something she shouldn't have." Later, they realized that they denied the diarrhea because they didn't want to face the fact that their beloved pet might have any problem, let alone a serious one. Meanwhile, the Pellerins described Daren as "healthy as a horse" right up until that very last day because, even though he didn't race around and couldn't eat just about anything he had as a pup, he never showed any serious signs of illness, either.

Further complicating matters, although most people define "chronic" to mean any problem that persists over a long period of time, "long" may mean different things to different people. To some, "a long time" means life-long, whereas to others it means lasting more than two weeks or a month. Still others define a chronic problem in terms of its outcome. Few of us would define a fractured leg that heals uneventfully as a chronic problem even though it may take six to eight weeks to heal. On the other hand, if that fractured bone became infected, it might rate as chronic if the infection didn't respond to medication within a week or two.

As with acute problems that may result in pet loss, chronic problems fall into one of three categories:

- Physical
- Behavioral
- Bond

Like every acute problem, every chronic one possesses a physical, a behavioral, and a bond component, and we ultimately need to take all three into account to get the whole picture. However, to gain the most comprehensive view of their combined role in pet loss, we first need to understand how each individual factor may affect your pet.

CHRONIC PHYSICAL PROBLEMS

Life-threatening, chronic physical problems typically involve the gradual failure of some major organ or organs over time until the animal finally dies. However, owners also may opt for euthanasia or decide to give up a pet with a non-life-threatening chronic physical problem because they can't deal with the situation for personal reasons.

Let's explore each of these categories in more detail to see what they can teach us about how and why chronic physical problems may lead to the loss of a pet, as well as ways to prevent such a loss.

LIFE-THREATENING
CHRONIC PHYSICAL PROBLEMS

In younger animals, chronic, life-threatening physical problems often begin as an assault on one organ, the effects of which then undermine the performance of other organs. Originally, Jasmine's medical symptoms arose from a malignant tumor in her intestinal tract. Later, however, her lungs and other organs became involved as the cancer spread. Further complicating matters, the treatment took its own toll on her liver and kidneys as well as on her immune system. And even though Jasmine lived for three years, which included good days as well as bad, her owners never could escape their awareness of her gradual deterioration.

Compare that sequence of events to what happened to Daren's aging organs, which failed so slowly and uniformly that he could compensate without showing any alarming signs of problems. Like most pet owners, the Pellerins could readily dismiss the signs that did appear as "normal" aging changes for two reasons: First, we expect older animals to slow down, so we don't view signs of this as problematic or solvable. Second, over time, many owners refocus their relationships with their pets based on the animals' personalities rather than their physical appearance. In the Pellerins' case, this transformation progressed so subtly that they took great offense when a friend who hadn't seen Daren for a few years exclaimed, "Gee, Daren's gotten so old!"

Life-threatening, chronic physical problems may arise from several sources aside from normal aging. Some, like certain diseases that cause debilitating heart, liver, or kidney problems, may possess a genetic component that more commonly affects individuals of certain species and breeds. Other problems, such as diabetes, may result more from being overweight than any species-specific tendency. Still others, such as those that involve the reproductive organs, may only affect males or females. And, finally, conditions that affect the animal's immune response, while not life-threatening in and of themselves, may leave the animal defenseless against other physical conditions that are.

Regardless of the organs that are affected or the course of the disease, all of the problems in this category share the capacity to shorten the animal's life as well as its quality of life, even with the very best treatment.

CHRONIC PHYSICAL PROBLEMS THAT CAUSE OWNER STRESS

Compare the physical problems we've talked about to those that follow:

- Blindness
- Deafness
- Loss of an eye or limb
- Continuing or recurrent skin or ear problems
- Curable pet diseases contagious to humans

None of these comprises anything that the veterinary medical community would consider a life-threatening problem. On the other hand, more than a few owners of animals have euthanized or given up pets who suffer from these problems .

"That's terrible!" both of the Macleods and all of the Pellerins exclaim in unison.

Before we condemn these folks, however, we need to put our emotions aside and consider these situations as objectively as possible. On the other hand, let me acknowledge that some people simply can't get past their emotions when it comes to owning a pet that, due to illness or injury, experiences some physical disability or impairment. As we noted in chapter three, some of these people simply can't bear the idea of owning an "imperfect" pet. However, others find these physical problems so frightening that they can't respond normally to an animal who develops them.

"Well, the idea of a one-eyed dog certainly makes *me* queasy!" exclaims one of the Pellerins' teenage daughters. "If Daren had lost an eye, I don't think I could've looked at him, much less petted him!"

In the Pellerin household, other family members probably could have taken up the slack, but an animal whose sole owner emotionally abandons it that way could suffer a great deal psychologically. Similarly, if the other Pellerins felt guilty, either about the daughter's behavior or anything about the circumstances that resulted in their pet's problem, they might feel obligated to spoil Daren to atone for this.

Admittedly, spoiling their pet might seem a far superior response when compared to ignoring or despising it, but such guilt-based displays may not fulfill the animal's physical and behavioral needs any better. For example, guilty owners of disabled pets may do things for the animal, such as carry or hand-feed it, rather than allow it to learn how to accomplish these activities on its own. By doing things for the pet that the animal could and should do on its own, these owners create two problems: First, they make the animal unnecessarily dependent on them. This, in turn, undermines the animal's confidence and sets the stage for behavioral and medical problems. Second, owner guilt almost always gives way to anger and resentment toward the animal over the long run, which the animal will experience even more difficulty handling thanks to its dependence on its owner.

Chronic low-grade problems such as those that involve ears or skin may undermine the relationship and, subsequently, the animal's life because they may require a substantial investment of time, money, and emotional energy from the owner. Unlike treating cancers and life-threatening diseases, treating these problems often doesn't provide us with much opportunity for heroics.

"I can understand that," Jim Macleod sheepishly admits several months after he condemned Tia Raynor for giving up her shar-pei. "When we were treating Jasmine's cancer, we got all kinds of support from our own veterinarian and the staff at the teaching hospital where we took her, as well as from a lot of our friends. Back then I remember getting really upset with Tia for complaining about having to give Fu a medicated bath every week, thinking I'd love to be in her position. Then when Tia went on vacation for a month and

I volunteered to do the job, I couldn't imagine how she'd managed to do it for more than a year with no end in sight. Add the fact that Fu started smelling again about four days after his bath, and I really can't blame her for giving him up."

> "*When we were treating Jasmine's cancer, we got all kinds of support from our own veterinarian and the staff at the teaching hospital where we took her, as well as from a lot of our friends.*"

Jim's remarks bring us to another potentially distressful aspect of chronic non-life-threatening pet problems: dealing with pet odors, discharges, or the administration of treatments that we may find repulsive. The mere idea of routinely cleaning the goop out of a bulldog's or shar-pei's repeatedly infected wrinkles, to say nothing of wiping any recurring discharge from the penis, vagina, or rectum of a less-than-fastidious cat causes some pet owners to recoil. For other owners, the thought of putting ointment or drops in their pet's eyes every day for the rest of the animal's life makes them feel light-headed.

Finally, chronic problems such as certain kinds of parasitic infestations that pose little danger to the pet but may affect susceptible people, may lead owners of afflicted animals to relinquish their pets. Owners who have immune-deficiency diseases or otherwise compromised immune responses obviously need to take any threat posed by such animals seriously. Other people with no known health problems may feel sufficiently threatened by the mere prospect of catching anything from a pet that they'll get rid of any animal who develops a transmissible condition. Regardless of the owner's specific problem, those who can't treat and keep the animal in a manner that assures both the owner's and the pet's health and well-being may choose to give up the pet.

AN OUNCE OF PREVENTION

Once we recognize that even apparently minor chronic physical problems can threaten an animal's life, then we can begin to consider ways to ensure that situations either don't reach this point, or that they reach it in a manner that takes both the animal's and the owner's needs into account. Owners who felt comfortable treating chronic medical problems right up to their pet's death, whether naturally or by euthanasia, credit two practices with their success:

1. Open and honest communication with the veterinarian(s) from beginning to end.

2. A willingness to view and accept their pet's problem as normal.

Never, ever underestimate the value of a frank and meaningful discussion with your veterinarian regarding what your pet's treatment will entail; what you can expect in terms of the animal's response (both physically and behaviorally); and what financial, physical, and emotional demands the treatment and any consequences of it will place upon you. Only by doing so can you act out of knowledge rather than out of emotions that won't sustain you over the long haul.

Often owners get so caught up in the whirlwind of diagnostic tests aimed at identifying the cause of the animal's condition that they can avoid facing what the problem really will mean to them and their pet. Aside from paying the bill for the tests and coping with any fears of the unknown during this period, these people can easily place the burden of this phase primarily on the veterinarian. Some owners (and veterinarians) also believe that the veterinarian should control the next phase: if and how to treat the problem. However, failure to become involved in the animal's care from the beginning can lead to confusion and misunderstanding further down the line.

"I agree," Jodie concurs as she recalls the last years with Jasmine. "I was all for doing whatever the veterinarian told us and didn't want to waste what I saw as critical time discussing things in detail. Luckily, Jim is much more methodical than I am and, before he gave permission for them to do anything to Jasmine, he insisted on knowing everything that was going to happen to her, why, and what we could expect. In retrospect, I know we fared a lot better than many people who treat their pets for long-term problems because we knew what we and Jasmine were in for from the beginning. Between ourselves, and with our veterinarians, we also discussed what we considered a quality life for her as well as ourselves because we didn't want our own feelings or confusion to result in her suffering needlessly when the end came."

Just as each of us has a different definition for a quality life for ourselves, we also maintain a unique definition of a quality life for our pets. When our pets suffer from life-threatening or potentially life-threatening conditions, whether or not others agree with our definition carries less weight than how this definition affects the treatment of the animal. Unfortunately, though, most of us don't give this a thought until *after* our pets develop a problem; then emotions rather than facts may cloud our judgment and cause us not to treat a problem we later wish we had, or to treat one we later regret we did.

"I can see how getting all the facts before treating any chronic problem makes things better all around," agrees Mr. Pellerin. "But I'm not sure how viewing an animal with terminal cancer or diabetes as 'normal' helps. Such serious problems surely shouldn't be taken lightly."

Viewing a pet with serious chronic problems as normal in no way means dismissing the severity of its situation. Rather, owners should view *treating* their animal's problems as a normal part of their lives, not unlike taking a shower or brushing their teeth. By doing so, administering medications and implementing any special dietary or exercise protocols becomes part of their daily schedule and, as such, carries little emotional charge. They don't love their pets any more or less because they must medicate them every single day because they don't see this care routing as a burden.

Ironically, as odd as this approach sounds to Mr. Pellerin, he and his family, like many owners of aging animals, automatically incorporated many of Daren's evolving age-related limitations or demands into their schedule with nary a thought. This typically happens, of course, because age-related changes often occur gradually and because we expect them as animals get older. None of the Pellerins gave it a second thought when the veterinarian recommended switching Daren to a senior diet; none of them questioned the old dog's morning stiffness on cold, damp days.

"Just like Grampa!" one of the Pellerin girls would tease the old dog as she slowed her pace for their daily walk.

When owners of younger pets that suffer from limiting physical conditions respond to their animals with that same degree of acceptance rather than agonizing over the unfairness of it all, they and their pets fare much better, too.

At the same time, because changes in all pets' health may creep up on us, taking a wellness-oriented approach rather than a problem-oriented one makes a lot of sense. Instead of conducting medical tests to determine the animal's problem, the wellness approach does it to establish a specific health database for each animal.

"What good does that do?" Jodie wants to know.

As much faith as many people invest in the ability of medical tests to diagnose physical problems, most tests remain relatively crude. A fair amount of organ damage may result before a blood test will register a problem; a significant number of malignant cells must amass before even the most sophisticated imaging equipment can detect them. What's more, the "normal" values used to judge these test results represent species averages; a particular breed, line, or individual animal normally may possess a higher or lower value.

"What difference does that make?" Mrs. Pellerin wonders as she leafs through Daren's uneventful medical records.

In a healthy animal, not much. However, when slowly evolving problems arise, such specific baseline data could enable the veterinarian to detect any changes sooner. For example, suppose that Daren's normal liver-function test values fell in the low–normal range and he experienced liver problems that raised those values into the high–normal range. Without test results collected from a healthy Daren with which to compare those new results, the veterinarian would miss this meaningful change.

Rather than taking a wellness approach, other owners of healthy animals, and especially healthy older pets, may adopt an "If it ain't broken, don't fix it" attitude. Because Daren essentially appeared normal right up until his last day, the Pellerins felt no need to seek veterinary care for him.

"He didn't have any problems!" Mrs. Pellerin protests. "He was a wonderful dog who lived a good long life and died quietly in his sleep!"

Mrs. Pellerin makes another valid point. Our technology-based medical system has focused so much on preventing death that for some people the idea that an individual could die "naturally" simply doesn't compute. While most of us don't claim immortality for ourselves or our pets, some of us still insist that when death occurs, regardless of the animal's age, there must be a specific cause for it—preferably one with a Latin name. Owners who don't want to hear that Rex or Fluffy died of old age, as well as owners like the Pellerins who do accept this cause, may find themselves in the awkward position of defending their beliefs at a most difficult time. (In chapter ten we'll talk about creating advance directives or living wills for pets, an exercise that will enable all pet owners, and especially those with aging animals, to work through end-of-life decisions beforehand so that they'll feel comfortable with their choices when the time comes.)

Although veterinarians often don't see the animal's behavior as a reason to treat or not to treat a chronic physical problem, some owners don't see it that way. Tia tolerated her shar-pei's nippiness and resistance to handling as long as he remained healthy. However, when she faced the prospect of regularly bathing such a dog for the rest of his life, she found that his negative behavior added a dimension to the situation that made the problem impossible for her to cope with.

CHRONIC BEHAVIORAL PROBLEMS

As with other chronic problems, chronic behavioral problems may pose life-threatening consequences in and of themselves as well as lead to an owner giving up an animal because of his or her negative feelings about the behavior. Additionally, owners of pets with chronic behavioral problems may suffer more than those whose animals succumb to chronic medical problems, for two reasons:

1. Many of these animals are physically healthy.

2. Treating behavioral problems carries more of a stigma than treating medical ones.

Whether right or wrong, when people see a healthy, good-looking animal they expect it to be well-behaved. Moreover, even though some people may condemn the behavior of certain breeds (such as rottweilers, pit bulls, and Siamese or Abyssinian cats) based on personal prejudice, those who spend good money to own such purebreds expect that money to buy them good behavior as well as that unique look.

"Doesn't it?" Jim Macleod wants to know as he pages through one of the cat magazines he and Jodie love to read.

It might, but it might not. In spite of the fact that temperament rates few, if any, points in many purebred show arenas, numerous breed descriptions give such glowing accounts about a particular breed's temperament that it seems nothing short of miraculous that these animals don't sport halos and wings. Nonetheless, a single breed may exhibit a tremendous range of behavior, even within a line or litter, and owners who neglect to address behavioral problems in their purebreds will fare worse than owners of mixed breeds who make this same mistake. Not only must these owners then live with a physically healthy animal whose behavioral problems might drive them up the wall, but they may have paid hundreds of dollars for this pleasure.

Even though I can safely say that behavioral problems remain the number one cause of canine and feline death, abandonment, or relinquishment in this country, I also know that seeking help for those problems carries a certain amount of stigma. Some of this no doubt springs from our deeply rooted fears of behavioral versus physical problems in members of our own species. We can muster all kinds of sympathy for the person with a hot virus or painful injury, but we shy away from those with "mental problems." Within the canine arena, most of us accept that a new pup should receive a certain amount of training. However, at the same time, most of us also believe that any idiot can train a dog, especially given the hundreds of books, videos, and television shows that guarantee to show us exactly how to do it. Once we invest in such a program, we expect the dog to behave itself for life.

> *Though behavioral problems remain the number one cause of canine and feline death, abandonment, or relinquishment in this country, seeking help for those problems carries a certain amount of stigma.*

Given these basic beliefs, it comes as little surprise that, for more than a few owners, admitting that their pet has a problem amounts to admitting that they failed to accomplish an idiot-simple task. Consequently, rather than dealing with the problem, they hope it will miraculously disappear. Perhaps Skippy will outgrow his biting when he gets his permanent teeth; maybe Sparky will stop barking when she and her owners move out of the city; surely Chloe will calm down after the kids go to college.

Unfortunately, though, such miracles rarely happen. The fundamental human–canine issues that lead to practically all negative canine behaviors will persist if the owner doesn't consciously confront and deal with them. Not only will failure to address these issues cause any negative behavior to persist, it most likely will get worse until it reaches life-threatening proportions.

Nonetheless, the idea of taking the dog to a "pet shrink," let alone making major changes in their own beliefs about why dogs act the way they do, may require a tremendous amount of effort as well as commitment to the pet on the part of the owner.

When on top of everything else, friends and relatives scoff at the owner who seeks professional help to resolve the animal's problems, that person may find it easier to live with the negative behavior or get rid of the dog.

For all of that, owners of problem dogs often fare much better than owners of problem cats when it comes to any stigma related to getting help. A person who seeks professional help for a feline behavioral problem more likely will face ridicule because of two erroneous beliefs about cats that pervade our society:

1. Cats can take care of themselves.

2. You can't train a cat.

Given these two commonly held myths, the conventional "wisdom" views a cat owner who seeks help as at least a bubble or two off plumb.

Unlike dogs, whose social behavior parallels that of humans in many ways, more solitary cats present us with such a unique behavioral repertoire that educating owners of problem cats about normal cat behavior often becomes a necessary first step. That, in turn, means that the owner may need to educate others involved in the problem about feline behavior, too. Unfortunately, the unique, almost schizophrenic nature of the human–feline bond often subjects owners who attempt such education to further ridicule. When a negative response comes from family members or friends, or if the commitment to the cat isn't strong enough to withstand the criticism, once again the owner may elect to either accept the negative behavior or get rid of the pet.

As you can tell from the discussion so far, chronic behavioral problems can potentially result in the animal's death or loss directly or indirectly through the strain they place on the human–animal relationship.

LIFE-THREATENING CHRONIC BEHAVIORAL PROBLEMS

In the last chapter, we discussed behavioral problems such as aggression, vocalizing, inappropriate elimination, or destructive chewing, digging, or scratching where a single incident might lead the owner to terminate the relationship. More often, though, owners tolerate this behavior for weeks, months, or even years until something suddenly turns that chronic problem into an acute one and forces the owners to deal with it. Most owners tolerate behavioral problems for one of three reasons:

1. They initially don't see the behavior as a problem.

2. They perceive any treatment as more problematic than the behavior itself.

3. They gain some benefit from owning an animal with behavioral problems.

Just as the signs of a slow-growing cancer in our pets may appear so gradually that they elude us for months or even years, behavioral problems can creep up on owners, too.

Consider what happened to Daren's littermate, Honey, who belonged to Mrs. Pellerin's niece, Nina Fredericks. From day one, everyone who knew Honey described her as "pushy." If she wanted attention, she'd nudge your hand or stick her face in yours. If that didn't work, she'd leap up and bark at you. Before Nina opened the door to take Honey for a walk, she had to brace herself lest the dog drag her through it. As time went on, Honey also took to growling when she didn't get her own way.

"The vet and the groomer said Honey growled at them for no reason, but they don't realize how upset she gets when you look at her a certain way." Nina made excuses even though she was beginning to feel uneasy about her pet's behavior.

When Honey's growls at the letter carrier and meter reader escalated to snapping, Nina explained, "Honey doesn't like strange men," but her uneasiness grew even more.

When Honey bit a neighbor's child who ran into the yard to retrieve a ball, Nina opted to get rid of the dog, saying, "She has too many problems."

In this situation, Nina's failure to respond to her pet's initial problem ultimately created two others. Not only did Honey's bad behavior escalate from irritating but minor chronic problems to major ones, but Nina's acceptance of the unpleasant but tolerable problems set the stage for ever more serious behavioral problems down the line.

"How can letting a dog nudge you make it bite?" Mrs. Pellerin asks.

By accepting all of Honey's behavior on the dog's terms rather than her own, Nina effectively ceded leadership of her and Honey's human–canine pack to the dog. As Honey grew older, she added more aggressive displays in an attempt to protect her territory. Thus, even though all of Honey's chronic problems appeared quite unrelated, they all sprang from the same cause: a lack of human leadership in the human–canine pack.

Unless a chronic problem sufficiently threatens their pet's life or themselves, many owners will choose to accept it rather than treat it, simply because of the time and energy it takes to resolve long-standing behavioral problems. Not only that, but many times the owner must change as much or more than the pet in order to solve the problem—something many owners don't want to do. When psychotropic drugs such as fluoxetine (Prozac) or buspirone (Buspar) first made their appearance on the behavioral scene, owners of animals with chronic aggression or elimination problems saw these as a gift from the gods: Praise be, all they had to do was give the dog or cat a pill once or twice a day to solve the problem! In reality, though, the drugs don't solve the problem, but merely eliminate its visible signs. As long as the animal stays on the medication (assuming it works in the first place), it behaves more acceptably. But unless the owner makes all the necessary corrective changes in themselves and their pets, the behavior will return when they discontinue the medication.

"So why not just keep the animal on the drug forever?" asks one of the Pellerin kids.

"Because the drugs are really expensive and you have to do regular blood and other tests to monitor the animal for negative side effects, and that adds even more to the cost," Nina volunteers. "I did consider drugs for Honey, but it didn't make sense to trade in her behavioral problems for medical ones."

In this situation, we see how Nina evolved from seeing her pet's problems as inconsequential to viewing them as overwhelming. Had she opted to ignore them and hope for the best because treating them involved too much work, she would have joined our second group of owners of pets with chronic problems: those who attempt to rearrange their lives to accommodate the animal's negative behavior. For some, that may mean living in dog-chewed or cat urine–soaked homes, and meeting their friends and doing all of their entertaining elsewhere. For others, it means locking the pet in the bedroom before they open the door to guests, staying away from the pet's "sensitive spots" (the animal's tummy or a favorite chair, for example), or adhering to any one of a number of habits they've devised to avoid confronting the problem.

Rather than treating or ignoring negative behaviors, a third group of owners will tolerate the displays because they believe doing so demonstrates their superior love for their pet. I won't get into the many ramifications of what I call the St. Francis Syndrome (which also can occur in physical and bond problems), except to say that these owners believe they gain more positive attention from owning misbehaved than well-behaved pets. If so, little reason exists for them to correct the problem.

Traditional thinking maintains that no pet will die of a chronic behavioral problem unless the owner chooses to put it down. However, most of the dogs who routinely chase cars eventually get hit, and sometimes deliberately by motorists tired of being harassed. Many animals who chew anything and everything eventually chew and swallow something toxic. If their injuries don't kill them outright, these animals' owners may opt to euthanize rather than treat them, saying, "What's the use? He'll only get hit (or eat something he shouldn't) again." Dogs and cats who routinely attack people or other animals may suddenly "disappear" from upscale neighborhoods or die of gunshot wounds in rural settings. Still other pets may focus on attacking another animal so single-mindedly that they don't realize that their quarry has led them right into the path of an oncoming truck.

Although animals suffering from chronic behavioral problems can come to some very gruesome ends, the very nature of these problems also greatly increases the probability that some change in the owner's life rather than the animal's behavior itself will lead the owner to terminate the relationship.

CHRONIC BEHAVIORAL
PROBLEMS THAT CAUSE OWNER STRESS

In the last chapter we saw how owners could instantly perceive once-tolerated behaviors as suddenly intolerable, precipitating a crisis. Now we must consider what can happen when owners accept negative behavior over a long period of time. In general, owners may euthanize or give up animals with chronic behavior problems when the behavior threatens

- The owner's other interactions with the pet
- The owner's interactions with other people

From the beginning, Tia described Fu's personality as "about as fun-loving as a toilet seat." She accepted this, however, because the naive breeder told Tia that what she viewed as Fu's intolerant and inflexible nature really reflected a prized canine temperament quality known as being "reserved." Tia could accept this as long as Fu remained healthy or allowed her to treat him with a minimum of hassles when he succumbed to a medical problem. However, when it became apparent that chronic medical problems would plague him forever, and that his personality would make treating him a nightmare, she called it quits.

In Tia's case, Fu's chronic medical problems made his negative behavior more of a liability than ever. Owners of healthy pets with strictly behavioral problems may become involved in a vicious cycle in which they punish the animal for the display, then feel guilty because they know they did nothing to prevent or treat it. This, in

Traditional thinking maintains that no pet will die of a chronic behavioral problem unless the owner chooses to put it down. However, most of the dogs who routinely chase cars eventually get hit . . .

turn, leads them to ignore the behavior or even spoil the animal to soothe their own guilty feelings, both of which simply reinforce the problem. Unfortunately, for all too many of these owners, the day comes when the cat's peeing on the bed or the dog's chewing the rug causes something to snap, and the owner reacts in such an inappropriate manner—perhaps flinging the pet against a wall or screaming at it to the point the poor animal flees in terror—that the owner feels horrified by the outburst. Fearing for the animal's safety as well as their own mental well-being, they give up the pet. Sadly, few will then disclose the pet's problem or their own less-than-ideal approach to it to any prospective new owners or shelter personnel, fearing that this admission will reflect badly on them or undermine the animal's chances of finding a good home.

In addition to previously tolerated negative behavior becoming intolerable when it interferes with the owner's image of him- or herself as a loving, qualified pet owner, it also may become unacceptable when it interferes with the owner's interactions with other people. As long as no one calls them on it, some people will allow their pets to break the rules—whether laws or simply unwritten social conventions—until they're caught in the act. Consequently, the owner of the dog who repeatedly takes off and refuses to come when called during their walks in the park may view her pet's behavior as a mild irritant for years—until she gets a ticket for violating local leash laws. Owners who rent their homes may never quite find the time to address their pets' destructive behaviors—until they receive a nasty note from the landlord pointing out that such animal behavior violates Section 8, Paragraph 2 of their lease. Faced with the seemingly overwhelming task of altering chronic behavior instantly, these owners may give up or euthanize the animal rather than run afoul of the law or lose their homes.

New people in the owner's life—particularly new love interests—also may cause owners to give up pets with chronic behavioral problems that the owners have tolerated up to that point. Although sometimes the new addition may come right out and say, "Either that #$*#@% barking dog goes or I do," owners more commonly give up their pets because they don't like what the animal's misbehavior might reveal about themselves to the new person.

For example, suppose you allow your cat to pee in your houseplants. You don't like this and suspect you could find a way to prevent the behavior, but you're just too busy. Plus you know other cat lovers who put up with this and even worse behavior. One day, you're chatting with your new boss whom you want to impress with your ability to handle a particularly challenging project. When the business talk gives way to casual conversation, another worker mentions cats.

"I love cats," the boss says to you. "But I can't stand cat fanatics. My sister has cats and she lets them pee in her houseplants. Can you believe that? What kind of a moron would put up with that? By the way, I pass right by your place on my way home. Mind if I stop in some day after work next week to see those charts you're working on for the big meeting?"

In this bit of fancy, we can see how situations may arise in which the owner's acceptance of problem pet behavior might undermine others' feelings about that person's competency in totally unrelated areas. Whether it's a valid connection or not, if owners care enough about what others think of them, this may undermine their relationship with the pet to the point that they give up the animal.

PREVENTING CHRONIC BEHAVIORAL PROBLEMS

Every chronic behavioral problem begins with one single episode that the owner chooses to ignore or to excuse rather than resolve. From then on it becomes easier to ignore or make excuses for the second, third, and successive episodes, too. The best way to prevent chronic behavioral problems from escalating to life-threatening proportions involves treating problems as they arise. Negative behaviors in pups or kittens that owners can eliminate in a matter of weeks will take months or more to resolve in an older animal.

If *anything* your pet does bothers you, deal with it. Don't dismiss it as normal behavior if you don't consider it normal. For example, Daren's and Honey's beagle genes lead them to sniff anything and everything, including certain areas of the human anatomy most folks consider private. Mrs. Pellerin decided that, normal beagle behavior or not, she wouldn't allow her dog to goose anyone. Nina, on the other hand, let Honey nose-search others because "that's what beagles do," even though she deplored the behavior. However, every time Honey displayed the behavior, it eroded her relationship with her owner. Although Nina didn't give up Honey because of her sniffing, the behavior earned the dog another black mark that added to the total as other problems arose.

Equally important, when you treat a chronic behavioral problem, do so because you believe it's the best thing to do for you and your pet. Don't treat the problem because the law, your neighbor, or your cousin says you should; don't treat the problem because the animal will die if you don't. Although all those reasons are terribly compelling, nothing but a sincere desire to create a well-behaved pet will generate the commitment necessary to resolve long-standing problems.

"Don't you think knowing you'll have to give up the animal or put it down if you don't solve the problem is a good enough reason?" asks Nina.

Perhaps it should be, but I know from experience working with many owners of pets with chronic behavioral problems that it isn't. Fear of loss and even of death itself doesn't come close to providing the quantity and quality of energy generated by a genuine love for that pet and a desire to live happily with it. No one likes to live with fear, and eventually owners who undertake a training program fueled by this emotion run into two problems:

1. They lack the energy they need to sustain them and their pets over the long haul.

2. They come to resent the animal and anyone who has tried to pressure them into treating it.

Needless to say, fear-based training doesn't resolve the animal's problem. In fact, it usually makes it worse.

As we've seen, the longer duration of chronic medical or behavioral problems makes it impossible to separate the relationship from the equation. Chronic medical problems may lead to chronic behavioral and bond problems as surely as the other way around, to the point that the components become so inextricably entwined we can't separate them. Still, three chronic bond problems do deserve special mention.

CHRONIC BOND PROBLEMS

Unlike chronic physical or behavioral problems that cause owners to euthanize or give up a pet, bond problems that elicit similar responses usually spring from the owner's very best, albeit often misguided, intentions. Put another way, these owners get pets for one of three questionable reasons:

- To fulfill a need or desire to be needed.
- To "elevate" an animal to the level of a person.
- To delight the kids or someone else incapable of caring for the pet.

In chapter three we saw how some owners may wake up one morning to the horrible realization that the pet they unwittingly allowed to take over their lives has become a humorless tyrant as well as a menace to society. However, others deliberately set out to create exactly such a relationship with their pets.

"Why would anyone do such a thing?" Jim says, shaking his head in amazement.

"I think I can understand how it could happen," Tia counters. "I never felt afraid to go anywhere when Fu was with me because just the way he carried himself and stared at people made them back off. If I'd lived in a crowded city rather than in a neighborhood with lots of kids where everyone knows everyone, I think I would have consciously or subconsciously wanted him to take care of me."

Had she wanted Fu to take care of her, Tia would have consciously or subconsciously rewarded those canine behaviors that supported this belief. As long as her lifestyle didn't conflict with Fu's behavior, the relationship would have remained mutually rewarding. However, if the day came when Tia wanted to admit someone to her home whom Fu considered a threat, the dog wouldn't have hesitated to override her wishes and threaten—or even attack—that person. Similarly, if she wanted to do something (such as yank him away from the visitor) that he found unacceptable, he wouldn't have hesitated to threaten or bite her, either.

> If anything *your pet does bothers you, deal with it. Don't dismiss it as normal behavior if you don't consider it normal.*

Sadly, when human–canine relationships collapse, the owners will euthanize or give up the dog, citing aggression as evidence of the animal's unpredictable and even psychotic nature. However, nothing could be further from the truth. In reality, the dog responded to the perceived intruder and his owner's interference in a perfectly predictable way given the nature of their particular human–animal bond: The *owner's* unpredictable response, not the dog's, caused the problem. Not only that, but we can even go so far as to say that the dog perceived any attack on the meddling owner as being for that person's benefit. After all, the dog is trying to protect her, something that she's communicated she wants done in countless different ways over the years. Given that long-standing relationship, how can he *not* give her a disciplinary nip to get her off his back so he can protect her from a big, brawny stranger?

Other times, owners swing in quite the opposite direction, reinforcing personality traits that make the animal highly dependent on them because it makes the owner feel good. Unfortunately, for many owners this means reinforcing pet fears that only they can quell. And although they may even realize what they're doing, they take such pleasure in soothing the frightened pet and protecting it from the thunderstorm, meter reader, or sound of the street sweeper that they perpetuate the dependent relationship.

Other owners may foster needy rituals that become so incorporated into their relationship with their pets that the success of the relationship comes to depend on those habits. For example, relationships that center around the owner cooking special foods for the pet or refusing to travel anywhere without the animal may become co-dependent over time. The owner can't bear not to cook for the animal any more than the pet will eat any other kind of food; the owner can't enjoy himself away from the pet any more than the pet can enjoy itself away from the owner.

Here again, as long as the owner and pet can remain within an environment where the owner can fulfill these special needs, no problems arise. However, if the owner can't soothe the frightened pet, cook the special food, or take the pet along, the very dependencies that defined the bond become the cause of its disintegration.

Another group of owners may relate to pets as child-like, usually somewhat dim-witted, fur-covered humanoids. These so-called anthropomorphic relationships usually develop for one of two reasons:

1. The owner actually wants a child but can't have one for some reason.

2. The owner believes that treating a pet like a human demonstrates a greater love and concern than treating it as a member of its own species.

Although often initiated with the highest ideals, bonds based on one or both of these owner beliefs invariably fail for the simple reason that animals *aren't* humans. They possess such unique and oftentimes wonderful physical and behavioral needs that treating them like humans, even in the very best human need–fulfilling ways, won't work. Over time, failure to meet the animal's species-specific needs may lead to physical and behavioral as well as bond problems. Owners who then try to treat those physical and behavioral problems the same way they would treat a person's problems may make them even worse.

In addition to chronic anthropomorphic relationships spelling trouble for the animal's long-term health and behavior, their often narrowly defined limits may cause problems, too. As totally engrossed as these owners may become in their pets' lives, few other people may share this view. When problems necessitate entrusting the pet's care to someone else, these owners may discover that no one wants to take on the job. Other times, the entrance of a Mr. or Ms. Right who raises the possibility of real babies, or the introduction of someone who doesn't agree that the owner's relationship with the pet is healthy, may cause the collapse of the human–animal relationship.

The tragedy of long-term relationships based on owner or animal neediness, or of those that treat animals as humans, lies in the irreparable harm that they can do to the animal over time. Consequently, when something changes such that the relationship no longer works for the owner, the chances of finding a new home with an owner willing to relate to the pet in that way— even if the animal would permit this, which many won't—are slim. That, in turn, means that animals raised in such environments will be euthanized if the owner can't maintain his or her half of the relationship for some reason.

Finally, buying pets for the kids or getting them as gifts for others may lead to chronic bond problems if the original purchaser doesn't intend to assume full responsibility for that animal from the beginning. Ideally, the kids or Grandma will so love the pet that they'll immediately take charge of it. However, expecting a four-year-old or an eighty-year-old to do this automatically puts an unreasonable strain on the human–animal relationship from day one. The recipients may not even want or like that particular animal. And even if they do, they may lack the necessary knowledge or skill to relate to it properly. Because of this, they may give the animal mixed signals, or the pet may become a source of frustration rather than joy. This, in turn, may lead the person who originally introduced the animal to feel guilty, and open a Pandora's box of complications that can sabotage any human–animal relationship. Over time, this lack of commitment to the animal will result in problems, any one of which could serve as the straw that breaks the already fragile relationship's back. The common result is that the owner gives up the pet.

As with all of the other problems we've discussed that lead to the loss of a pet, prevention can save everyone a lot of heartache.

PREVENTING CHRONIC
BOND PROBLEMS

As complex as bond problems can become, we can sum up how to prevent them with two simple rules that echo throughout the preceding pages.

1. Never get a pet for any reason other than because you sincerely want one.

2. Always remember that each animal possesses its own needs, and that responsible pet ownership involves knowing and meeting those needs as well as your own.

If these two basic principles form the foundation of the human–animal relationship, then the likelihood of losing a pet because of a chronic bond problem decreases significantly, and the owner's chance of coping with such a loss without regret should it occur increases dramatically.

Now that we know what happens to pets that die or are given up, the reasons this happens, and ways to avoid being caught in this situation, we turn our attention to the different ways we respond to the loss of a pet.

CHAPTER FIVE

GUILT PLUS FIVE

Pet Loss and the Healing Process

> *Healing is a matter of time, but it is sometimes also a matter of opportunity.*
>
> —HIPPOCRATES
> *Precepts*

"I'M GETTING really worried about my mom," Tony Robichaud confesses to his coworker, Chris Perkins. "Her old Scottish terrier just died, but instead of dealing with it, Mom's been on an emotional roller coaster. One day she goes on and on about all the things she should have done to keep Dundee alive. The next day she's ranting about the vet, saying he's incompetent and that she should have taken Dundee to someone else. No sooner does she finally seem to accept things than the whole cycle starts all over again. I tell you, much as I liked Dundee, I wish Mom would get over this!"

"Don't hold your breath," commiserates Chris. "My husband still can't accept the fact that our cat Tipper is dead, and we had her put to sleep more than six months ago."

"I can understand that," chimes in their supervisor, Lolly Goodwin. "My cat, Walter, disappeared five years ago and I still can't pass the field where I last saw him without getting all weepy."

IN THIS chapter we begin our exploration of the different ways people respond to pet loss. Most grief counselors now accept the groundbreaking work of physician Elisabeth Kübler-Ross, who described the five stages people go through as they come to terms with their own impending death or that of a loved one:

- Denial
- Anger
- Bargaining
- Depression
- Acceptance

Although traditionally referred to as the grieving process, I find that terminology misleading for two reasons. First, these stages may or may not represent a linear sequence, depending on the individual. Some owners zip through denial, anger, and bargaining, then cycle through anger and bargaining again before reaching depression. Other owners get stuck at one stage or another, sometimes for an extended period, while others never move beyond a certain stage at all. Second, because the sequence ideally ends with the acceptance of the loss of a loved one, a comforting rather than a sad outcome, I prefer to think of this as a healing rather than a grieving process.

In addition to working through this sequence, owners facing the loss of a pet by any means also may experience a certain amount of guilt. Rather than functioning as a separate stage, however, that guilt may permeate the whole process, making it more difficult for owners to reach acceptance. Consequently, before we can understand the various stages of the healing process and how to negotiate them, we first need to understand how guilt can rear its ugly head every step of the way.

GUILTY UNTIL PROVEN INNOCENT

For years, I've maintained that guilt more than any other emotion determines the true nature of our bonds with our pets. In the last three decades, as more and more women entered the workforce by choice, and as more couples realize it takes two incomes just to make ends meet, that guilt has reached epidemic proportions. For many people, owning a pet represents a major conflict between what their minds and their hearts tell them or, more specifically, between the two conflicting messages that arise from their hearts and minds.

All animal lovers intuitively know what science is just beginning to prove: the more complex our lives, the more animal companionship may help smooth the rough spots, giving our mental and physical health a boost. At the same time, though, we're often left feeling guilty about how we treat the furry or feathered friend who bestows these wonderful benefits: We leave Sugar alone for hours at a time; we feed her the same dull-looking food, day in and day out; we go on vacation and leave her with some stranger; we get involved in an important project or new partner and pay even less attention to her than before.

If such guilty feelings routinely influence our relationships with our pets, it should come as no surprise that guilt may attack with a vengeance when we lose a pet by any means.

THE NATURE OF GUILT
STEMMING FROM PET LOSS

Consider what happened to Tony Robichaud's mother, Ellie, and her old Scottish terrier, Dundee, whom she got shortly after Tony and his sister left home.

"Ellie's suffering from empty-nest syndrome, so she replaced the kids with a dog," her husband, Jack, jokingly told their friends at the time.

Ellie doted on Dundee from the moment she got him. They went on long walks together and he became her constant companion and confidante as she worked in her garden, baked and cooked for the holidays, or redecorated the house.

However, ten years later Jack retired and the couple began to make good on their promise to see as much of the world as they could. Shortly after they returned home from a particularly wonderful trip, twelve-year-old Dundee collapsed. Tests revealed a large, inoperable mass on his liver, and he died less than a month later. Instantly, and like many owners, Ellie immediately felt overwhelmed by guilt.

"Oh, why did I ever leave you?" she softly crooned to the old dog during his last days and after he died. "If only I'd been here, this never would have happened."

Similarly, Chris Perkins's husband, Bill, can't get past the fact that he took the family cat, Tipper, to the veterinary clinic and held her while the veterinarian euthanized her.

"I know I did the right thing," he insists. "But I just feel so guilty about doing it."

In spite of the fact that Tony considers his mother's

> *For many people, owning a pet represents a major conflict between what their minds and their hearts tell them or, more specifically, between the two conflicting messages that arise from their hearts and minds.*

reaction to Dundee's death excessive, he can easily summon reasons why he should feel guilty about giving up his dog, Leo, because of the animal's behavioral problems. And what pet owner *can't* sympathize with the guilt experienced by Lolly Goodwin and other owners of pets that one day disappear? Thoughts such as "If only I hadn't let him out that morning," "I should have looked for him longer," or "If only I'd put an ID tag on him" haunt them.

Given guilt's universality, we can't help but ask the obvious question: What purpose does guilt play in the healing process?

GUILT'S ROLE IN THE HEALING PROCESS

As understandable and even natural as all these guilty owner responses seem, does guilt help or hinder the healing process? Based on more than twenty-five years of interactions with owners coping with the loss of a pet, I believe that, overall, guilt does more harm than good.

"You don't see acknowledging the fact that you really screwed up to the point that it cost your pet its life a good thing?" Bill Perkins asks incredulously.

I do see acknowledging that fact as absolutely crucial for the success of any relationships with any *future* pets, but most owners who acknowledge their error—and avoid repeating it—eventually let go of the guilt. Those who persistently link guilt to a lost pet fail to recognize three realities:

1. We can't change the past.

2. Guilt ultimately leads to resentment.

3. Unresolved guilt from one relationship may plague future ones.

We lose pets, sometimes under the most horrible conditions. Once we see the body, turn the animal over to someone else, or give up the search, our physical relationship with that pet ceases to exist. We may still think about the animal; we may still sense its presence in some other way; we may even actually see or think we see it with someone else. But we no longer routinely share the same physical space. Given that fact, ruminating over what we should have done with, for, or to that particular animal serves no purpose. The issue isn't what we did in the past, but what we intend to do now to ensure that we won't make the same mistakes again with another animal.

Unresolved guilt ultimately leads to resentment. Admittedly, all owners who believe they failed their pets may initially gain something positive from the guilt. For example, when Tony gave up his one-year-old dog, Leo, because his landlord threatened to evict him and his constantly barking and destructive, chewing pet, Tony found the tongue-lashing his neighbor gave him cathartic.

"I knew it was my fault that Leo had those problems," he conceded. "And it seemed only right that my neighbor would rake me over the coals for what I'd done."

Later, however, he came to resent the neighbor's continued references to Leo's "despicable behavior."

"It got so bad, I'd just look at Leo's picture and get pissed off at my neighbor instead of remembering what a wonderful pet Leo was in many ways," Tony says, describing the painful interlude. "Later I realized that my neighbor really didn't care much about me at all. Otherwise, she would have helped rather than criticized me."

Unfortunately, a lot of people who consider themselves animal lovers, including those who work within the animal care realm (veterinarians, vet techs, and shelter and rescue group personnel, for example) dispense after-the-fact criticism a lot more freely than before-the-fact useful advice. I suspect this is because they don't know what else to say. Compare the response, "Any moron can teach a dog not to chew or bark, if he really wanted to!" to "How terrible for you to lose/give up your pet. Tell me what happened. Maybe we can figure out some way to make sure it doesn't happen again." Which response requires the most knowledge and genuine caring?

As if all this weren't bad enough, unresolved guilt with one animal may plague future relationships with animals, too. After Dundee's death, Ellie clings so tenaciously to the idea that her absence somehow caused the Scotty's cancer that she refuses to leave her new dog alone. Not only does her constant attention make the new pet overly dependent and create dependency-related medical and behavioral problems, it puts a considerable strain on Ellie's relationship with her husband.

"We can't go anywhere because of the blasted dog!" Jack angrily fumes to Tony.

Meanwhile Ellie uses her new dog's recurrent health and behavioral problems as proof that something horrible will happen if she leaves her pet, totally unaware that her unresolved guilt about her relationship with Dundee has actually created this problem.

While guilt can undermine the healing process in many ways, its most harmful effect is that it causes us to get stuck at one stage or another so that we never achieve the peace that comes with acceptance. Owners who become trapped by guilt but finally manage to extricate

themselves describe their guilt-driven period as hell—
hardly the outcome any of us wish to associate with the
loss of a loved one.

DEALING WITH GUILT

Without a doubt, anything owners can do to avoid guilt
in their relationship with their pets *before* they lose them
will greatly limit the amount of guilt and the time it takes
to deal with it when they do lose the animal. As always,
knowledge serves as our best protection from negative
emotions. The more owners involve themselves in their
pet's health and behavior, the more they see the relationship as a series of conscious, knowledge-based choices
they make for their pet's and their own benefits, and the
fewer regrets they'll experience.

"What if you didn't make those choices?" asks Tony.
"How do you deal with the guilt then?"

Sometimes the loss hits us so hard and so fast that the
guilt sets in before we realize what happened. In these
situations I always recall some wonderful advice about
dealing with pain: Keep breathing. When pain hits, we
often automatically gasp in surprise, setting into motion
a whole flood of physiological responses that make the
pain worse rather than better. But if we can just keep
breathing, slowly, deeply, and evenly, we can breathe
through the pain. Giving into guilt at the moment of crisis is a lot like gasping and then holding your breath: Not
only does it make the loss hurt even more, it makes
it impossible to accept the loss and feel comfortable
building a new relationship with a new pet.

Fortunately, guilt produces such potent negative thoughts that once we recognize them, we can focus on eliminating them. Phrases such as "if only" or "I should have" often signal a guilt-based rather than knowledge-based assessment of the situation. As soon as you notice these phrases recurring in your thoughts about your pet, stop and ask yourself these questions:

- What am I gaining from this line of thinking that will benefit me and any future pet?

- If I'm not gaining anything, what must I do to remedy that?

If the mere act of castigating yourself makes you feel better, then nothing I can say will comfort you. On the other hand, if you don't like the way guilt makes you feel about yourself and how it negatively affects your memories of your former pet, then consider ways to alleviate it. This may mean reading books about pet selection, a particular breed of animal, pet first aid, behavioral problems, traveling with pets, or any one of hundreds of topics that may help you avoid the premature loss of a pet in the future. Educating yourself will also strengthen your ability to cope with the death of a pet from natural causes.

That knowledge alone will allow you to breathe easier, whether you get a new pet or not.

Now that we recognize how guilt can cast a shadow over the entire healing process following the loss of a pet, let's examine how each of Kübler-Ross's five stages play out in the human–animal arena.

SAY IT ISN'T SO

Because fear of our own deaths represents the ultimate fear, I like to equate denial with the freeze fear response. Nonetheless, recognizing that our physical relationship with a pet ends once we see its dead body, relinquish ownership of that pet to someone else, or give up the search, it would seem that denial wouldn't play much of a role. Ellie's husband buried Dundee in the backyard; Bill held Tipper while the veterinarian euthanized her; Tony signed the papers, paid the fee, and handed Leo to the volunteer at the animal shelter; and Lolly gave up the search for Walter. It all seems so concrete: What's to deny?

Logic, of course, may fall by the wayside when we lose a loved one, and each kind of loss provides ample opportunities for denial.

DENIAL AND NATURAL DEATH

From the instant Ellie returned home from her trip and noticed something wrong with Dundee until he died a month later, she felt caught up in a whirlwind of modern veterinary medicine. Each day brought new tests or results from previous ones, consultations with specialists, and all the ups and downs inherent in life with an acute, terminally ill loved one. For as much as death lurked around every corner, though, the mere intensity of the activity generated a sense of vitality. With all these marvelous tests, equipment, and specialists, how could Dundee possibly die? It just couldn't happen. If Ellie felt that way about the power of medical science to cure her old dog, you can imagine how owners of critically ill or injured young animals might find their pets' deaths even more incomprehensible.

Chronic problems that cut a young animal's life short also produce similar feelings of denial when circumstances force owners to realize that, regardless of what they might have wanted to believe, the problem simply couldn't go on forever. Each day it persists, it tosses another grain of sand into the smooth workings of the animal's physiology and/or behavior until it brings the entire system to a grinding halt. However, instead of viewing each day's little assaults as leading inexorably toward the end, busy owners with complex lives and problem pets use each day they survive in that state as proof that things can go on that way forever. When reality suddenly intrudes and that fantasy collapses, we find it difficult to accept.

DENIAL AND EUTHANASIA

You would think that euthanizing a pet would eliminate any chance for denial, and yet the choice provides owners with the most reasons for denial. Although our society is slowly making a shift toward allowing people to die without the intervention of modern medical heroics, we still find the idea of choosing to end our own or a loved one's life quite unnerving. Even if we discuss it, we often focus the discussion on physical pain and suffering: Just as we often deny the existence of "mental" problems and their treatment, we find it difficult to accept the idea of ending the life of a physically healthy individual who suffers unbearable mental anguish.

Nonetheless, animals with medical, behavioral, or bond problems that the owner believes are terminal are routinely euthanized, and the fact that the animal's death resulted from a conscious owner choice makes these folks particularly susceptible to denial.

When the day came that even the most heroic treatments couldn't keep Tipper's old kidneys functioning anymore, Bill couldn't believe it. In a daze, he heard the veterinarian pronounce the awful words, "No hope," heard himself requesting euthanasia for his beloved pet, signed the necessary paperwork, and stood there and held her while she died, all as if in a trance. When the veterinary staff asked if he wanted to talk about it, he shook his head. When he stood alone in the parking lot of the clinic, he felt as if he'd been hit by a truck.

"I just couldn't believe that she was dead," he said later. "And sometimes I still don't."

Owners who opt to euthanize their pets because of behavioral or bond problems may suffer even more because of what others may say about those who euthanize physically healthy animals, no matter how severe the animal's other problems may be. The more negative the situation, the more reason to deny it; owners who are hassled by friends, animal care professionals, or others regarding the choice of euthanasia may find plenty of reasons to try to put the entire event out of their minds.

Many who experience the loss of a pet to death or euthanasia can imagine nothing worse, but many of those who give up their pets can.

DENIAL RELATED
TO GIVING UP A PET

Because most folks give up animals with behavioral or bond problems rather than medical ones—and because these problems rarely provide us with something nice and neat to blame, like a virus or bacteria—giving up an otherwise healthy pet can leave many owners in a state of shock.

Consider what happened to Tony. All during his brief relationship with Leo, Tony considered his pet an extraordinarily healthy, rambunctious pup with "a few quirks," but certainly no serious problems. When Tony's landlord threatened to evict him unless he got rid of the dog, Tony found himself in the horrendous position of having to give up, and maybe even cause the death of, a pet whose problem he didn't even acknowledge as real. Faced with such a prospect, can we blame him for trying to deny it ever happened?

"I did everything I could for the dog," Tony tells a friend. "But it just didn't work out."

Bond problems that lead to pet loss provide fertile ground for owner denial because the responsibility for mucked-up relationships rests primarily on human shoulders. We can blame phys-

> Although our society is slowly making a shift toward allowing people to die without the intervention of modern medical heroics, we still find the idea of choosing to end our own or a loved one's life quite unnerving.

ical ailments and injuries on germs and careless drivers; we can attribute behavioral problems to the animal's breeding or early experiences ("I just know she was abused before I got her. That's why nothing I did to help her ever worked."). However, we can't blame a relationship-gone-sour on anything but ourselves. True, we can try to shift some of the responsibility to the pet, but never all of it.

Given the difficulty of extricating ourselves from behavioral or bond problems, we can appreciate why many owners who give up their pets for these reasons may prefer to deny the problems ever existed. Instead, the owner rationalizes:

- "He's a great cat, but my son has allergies."
- "My new landlord doesn't allow pets."
- "I'm afraid he'll hurt the new baby."

After owners repeat these reasons to themselves and others often enough, they begin to believe them. Others may even project the choice to give up the pet onto the pet itself.

"I could tell that Leo wasn't happy living with me by the way he was acting," Tony explains to a coworker. "He really wanted to be in a different home."

In this situation, not only does Tony deny getting rid of his pet, he defines the event as a benevolent gesture on his part. Just as denial initially may comfort those who give up their pets, owners whose animals disappear may be in denial leading up to or just after their loss, too.

DENIAL AND THE LOST PET

Unlike owners who know exactly when their relationship with their pets ended, those whose pets disappear have no such assurances. The first night Walter didn't come home, Lolly felt concerned, but not unduly upset. Like many free-roaming animals, Walter had disappeared before and always came back a few days later none the worse for wear. Why wouldn't the same thing happen this time? In these situations, denial offers the most comforting as well as logical response because the other alternatives—that the pet is dead or otherwise gone for good—seem so unthinkable.

While denial attends all forms of pet loss, it can trap owners whose pets disappear for two reasons. First, denial may offer a better option than dealing with the guilt that may plague these owners for permitting the lack of supervision that enabled their pets to disappear. Second, the lack of physical proof of the animal's demise gives its owner a justifiable and socially acceptable reason to deny the loss.

DEALING WITH DENIAL

The greatest challenge when dealing with denial of your loss involves recognizing that:

- You are in denial
- Denial constitutes a necessary first step in the healing process
- If you can't get beyond denial, guilt may be hindering the healing process

Although it still may seem ludicrous that a person confronted with a pet's death could deny the fact, remember that denial represents a fear-based freeze response. Fear drives us to opt for denial for one of two reasons:

1. We feel so stunned by the loss we can't think of anything at all.
2. We feel that we can't cope with the alternatives.

Those who describe the frightening alternatives that they preferred to deny rather than face often mention:

- Dealing with the disposal of the animal's body
- Explaining to others the circumstances surrounding the animal's loss
- Facing life without the animal's presence
- Living with any guilt related to the animal's loss

Consequently, if you consciously consider all of these fears and any others that might plague you *before* you lose your pet, you won't feel quite so paralyzed by them when that day actually arrives. Knowledge builds confidence: The more knowledge you possess about all aspects of pet loss, the more confidence and the less fear you'll experience when you have to face that loss.

Dealing with guilt and denial understandably could lead to anger. However, this difficult emotion comes into play for other reasons at this time, too.

THE SOUND AND THE FURY

If we haven't come to grips with the loss of a pet by adopting a fear-based freeze response and denying it, the fear-based fight response in the form of anger provides the next most logical option. But anger aimed at whom? Owners typically direct their anger at four targets when pet loss occurs:

- Themselves
- The animal
- Others involved in the animal's loss
- Circumstances perceived as beyond the owner's control

The specific form the anger takes as well as its targets may vary considerably depending on the situation, but a few basic patterns emerge. Let's return to our grieving owners to see what their experiences can teach us about anger.

ANGER AND NATURAL DEATH

When circumstances made it impossible to deny Dundee's death any longer, Ellie flew into a rage. She began by berating herself for ever leaving her beloved pet, for missing early warning signs, and for failing him in a host of other real and imagined ways during their life together. When that didn't comfort her, she then attacked Dundee, mentally reproaching him for abandoning her when she loved him so much, for not letting her know about his problems, and for countless other real and imagined failures on his part.

Still finding no comfort from these chaotic thoughts, she attacked Dundee's regular veterinarian—"Why didn't he notice Dundee had problems sooner when we could have done something?"—and then the specialists—"All those sophisticated tests and all that money I spent, for what? So they could tell me they couldn't do anything!" Even her husband weighed in for more than his share of harsh words for making her "gallivant around the world" when Dundee needed her at home.

In addition to railing against veterinarians who can't save their pets, owners of free-roaming animals that are hit by cars, shot, poisoned, or that otherwise come to tragic ends almost invariably lash out at the drivers, hunters, game wardens, neighbors, road crews, or anyone else with whom they can even tenuously link the animal's death.

For those of us who live with a pet that suffers chronic problems, every day the animal survives fortifies our beliefs that either the problem doesn't really exist, or somehow we and our pet have managed to beat the odds so we needn't worry about it. When we must finally deal with the problem's existence as well as its severity and contribution to the animal's death, we feel frustrated and angry.

Here again owners may verbally attack veterinarians, technicians and others in the animal healthcare community, family members, friends, and anyone else they can blame for the animal's death, no matter how flimsy the evidence.

When animals die as a result of euthanasia, these basic forms of anger take on another dimension entirely.

ANGER AND EUTHANASIA

Few people like to make life-and-death decisions, and fewer still willingly accept the responsibility for these choices. Consequently, owners who find themselves in the position of requesting euthanasia for a beloved pet also can feel mad as hell.

During the weeks following Tipper's euthanasia, Bill mentally replayed his pet's declining years, seeking evidence of any possible mistake he may have made, then mercilessly rebuking himself for making it. In addition, his wife, Chris, their kids, and the veterinarian who treated Tipper also received their share of his rage, too. According to Bill, the other family members didn't medicate Tipper as conscientiously as he did, and the veterinarian didn't treat the cat as aggressively as Bill thought was needed on several occasions.

However, in spite of the often highly specific, angry accusations Bill flung at himself and others during this time, he reserved the most hurtful one for his pet: "If you really loved me, how could you die and leave me?" Because he formulated the question to his deceased pet in a manner that precluded any loving explanation for her death, it merely reinforced rather than dissipated his anger.

Owners who choose to euthanize a pet with behavioral problems after they seek professional help and learn exactly what caused the behavior and what it will take to correct it commonly express anger first at themselves, and then at the professional who tried to help. Owners who didn't seek help more commonly rant at the breeder or pet store that sold them the animal, some other person they insist abused and "ruined" the animal before they got it, the neighbors who called the police or animal control officer to file the complaint, and the officer who responded to that call, among others.

Because many of the relationships that lead to pet euthanasia fall into the realm of what many nonanimal folks and even some animal lovers consider beyond the fringe, owners who create such relationships may experience a great deal of fear-based anger at this time, too. For one thing, the fear of exposure invariably looms when these relationships deteriorate to the point to which the owner feels obligated to give up the pet. It's one thing to say, "I had Snookums put to sleep because he had terminal cancer." It's quite another to say, "I had Snookums put down because he sucked my toes and I didn't want my new boyfriend to find out about it."

Those lacking an understanding of the ramifications of the human–animal bond might easily condemn these owners as well as question their mental stability. However, I do hope that as we delve more deeply into the human response in the chapters ahead, you'll begin to feel a greater tolerance for the complexity of the bond. For now, suffice it to say that the intolerance of these unknowledgeable people may terrify owners who find themselves in this position. As a

> *Few people like to make life-and-death decisions, and fewer still willingly accept the responsibility for these choices.*

result, one real or imagined insensitive word from an animal healthcare professional, friend, or even a stranger may trigger a very angry outburst from the owner.

ANGER RELATED TO GIVING UP A PET

After Tony gave up Leo, he went through a period during which he treated anyone who asked what had happened to his dog to a scathing diatribe about his "animal-hating" landlord. Because, like many owners, he only thought of physical problems as real, he found it relatively easy to deny Leo's behavioral problems and, thus, the need to do anything about them. When ultimately faced with giving up the pet as a result of those problems, owners like Tony often experience considerable fear-induced anger for one or both of the following reasons:

1. Unlike most owners of animals with physical problems, these owners may not know what caused their pets' problems.

2. They may have no clue where they can gain that knowledge.

In these situations, neighbors, law enforcement officers, and shelter workers who offer criticism rather than helpful information can find themselves on the receiving end of more than their share of owner anger, too.

Owners who form bonds with their pets that ultimately lead them to give up the animal also lash out at themselves, their pets, others, and circumstances they view as beyond their control—such as getting a new job or moving to a new house. And, once again, how much of the anger gets aimed at others depends on how much responsibility the owner wishes to accept for the nature of the relationship. Those who recognize how their own behavior contributed to the problem become more angry at themselves; those who see their approach as acceptable will blame the pet and others. I can still recall the man who furiously pounded my desk and shouted, "It's not fair! I treated him exactly the way I treated all my other dogs and I never had any problems with them! What the hell's wrong with the dogs they're breeding nowadays? I took him to the best trainers in the state. How could they screw him up so bad?" Sadly, his remarks remain with me because I've heard similar laments so many times.

When pets disappear without a trace, we can find still other reasons to feel angry.

ANGER AND THE LOST PET

Once again these owners must add uncertainty to this stage of the healing process. And just as this uncertainty may keep them in denial longer, it also may prolong their frustration and anger. In addition to lashing out at all of the vehicles and drivers; predatory animals; and devious humans wielding guns, traps, rocks, and poisons that Lolly imagines might have attacked Walter, she fears criticism on three fronts:

1. How could anyone possibly allow a pet to disappear?

2. What kind of person would give up looking for a lost pet?

3. What sorry situation could make the pet run away?

Even when owners admit the validity of such accusations, they may react with an angry outburst. As in other cases of loss-related anger, though, owners may direct their anger at seemingly unrelated targets. Thus, even though Lolly's friends congratulated her for handling Walter's loss so well, the workers she hired to repaint her home and whom she browbeat unmercifully following her pet's disappearance considered her a nutcase.

"You needn't remind me how crazy anger makes me feel and act," Lolly concedes. "The question is, what can I do to get rid of it?"

DISSIPATING ANGER IN THE HEALING PROCESS

Because anger constitutes a normal stage of the healing process, no one facing the loss of a beloved pet can escape it entirely. On the other hand, recognizing it as a fear-based response rather than a righteous or courageous one will help keep it in its proper perspective. When the urge to blow up at someone strikes you, stop and ask yourself: "Am I really angry at this person or am I afraid that I can't cope with the loss of my pet?" In the latter case, take some more of those slow, deep, and even breaths to give knowledge a chance to replace the fear, or to allow you to do what you need to alleviate that fear.

Additionally, bear in mind that other family members and those who knew and loved the pet are also grieving, but maybe not in the same way you are. When Jack, in denial, turns on the television within minutes of burying Dundee, Ellie flies into a rage.

"How can you watch some stupid football game?" she screams at him. "Don't you give a damn about me or Dundee?"

When Chris and Bill Perkins find themselves shouting at each other about some minor car repair Chris forgot to have done the day after Tipper died, they don't realize until later that the cat's death, not the car's squeaky door hinge, precipitated the argument.

From these examples, we can appreciate how the sheer intensity of the anger-versus-denial phase of the healing process may lead us to forget its true source: our fear that we'll be unable to cope with the loss of a loved one. Because of this, we also can understand why we'd feel driven to try to bargain our way out of it.

BARGAIN HUNTING

Think of the bargaining phase of the healing process as the fear-based flight response, an attempt to buy relief from the anger and make our peace with the loss without going back into denial again.

"What's to bargain about?" Tony asks. "Dead is dead. Gone is gone."

True, and that's why the root cause of the pet's loss— acute or chronic problems—doesn't affect bargaining nearly as much as whether the animal dies naturally or from euthanasia, we give it up, or it disappears.

BARGAINING AND NATURAL DEATH

When faced with a terminally ill pet, bargaining initially may take the form of seeking second opinions, taking the animal to a state-of-the-art facility for more sophisticated care, or even volunteering the animal for some new experimental treatment.

"I knew that last treatment wouldn't save Dundee," Ellie admits later. "But I felt like I had to do something more."

After Dundee dies, Ellie turns her post-death choices into bargaining sessions. She can't seem to make a choice for fear of the final goodbye, so she bargains for more time. She asks the veterinarian to keep Dundee's body until she can decide whether to bury or cremate him, carefully weighing the pros and cons of each option. Once she decides on burial, she ponders the question of where to bury him: at home or in the local pet cemetery? If at home, where exactly? In the woods behind the house where he loved to run or under the apple tree where he used to nap in the summer? Should she buy a casket for him or ask Jack to make a plain wooden box? Should she bury his collar or save it to remember him by?

> *Because anger constitutes a normal stage of the healing process, no one facing the loss of a beloved pet can escape it entirely.*

In conjunction with this bargaining, Ellie tells herself, "It's all for the best. Dundee's not suffering any more," in hopes of convincing herself that death offered the best solution given her pet's problems.

To a nonanimal lover such bargaining may sound ludicrous, but for those who have lost a pet to death, such deliberations put a measure of control back into our lives because they give us something concrete to do. Working through the probabilities and making the best choices allows us to think rather than emote; bargaining allows us to pick up a saw and hammer or shovel, to climb a special mountain or walk a special beach and sprinkle ashes, to do something tangible to dissipate the uncertainty of death.

Rather than performing rituals that enable them to create a consolidated, final image of the pet, other owners take exactly the opposite approach, methodically removing every trace of the animal's presence from their lives. Even though I can't prove this, I suspect that these people feel the greatest guilt about their relationships with their pets, too, and removing all evidence of the animal becomes a symbolic attempt to erase that realization from their minds.

In the case of euthanasia, the bargaining becomes even more personal.

BARGAINING AND EUTHANASIA

I can think of nothing I've encountered in veterinary practice that lays open the soul more than the choice to euthanize a beloved pet. Those who make this choice for a pet with a terminal illness or injury at least can claim whatever comfort comes from the awareness that society generally supports this as a caring act. Euthanizing a pet for lesser problems, however, can send owners down a very lonely and dark path that can get even darker in the days following the pet's death.

When Bill called a family conference to discuss whether to let Tipper die naturally or ask the veterinarian to euthanize her, Bill actually found a few hours' relief while discussing this sad choice openly with his wife and children.

"We talked about what euthanasia involved and what lay ahead for Tipper if we didn't do it," Bill recalls later. "We all agreed that the best thing for Tipper would be if we let her go."

After Tipper's death, the family still agrees that they did the right thing, but each one rationalizes it in their own way. Bill views euthanizing Tipper as a way of protecting his pet from unnecessary pain and suffering and death in some clinic away from her family. The family's young children see letting the cat go as a way of relieving the tension that arose in the house when Tipper's condition worsened. And Chris believes that letting Tipper go by choice has sustained her quality relationship with her pet.

"I loved that cat as much as Bill did, but in a different way," she explains later. "Toward the end, though, I was the one who had to clean up the vomit and diarrhea, not Bill, and I didn't like the way that was making me feel about her or him. Maybe a stronger person could have handled it, but I couldn't with my job, the kids, and everything else. This way, most of my memories of her are really good ones."

In all cases of euthanasia, we strike bargains with ourselves that permit us to make this choice and then accept the death that results. As we'll discuss in chapters eight and nine, we sometimes feel obligated to exclude children, the elderly, or others we judge as unable to participate in this process in one way or another. However, fear rather than concern for their welfare usually compels us to take this path. In reality, for most people, the more they involve themselves in the process of euthanasia, the better they can handle this phase of the healing process. Those who opt to divorce themselves from the euthanasia process usually do so because of some unresolved guilt regarding their relationship with the animal.

Compared to owners coping with natural death or euthanasia, owners who give up their pets can paint rosier scenarios for their pets as well as themselves. However, such bargains might not save them much agony in the long run.

BARGAINING RELATED TO GIVING UP A PET

Owners who give up their pets almost invariably try to convince themselves that a good person adopted the animal and provides it with a quality of life far superior to anything they, themselves, could offer. First they remind themselves of the pet's many fine qualities.

"Leo was such a great dog, I can't imagine someone not adopting him right away," Tony tells Chris. "Plus he had that wonderful silvery gray coat that people admired so much. And remember how happy he was to see everyone? Everyone loved that about him, too."

At the same time, though, a lot of these owners also acknowledge that they failed their pets in some way. To cope with this, they strike mental bargains with themselves that include the new owner making up for these shortcomings, often in a way that they never could.

"I saw a show on television about dogs who climb ladders, walk on balance beams, and go through all kinds of obstacles. Wouldn't it be great if Leo's new owner teaches him something like that?" Tony asks Chris. "I never had time, plus there was no room at my place, but I know a lot of people around town who do have the time and space to do stuff like that."

Meanwhile owners of aggressive animals envision their former pets finding work with law enforcement officers or saving their new owners from muggers or thieves.

Unfortunately, some owners don't succeed in mustering such rosy visions during this phase, and instead succumb to images of one worst-case scenario after another involving their former pets. Here again, I suspect that these upsetting rather than comforting responses arise from owner guilt about the quality of their relationship with the animal.

Such negative feelings often affect the bargains that owners of disappeared pets strike, too.

BARGAINING AND THE LOST PET

Owners whose pets disappear may envision the same negative images that afflict those who give up their pets, but their positive bargains more commonly involve envisioning the lost pet living with someone who loves it and cares for it exactly as they did, rather than with someone who does the job better.

"Every time I imagine Walter with someone else, I picture that person scratching the white patch of fur under his chin and feeding him tiny pieces of cantaloupe just like I used to," admits Lolly. "Maybe it sounds stupid, but that thought comforts me a lot."

As with given-up pets, lost pets create a dilemma for their owner in that, unlike natural death and euthanasia, the situation confers no sense of finality. No matter how clearly Lolly envisions that perfect new home that frees her from all her fears of Walter lying dead or living with someone who abuses him, the image of one day encountering him with some other, loving owner always lurks in the back of her mind.

"What would I do if I met the person who found Walter and took him in?" Lolly asks herself as she drives by the meadow where she last saw him. "Would I want him back? What if he didn't recognize me? I think that would be worse than knowing he was dead. Or what if his new owners really love him. How could I take him away from them?"

Whereas the bargains of owners of dead animals or those officially given up to others may enable these people to escape denial and anger by providing something concrete to cling to, the bargains struck by owners of lost animals may lead straight down the road to depression.

However, before we discuss depression, let's consider ways to keep from becoming trapped in the bargaining stage.

DISSIPATING THE
URGE TO BARGAIN

Of the first three stages of the healing process, bargaining greatly appeals to many owners because it allows us to actively rationalize the animal's loss. This, in turn, makes us feel as if we're doing something more thoughtful and constructive than engaging in denial or anger.

In my experience, the amount of guilt an owner feels once again will determine the duration of the bargaining phase. The more guilt owners feel about the animal's loss, the more obligated they'll feel to rationalize the loss to themselves and others. Intellectually inclined owners will stay in this stage longer, whereas owners who feel more comfortable with their emotions than their thoughts may quickly abandon it in favor of more denial and anger. On the other hand, those who worked through all of their choices *before* the animal died, was given up, or disappeared experience the least guilt and thus get through this stage the fastest.

"How can you prepare for the disappearance of a pet?" Lolly asks hotly. "Nobody plans a disappearance. It just happens."

As we saw in chapter two, although pets may disappear for reasons totally beyond their owners' control, far more often the owner's actions contribute to the animal's loss in one way or another. If the owner can't accept that, then the chances of accepting the pet's loss diminish accordingly.

Once we come to the end of the bargaining phase, we realize that we've exhausted all of our fear-based options. If we make it this far and refuse to give in to our fears, what happens next?

THE DARK BEFORE THE DAWN

Those of us who reach the depression stage in some ways face a lot tougher row to hoe today than thirty years ago. Back then, people typically viewed depression as a normal part of life. Problems arose, they knocked us for a loop, we went through a period when we thought we couldn't deal with them, most of us somehow did, and life went on. Today, however, media attention and the widespread use of psychotropic drugs have created the impression that *all* depression, not just that which meets strict medical criteria, is pathological. Because of this, owners who experience depression following the loss of a pet must deal with the pervasive belief that it represents something physically or mentally *wrong* with them rather than a normal response.

"True, but don't some people get clinically depressed when they lose a pet?" Chris counters. "I know I was really worried about Bill there for a while."

This may happen, and if it does, a complete physical and mental health workup by a qualified professional most certainly should head your list of priorities at this time. If you choose this route, I strongly recommend seeking out a health professional with solid working knowledge of the human–animal bond who also recognizes that the grieving process associated with the loss of a beloved pet runs the same course as that of the loss of a beloved person. A professional who lacks this knowledge and an appreciation of the value of animal companionship could erroneously view anyone grieving the loss of a pet as mentally or emotionally unstable, thereby undermining rather than facilitating the owner's acceptance of the loss.

As far as taking some mood-altering drug prescribed by your family physician in response to your remarks about feeling down since the cat died, bear in mind that taking a drug to relieve the normal depression associated with loss, like taking a few drinks, may dull or eliminate the symptoms for a while, but it won't help resolve the cause. Only facing the monster that causes the depression can do that.

And how do we do that? Once we exhaust the only fear-based responses available, we can either cycle through some or all of them again or we can face the reality that no amount of denial, anger, or bargaining can ever bring back the beloved animal. Needless to say, when that realization hits, most of us find it pretty depressing.

DEPRESSION AND NATURAL DEATH

"I remember very clearly the day I hit the depression stage after Dundee died because it scared me witless," Ellie says, describing her foray into this dark valley. "I was planting some pansies under the apple tree and thinking how easy it was to dig in the soil when I realized that I was digging in the spot where Jack had buried Dundee. A black cloud suddenly engulfed me and I knew Dundee was gone for good. I started to cry so hard I thought I'd never be able to stop."

Other owners tell of feeling so cold and numb they couldn't even cry, a reaction they considered even more terrifying. In fact, research indicates that's probably true. The tears of grief, unlike those caused by pain or irritation, contain the biochemical waste products associated with this emotional state. People who cry rid their bodies of these chemicals more quickly than those who don't.

In all cases, though, the often initially mind-numbing realization that, no matter how hard we try, no matter how hard we pray, or how much faith we place in medical science, we can't bring that animal back to life washes over us again and again.

"I tried to talk myself out of it at first because it was so horrible," Ellie admits. "But I'd already tried to deny Dundee's death before so I knew that wouldn't work. The same thing happened when I tried to get angry. Normally I don't like to pick fights, and I felt so depressed it just didn't seem worth the effort to do that anymore, either. I did think about fixing myself a stiff drink to knock me out so at least I could sleep through it, but it was only nine o'clock in the morning, plus I don't like to drink. So I just kept sobbing and working in the garden instead. It took me about a week to get over it. The first two days were awful, but then each day got a little better."

Ellie chose a more extroverted approach to depression, openly sobbing and forcing herself to work in the garden both she and Dundee loved, and calling sympathetic friends to pour out her grief to them. Others take the opposite approach, withdrawing from everyone and everything that reminds them of the deceased pet. While

such introverted behavior rings mental-health warning bells, this approach does work for some people.
However, like Ellie and other extroverts, not all intro-
verts shut themselves off from the reality of their pet's
death. Instead, they use this
period of physical, mental,
and emotional retreat from
others to face that reality
once and for all without dis-
traction. If, on the other
hand, they truly want and
need to talk through their
feelings with others but worry that others won't understand how acutely they feel the loss, then an introverted
approach will prolong rather than enhance the healing
process.

> "I remember very
> clearly the day I
> hit the depression
> stage after Dundee
> died because it
> scared me witless."

   Although some people deal with this stage all at
once, others make brief forays into it, then retreat to one
of the preceding stages for respite. However, for most
people, the utter finality of death eventually enables
them to find their way through it.

DEPRESSION AND EUTHANASIA

Owners who euthanize their pets must cope with all the
depressing thoughts that assail owners who lose their
pets to natural death, plus one more: They must accept
that they made the choice to end the animal's life.

   "That was the part that hit me the hardest." Bill
shakes his head vigorously in agreement. "Even though I
knew I did the right thing, I kept recycling that same
thought over and over again: I killed the animal I loved

more than any other on this earth, one I loved more than
most people."

Needless to say, for owners who don't believe they
did the right thing when they requested euthanasia for
their pets, the depression may become even more intense. Where owners like Bill whose pets suffered from
terminal diseases or illnesses often can focus all of their
efforts on working through their own complicity in their
pet's death for almost universally accepted reasons, those
who opt for euthanasia for treatable conditions don't
fare nearly as well. In addition to coming to grips with
the animal's death, they also need to make their peace
with their choice not to find the time, money, or energy
to treat that pet, a choice that garners far less support
from other people. These owners also must sometimes
deal with the fact that their choice to euthanize the pet
ran counter to the wishes of other members of the
household or those whose opinions they value.

Still, even with these additional complications, euthanasia does provide the finality of death, something the
owners of given-up or lost pets may never experience.

DEPRESSION AND THE GIVEN-UP OR LOST PET

The same uncertainty that haunts owners who give up or
lose pets from day one continues to plague them when
they reach the depression stage. The day Tony saw a new
animal rights billboard on the highway with the statistics
about all the unwanted pets who die in shelters, he almost lost control of his car.

"I felt like I was going to throw up," he says, of the
harrowing event. "Suddenly all my fantasies about Leo in

this great new home with people who really loved him vaporized. I couldn't think. I couldn't do anything. I pulled over to the side of the road and just sat there staring at that billboard. I sometimes think I'd still be sitting there if a cop hadn't stopped and asked me if I was all right."

Lolly describes her own descent into depression.

"I thought I was doing pretty well until I saw a dead cat lying by the side of the road," she reports. "It looked a lot like Walter and in an instant all my fantasies flew out the window, too. For a while after that, I became obsessed with looking for road kill, simultaneously dreading and hoping I'd find his body so I'd at least know what happened to him. It seems so crazy now, but I couldn't help myself."

Just as owners who lose their pets to death must face the fact that they'll never see that animal alive again, owners who give up their pets or those whose pets disappear ultimately must deal with the realization that something terrible, including death, might have befallen their pets, too. Moreover, like those who opt for euthanasia, owners who relinquish their pets for any reason play an active role in the event. Because of this, nothing can ever completely absolve them of any negative consequences of that choice. And, as we've seen, owners share complicity in most cases of disappeared or lost pets, too.

Once again, owners who give up pets to escape treating treatable problems or make the choice to let them roam with the least amount of forethought may experience far deeper and longer-lasting depression than those who give up their pets or let them run loose on the firm belief that this represents the best thing for them and the animal. Similarly, those who have thought through what could happen to their pets—the worst as well as the best—don't suffer nearly as much depression as those who haven't imagined this spectrum of possibilities. Owners who fail to take the time to address these issues beforehand more readily fall prey to guilt and its negative effects on the healing process. Unlike denial, anger, and bargaining, which allow us to project guilt and fear away from ourselves, feeling depressed can seem like being stuck in a black hole with nothing but our worst fears.

Fortunately, we needn't wallow in that abyss forever.

DISSIPATING DEPRESSION

When Ellie later analyzes her thoughts during her period of depression, she realizes that more of them related to guilt than the actual death of her dog, an experience that many people whose pets die share. This makes sense. If we couple the belief that we somehow let our pets down with the awareness that we'll never have a chance to right that wrong, how can we not feel hopeless? If we feel that way, successfully negotiating this most grueling phase of the healing process requires that we deal with any residual guilt as well as the depression.

Owners who completed this part of the journey in relatively good shape offer these suggestions:

- Recognize your feelings as normal
- Talk or cry it out with sympathetic but knowledgeable people
- Stay active

- Remember that others who loved the pet may be experiencing the same or other phases of the healing process
- Laugh

Think of the onset of depression as the ultimate freeze state. You can allow it to paralyze you, retreat from it into one of the preceding stages of the healing process, or move through it to acceptance. A conscious choice to move in either direction will serve you much better than doing nothing at all.

"Isn't a step backward, well, a step backward?" Bill wants to know.

Not if you acknowledge that you choose to do this. That puts you in control of the situation rather than making you a victim of it.

If you move forward to meet the pain and darkness, nothing says you need to do it alone. Talk or cry it out with a friend or counselor, but choose this person wisely. When Tony told his best friend how horrible he felt about giving up Leo, that well-meaning but naive person sincerely assured him that she understood how Tony could give up his dog because she knew Tony had done everything possible for his pet. While this response sounds sympathy-card perfect, it completely ignores the fact that Tony, like a lot of grieving owners, doesn't believe that at all. This, in turn, creates a terrible predicament for Tony: Should he nod his head in agreement even though he doesn't agree, or should he tell his friend that she doesn't know what she's talking about and risk alienating her at a time when he needs her the most?

Owners who encounter similar responses from naive professional counselors also wind up *paying* for this inappropriate advice.

Compare such a discussion based on false beliefs to the one that occurred between Chris and Bill. When Chris tries to put words into Bill's mouth regarding all he'd done for Tipper, he cuts her off.

"Maybe *you* think I did everything possible, but right now I don't," he insists.

"All right, I can accept that," she counters. "But Tipper is gone and nothing you say or do will bring her back. So let's take a walk and you can tell me what you'd do differently the next time."

"Who says there's going to be a next time?" Bill asks almost defensively.

"If not for you, maybe for one of the kids," Chris reminds him. "They miss Tipper as much as you do, if not in the same way. If you think you made a lot of mistakes, I think we'd like to know what they are so we don't repeat them."

Through these few simple statements, Chris acknowledges Bill's feelings as real, reminds him about the rest of his family, and invites him to take an active rather than reactive approach to making peace with Tipper's death.

Another rarely discussed but extremely helpful friend with whom to share one's feelings at this time is the deceased, given-up, or lost pet.

A shy smile lights up Lolly's face.

"I thought I was the only one who did that," she murmurs softly, then speaks more confidently. "I realized that what was killing me was the guilt, and it didn't matter what anyone said about it because I hadn't let *them* down. I'd let Walter down, or at least that's the way I saw it. One day I saw the chipmunk Walter tried for years to catch and I automatically said, 'Look Walter, there's your playmate,' like I always did. Then I imagined I heard him answer, 'Yeah, and now that he can't see me, I'm gonna get him!' I laughed and we kept talking. I don't know, maybe I made the whole thing up or maybe I was even crazy for a while, but it felt good to tell him how sorry I was for not taking better care of him and that I loved him very much. And then he said, 'It's all right. I forgive you. And I love you very much, too.' And that was it. It seems so stupid and yet. . . ."

And yet this approach worked for Lolly and a lot of owners who trust the love they shared with that animal to see them through the healing process.

"Think I should go into business as a cat psychic?" Lolly laughs. Which brings us to one of the best ways to deal with depression following the loss of a pet: humor.

No matter how hard it may seem or how feeble the first attempts, anything you can do to bring a smile to your face during this time can help tremendously. Rather than representing some sunny-side-up pop psychology, this approach springs from our deeply embedded evolutionary roots: playful animals clearly communicate to every living being—including to themselves—that they can cope.

"I don't understand," Bill shakes his head in confusion. "How does that work?"

Play requires energy above and beyond that necessary to survive. Those who play demonstrate that, no matter how bad the situation may look to others, they can deal with it, and they possess the excess energy needed to amuse themselves, too. In the physical realm, such playful displays may actually cause predators to back off, not wanting to risk harming themselves by taking on such an obviously fit individual. In the mental realm, we can use play to trick minds that believe they can't cope into believing they can. And, just as we can do this with our pets when they get uptight, we can do the same thing with ourselves.

In fact, for many owners dealing with depression, that first smile or chuckle is the first sign of acceptance.

THE LIGHT AT THE END OF THE TUNNEL

After experiencing all the mind- and spirit-exhausting effects of guilt and the first four fear-based steps of the healing process, acceptance seems so light and airy, so ephemeral by comparison, that it may take us a while to notice it at all.

"I know what you mean," Ellie agrees as she waters the lovely display of pansies over Dundee's grave. The new pup sits on Jack's lap as he plots the itinerary for his and Ellie's next trip. "I noticed right away when I didn't feel so depressed, but I didn't feel any great exhilaration replace it. It felt more like relief, and at first I thought it was just relief from the depression. Later, though, I realized that it was relief from all my fears about Dundee and what I'd do without him. That brought a certain peace. It's hard to explain. I still feel sad and miss him at times, but it's all right."

Other people provide similarly nebulous descriptions of this stage, noting how almost anticlimactic it seems after all they'd gone through to get there. Given the low-key, albeit all-inclusive, statement that acceptance makes after all the emotional intensity that led up to it, would owners who experienced this process go through it again?

> *No matter how hard it may seem or how feeble the first attempts, anything you can do to bring a smile to your face during this time can help tremendously.*

"Absolutely," Bill, like many in this group, answers without hesitation. "I'm convinced that the reason most of us go through the cycle, even at its worst, is because it's the best way to do it. I learned so much about myself and guilt and fear, I don't see how I could have done it any other way. The next time it happens, though," Bill adds, rubbing the ears of the kitten he holds in his lap, "I know I'll do things differently."

Tony nods in agreement, a faraway look in his eye as he watches owners and their dogs romping in the park. "In a way, I think that's the greatest gift Leo gave me."

All owners who make it to this stage would heartily agree.

Phew! Even dry-running the healing process takes a lot of energy, doesn't it? Now that we know the basics, let's explore how some unique human characteristics also may affect how we deal with the loss of a pet.

CHAPTER SIX

THE FEMININE TOUCH

Pet Loss and Human Nurturing

> *O gentle cat,*
> *How shall I part with thee . . .*
> *When you are not in my delighted eye!*
> *How shall I eat when you are not beside*
> *To share the bit? How shall I ever sleep*
> *While I no more your lulling murmurs hear?*
>
> —JAMES THOMPSON
> (A SCOTTIST POET)

IT SURPRISED no one to learn that Athena Ludlow had won the coveted Mother of the Year award in her community—especially not her children who remembered her nursing them through every physical, mental, and emotional trauma that befell them. After the kids left home, though, Athena finally found the time to indulge her great love of animals. As a registered wildlife rehabilitator, she nursed numerous wild creatures back to health, but the lion's share of her maternal instincts went into the care of Julio, a scruffy old cat she took in as a stray. When Julio died two years later, Athena felt lost and bewildered.

"I know all about the stages of grief, but I'm feeling something more than that," she said, trying to explain her feelings at a family gathering that included her cousins, Jeremy Marchak and Rita Andrews, and her sister-in-law, Callie Ludlow.

"I felt the same way after I put Noah to sleep," Jeremy admitted, referring to his greyhound who got hit by a car. "I not only lost him, I lost a part of myself."

Rita murmured something sympathetic, a little hesitant to mention that, of all the things she missed since she gave up her dog, Hugo, she missed the feel of him the most: his tongue licking her fingertips, the pressure of his body against the small of her back as she slept, the tickle of his breath on her eyelids when he woke her up in the morning.

HAD I written this book twenty years ago, I probably would have devoted this and the next chapter to the different ways men and women respond to the loss of a pet. However, conversations with countless pet owners over the years have convinced me that what we traditionally think of as typically female or male responses to pet loss relate a lot more to a person's mind-set than his or her gender.

The very word "animal" contributes to our often deeply intimate but quite varied feelings about our pets.

We can agree that the word comes from the feminine Latin term *anima*, but beyond that things get complicated. More traditional texts note that *anima* comes from the masculine *animus*, Latin for "breath" and "soul." However, according to the *Woman's Encyclopedia of Myths and Secrets* by Barbara Walker (HarperCollins, 1983), *anima* comes from the roots *an* and *ma*, which means "heavenly mother" and refers to a time when all souls emanated from a single feminine being. The sixteenth-century philosopher Guillaume Postel seemed to point us toward a less gender-biased approach when he suggested that every soul possessed a male and female half, the *anima* and the *animus*. While definitely an improvement over the Christian view put forward in the Council of Nantes in 660 A.D. that proclaimed women "soulless brutes," Postel unfortunately also maintained that Christ only redeemed the male half of the soul; the feminine half awaited a female savior. Later, Swiss psychologist Carl Jung revived the two Latin terms to describe the more logical (male-like, left brain) and intuitive/creative (female-like, right brain) behaviors found to one degree or another in every individual.

Today our relationships with animals and our own physical natures remain as paradoxically entwined as ever. When I think of my relationships with my current collection of pets as well as with other animals over the years, I can't deny the roles played by the animals' and my own physical natures. Moreover, given my awareness of the human–animal bond, I can't ignore how naturally this came about. Nonetheless, when I attempt to analyze this aspect of my fascination for and kinship with my pets, let alone explain it to others, I can almost feel the centuries of monotheistic conditioning nagging at me, questioning the pleasure I find in nonhuman companionship.

When such paradoxical thoughts assail people who share their lives with pets under the best of circumstances, does it come as any surprise that trying to understand these feelings can complicate the situation when they lose a pet, too?

To get to the heart of this issue, let's begin with a discussion of the feminine half of the soul. For convenience, think of the feminine part of yourself as consisting of two major components: your nurturing and sensory instincts. Each of these components, in turn, consists of elements that may come into play when you lose a pet. Nurturing functions that arise in our relationships with our pets may go in one of two directions:

1. We nurture the animal.

2. The animal nurtures us.

Rather than relating to any specific function, these kinds of relationships have more to do with our responses to close physical contact with our pets or theirs with us. These relationships, too, may flow in one of two directions:

1. We perceive the pet as a source of physical pleasure.

2. The animal relates to us in physical ways.

For example, Athena and Julio exchanged sight, sound, scent, touch, and taste sensory data with each other every day. However, that sensory data didn't just trigger Athena to notice the color of Julio's eyes or the scent of his fur. His trusting expression reminded her of her children's expressions when they were young and elicited a whole host of memories regarding them, as well as all of the positive physiological changes such fond memories precipitate. The mere scent of his fur not only evoked the image of her mother's cat, but also of her mother, unleashing a completely different cascade of psychological and physiological sensations. And surely all owners can provide examples of sights, sounds, scents, touches, or tastes capable of precipitating an equally complex set of physical and behavioral changes in their pets.

Both the frequency and magnitude of such nurturing and personal interactions virtually guarantees that a noticeable psychological and physiological void will appear when we lose our pets. The intimacy of those interactions also guarantees that those unfamiliar with the true nature of the human–animal bond may succumb to the temptation to erroneously view such feelings within a highly limited and not at all representational sexual context. Not only could such a narrow view cause these people to experience totally inappropriate and unnecessary guilt, it also might keep them from discussing these quite natural feelings with others, both of which could greatly hinder the healing process following pet loss.

To understand how the different forms of pet loss may affect our feminine selves, we need to understand all of these components. For the sake of clarity, I will present each of the these elements separately in this chapter. Because we may possess many or all of these qualities and may express one orientation at one time and a different one at other times, my examples will demonstrate how these can play out in the same human–animal relationship.

THE OWNER AS PET PARENT

Because all pets require some degree of nurturing, most pet owners probably possess some parenting instincts or they wouldn't get a pet in the first place. Ideally, however, when we interact with our pets, one word governs our actions: balance. In addition to always striving to meet their needs as well as our own, we also should strive to balance any desire to nurture them and encourage their dependence on us with the desire to build their independence. As you might expect, however, the more our nurturing instincts compel us to view our pets as our babies, the more difficulty we experience when we lose them.

Please note that in the following discussion I use the word "maternal" to describe this form of nurturing even though men and boys as well as women and girls may experience these feelings for their pets. I do this because the more generic, perhaps more politically correct, term "parental," by tradition, doesn't convey the more intimate emotions inherent in the maternal response.

Maternal Instincts
and Natural Death

Previous chapters discussed some of the traumas that can befall any owners who treat their pets like furry humanoids, and we can multiply those a thousandfold for owners with strong maternal instincts. When Athena lost Julio, she felt exactly as she would have if one of her children had died.

"I'm almost ashamed to say I felt worse in a way because Julio always stayed my baby while my children grew up and had lives of their own," Athena tentatively confesses.

Although some people might find this idea initially shocking, those who relate to animals in this manner recognize this fact as undeniably true. Additionally, of the various orientations we may adopt toward our pets, a maternal one takes the most time and energy. From the moment Julio first appeared on Athena's doorstep as a scrawny stray, she gave him the same quality care that earned her that coveted Mother of the Year award. When the feline immune deficiency virus (FIV) undermined his immune response and he succumbed to one infection after another until he finally died, she spent hours every day attending to his needs.

Like many owners with strong maternal instincts who take a more anthropomorphic view of their pets, Julio's death hit Athena hard because:

- She lost the emotional equivalent of her baby
- She lost a major source of meaning in her own life

Only those who have experienced the death of a young child can begin to comprehend what some owners feel when their pets die. Furthermore, unlike parents who lose a child and receive a great outpouring of sympathy from family and friends, maternal nurturers whose pets die often feel compelled to suffer their grief in silence.

"I felt like I was dying inside," Athena admits later. "But when I broached the subject to one of my sons, he said, 'Gee, Mom, Julio was only a cat.' That hurt me so deeply I decided not to say anything more."

In addition to feeling she can't talk to anyone about her feelings, Athena also faces empty hours each day that she once filled interacting with Julio. Consequently, at a time when she needs meaningful activity the most to occupy her mind and give her a sense of worth, she finds herself with little to do. Compared with taking care of her dying cat, most activities (such as going shopping or to a movie) seem at least frivolous if not downright disrespectful.

"How can I possibly go to the county fair at a time like this?" she wonders aloud after refusing an invitation from a well-meaning friend.

Maternal owners who lose pets to acute illness or traumatic injury fare even worse because they believe their maternal feelings should protect their animals from such terminal conditions. Consequently, in addition to coping with all the agony of losing a surrogate child and finding themselves with more than enough time to dwell on it, these owners often add a large dose of guilt to the process.

Owner guilt becomes even more intense when the person has a strong emotion-based maternal instinct toward a pet with a behavioral problem that ultimately leads to its death. Owners who believe that tolerating treatable behavioral problems indicates greater love often fall prey to this fate. The doting owner whose dog routinely bolts "just like a kid" every time the door opens can hardly contain his grief when a car strikes and kills his beloved pet. Because the owner believes that spoiling his dog as an overindulgent parent represents the most loving approach, when his dog pays the price he felt feels betrayed along with everything else.

From the moment Julio first appeared on Athena's doorstep as a scrawny stray, she gave him the same quality care that earned her that coveted Mother of the Year award.

Pets who die as the result of bond problems leave their owners feeling pretty lost and abandoned, too. I've mentioned situations in which owners create such highly dependent pets within such highly controlled owner limits that when the owners can no longer maintain those limits, the animal and/or the relationship crumbles. Animals who refuse to eat or drink and succumb to life-threatening ailments when separated from their owners come to mind here, as do those who could survive those ailments with sophisticated medical care—if they could survive away from their owners long enough to receive it. Because the relationship is the problem rather than merely a contributing factor, maternal owners who foster such relationships often find it much more difficult to divorce themselves from their role in the animal's death. That, in turn, increases the amount of guilt associated with the animal's demise.

MATERNAL INSTINCTS
AND EUTHANASIA

If we as parents find the idea of losing a baby to death incomprehensible, the idea of euthanizing a baby strikes us as even more unfathomable. When Jeremy faced this choice after Noah got hit by a car, his view of himself as the greyhound's nurturing parent made this excruciatingly painful for him to do. Even the veterinarian's heartfelt assurance that nothing could be done to save Noah and that the animal suffered greatly did little to relieve Jeremy's feelings that he'd failed his dog when it needed him most.

Because maternal owners more commonly view their pets as children and project their own human thoughts and emotions—including any fears—onto them, owners who don't work through their beliefs about euthanasia prior to the fateful day may find themselves on the receiving end of a megadose of fear and guilt. Answering the question, "What kind of person would euthanize his or her own baby?" gives rise to extremely difficult and unpleasant thoughts and feelings. When forced to confront these feelings about our pets under the worst of conditions, the event can take on nightmare proportions.

Once again, pets who are euthanized because of behavioral problems can generate even more guilt among their owners. Owners who erroneously seek to fill the role of overindulgent mom rather than knowledgeable leader for their dogs often experience an almost crushing sense of betrayal when their pets begin to display inappropriate and even unmanageable aggression. It may reach the point where the owners feel obligated to put the animals down. I recall one of the sweetest, most loving guys you could imagine telling me over and over again, "I thought he was my best friend. How could he possibly bite me when I loved him so much?" Although the most fundamental principles of animal behavior make it quite clear that this man's failure to communicate leadership led the dog to bite him, no amount of information could convince him that his pet hadn't rejected his love.

Maternal owners who euthanize pets because of bond problems also must cope with increased feelings of guilt as well as betrayal when their "Love will conquer all" or "Mother knows best" approach fails. In a case where medical problems raise the issue of euthanasia, most pet owners seek professional input and thus may receive guidance that will keep maternal views from undermining the pet's physical health. However, bond problems may go undetected until they reach crisis proportions. When this happens, owners who feel compelled to euthanize the animal must face life without the pet plus the awareness that love does *not* always conquer all and that mother does *not* always know best. These are hardly comforting thoughts at such a difficult time.

Because so much of a maternal relationship involves actively molding the animal to meet our own ideal image, owners with strong maternal feelings who give up their pets must work through a number of issues to reach acceptance of that choice, too.

MATERNAL INSTINCTS
AND GIVING UP A PET

Chapter five discussed how owners who give up their pets must deal with the additional burden of the unknown, which becomes a particularly personal issue for maternal owners.

"When I gave up Hugo, I felt like one of those women who gives up her baby for adoption," Rita admits hesitantly.

And that wasn't the worst of it for Rita and others like her who find themselves in this position. On the one hand, her maternal instincts urge her to hope that any new owners will care for Hugo with the same love and care that she showered upon him. On the other hand, if she did such a bang-up job, how come she couldn't keep him herself?

Rita gave up Hugo because she eventually found his "neediness" maddening, even though her own maternal instincts led her to reinforce this behavior at first. Like all maternally inclined owners who give up their pets because of bond problems, Rita suffered for all the reasons mentioned so far, plus the fact that giving up her pet made her a bad parent in her own eyes. Obviously, the more maternal our view of our pets, the more we'll feel like an unfit parent if we must give them up. Once we make that connection, given the anthropomorphic nature of these relationships, we may easily fall prey to images of our pets languishing in substandard foster homes or the animal equivalent of reform school.

If taking a maternal approach to an older animal can elicit such feelings, owners who take a similar view toward the young that result from planned or unplanned matings may suffer greatly, too. In this situation, the fact that the owner tends to these young from day one may enhance any maternal feelings tremendously, making it very difficult for that person to let the animals go to new homes. Some of these owners cloak their feelings by insisting that they just want the animals to go to good homes, but no home other than their own ever seems good enough. In some cases, the owners wind up keeping all the young themselves; in the worst cases, the owners delay until the animals reach an age when they hold little maternal appeal for anyone—including the owner—and the owner gives them up to a shelter because it's so much work to care for them all.

Owners with strong maternal tendencies who give up their older pets may take the human adoption or foster child analogy even further, fantasizing about their given-up pets' new owners seeking them out, much as children may seek out their biological parents as they grow older. Such images comfort some, whereas others see such reunions as a potential source of pain. In the latter case, the notion that the animal fares worse might plague them, while others find it difficult to handle the idea that their pet might fare better with someone else.

Here again, the very intimacy of the maternal response may make it difficult for owners to voice their fears when they give up their pet. Because we know fear drives the first four stages of the healing process, the greater the fear, the longer it takes to accept the animal's loss. And when the animal becomes physically lost, those fears may become even greater.

MATERNAL INSTINCTS AND THE LOST PET

Like other nurturers, Callie Ludlow immediately invoked a human-baby analogy when her cat, Marcroft, disappeared. Then she fell prey to the belief that someone abducted her pet. After all, what pet in its right mind would deliberately leave a loving mother? Because mother knows best, no other option could possibly exist. Nor could Marcroft simply have wandered off and voluntarily taken up with someone else. But then again, if Marcroft didn't wander off and wasn't abducted, then he must be dead, an option that blew Callie's mother-knows-best belief out of the water, too.

Unfortunately, pet abduction theories usually generate as much enthusiasm from others, including the law enforcement community, as tales of alien abduction. This in no way means that pet abductions don't occur, but it does mean that when we consider this possibility, it should be based on solid facts rather than on maternal instincts that refuse to consider any other possibility, no matter how much more valid.

By the same token, although any search mounted for a lost pet should take into account any maternal instincts about the pet's possible whereabouts, these, too, should spring from solid fact. Compare the following two owner hunches regarding a lost pet's possible whereabouts:

"I'm going to call Athena and ask her to look around her neighborhood for Marcroft because today is Tuesday,

we always visited her every Tuesday, and he enjoys going there so much."

or

"I'm going to call Athena and ask her to look for Marcroft because I'm sure he heard me tell her I planned to visit her today and he knew how excited I was about seeing her again."

In the first case, a regular trip a pet and owner perceive positively could legitimately give rise to the notion that the animal might undertake the journey on its own. In the second case, the owner's response expresses unfounded speculation about what might go on in the animal's mind.

Given how intimately our maternal instincts may urge us to interact with our pets and scramble our thoughts when we lose them by any means, can we do anything to keep these feelings from overwhelming us before and after the fact?

DEALING WITH MATERNAL INSTINCTS

Let's begin with a recap of the three most salient points about the maternal view.

First, there's nothing wrong with taking a maternal view toward a pet, per se. Problems only arise when that view results strictly from human feelings rather than from solid knowledge of a given animal's unique needs.

Second, a strongly maternal approach takes a lot of time. Whether the pet actually requires a lot of maternal care because of medical problems or because the owner simply enjoys filling his or her time this way, the fact remains that the loss of that pet will create a greater void than if such care had not occurred.

Third, owners who define their relationship with their pets in terms of their maternal responses to the animal will find themselves without a function and without a pet when that animal dies, is given up, or disappears. Because staying active plays such an important part in the healing process, those whose activities centered almost exclusively around their pets find themselves feeling doubly lost.

> There's nothing wrong with taking a maternal view toward a pet. Problems only arise when that view results strictly from human feelings rather than from solid knowledge of a given animal's unique needs.

Putting these three points together brings us back to a concept I introduced earlier: balance. If we relate to our pets in a manner that expresses maternal concern because it fulfills the animal's needs as well as our own, and if this awareness results from solid facts about that animal's physical and behavioral needs rather than some unsubstantiated beliefs, then maternal feelings probably won't complicate the healing process when we lose that pet. In fact, the awareness that we did the right thing, both for the animal and ourselves, will help fill the void at this time and allow us to accept the pet's loss more easily.

On the other hand, if we allow blind maternal instinct to guide us, then we must deal with the additional negative consequences that may arise when that instinct contributes to the animal's loss.

It seems so natural to think of our pets as our babies that it doesn't quite make sense that sometimes we may expect our pets to baby us—sometimes at the same time that we baby them. Nonetheless, many owners experience exactly such contradictory feelings about their pets.

THE PET AS PROTECTOR

It's hard to imagine owners admitting that they view their pets as parental figures, but a significant number of us do, at least occasionally. Generally we view our pets as protectors of one sort or another. Typically, this idea elicits images of a Doberman, rottweiler, or German shepherd dog snarling at miscreants lurking outside the owner's home. However, as we shall see, we may rely on our pets to protect us in less dramatic ways, too.

Let's examine each major form of pet loss through this particular human–animal lens to see what it reveals about the healing process.

DEPENDENT OWNERS AND NATURAL PET DEATH

Owners who rely on their pets to protect them physically find themselves in a major bind if those animals succumb to life-threatening illness or injury: The ill or injured animal obviously can't protect them very well anymore, and if it dies it can't protect them at all. Even though Athena spent most of her time mothering Julio, after he died she realized how much she depended on the cat to alert her to the presence of people or other animals in the yard.

"He always gave this funny little yowl any time someone came up the driveway," she explains. "After he died, I found myself running to look out the front window every time I heard the least little sound, thinking there was someone out there. Until then, I never realized how much I relied on him to tell me this."

And did Athena expect the old, ten-pound cat to protect her?

"Yes, I did, but I have no idea why," she admits, bemused. "Even though he was my baby, I always thought he'd defend me if someone or something ever threatened to harm me."

At the other end of the spectrum from pets like Julio whose owners gradually and even subconsciously assign them a protective role over time, we find animals whose owners get them specifically for protection. While finding herself without Julio's protection contributes to the mosaic of Athena's grief over his loss, owners who see protection as their pet's primary function may feel extremely vulnerable.

"I saw that when my neighbor's rottweiler died," Athena chimes in. "She got so paranoid about someone breaking into her house, she went out and bought a gun. I was scared to death that she'd accidentally shoot the meter reader or the paper boy!"

Athena's neighbor feared for her physical safety after her pet's death, but other owners who depend on their pets to protect them from life's various emotional crises fear for their mental health. To understand how this works, imagine receiving some bad news, such as the unexpected death of a dear friend, with and without your pet at hand. Which scenario comforts you the most?

"Oh, with the pet, definitely!" Athena replies without a moment's hesitation.

Imagine actively enhancing this aspect of your relationship with your pet and then facing one particular piece of bad news—the death of that pet—without the benefit of animal companionship.

"I'd be devastated," Athena again replies without hesitation. "Absolutely devastated. I'd feel completely lost and abandoned."

Just like a child who loses a parent.

When such feelings dominate a relationship, we can appreciate how difficult the idea of accepting the animal's loss becomes. When owners contribute to the pet's death by tolerating life-threatening behavioral or bond problems, the sense of loss becomes more acute. In these situations, the owner must face the fact that they inadvertently or deliberately destroyed their own source of protection.

DEPENDENT OWNERS AND EUTHANASIA

As a single dad living in a low-income, inner-city community, Jeremy Andrews had come to rely on his greyhound, Noah, to protect him and his two children.

"Of course, most of the time he was a complete marshmallow," Jeremy admits. "But he could curl your hair with his bark, and he was big and fast. Anyone who didn't know him would think twice about breaking into our apartment or messing with us when we walked him."

When Noah got hit by a car and sustained massive injuries, Jeremy and his kids' world collapsed.

"At first I wanted to tell the vet to do everything possible to save him, even if he'd be an invalid and even if I couldn't afford it," Jeremy says. "I just couldn't imagine not having him there to protect me and the kids."

As a single dad living in a low-income, inner-city community, Jeremy Andrews had come to rely on his greyhound, Noah, to protect him and his two children. When Noah got hit by a car and sustained massive injuries, Jeremy and his kids' world collapsed.

Whether owners rely on their pets to protect them from life's physical, mental, and/or emotional threats, the idea of making a conscious choice to terminate that protection via euthanasia means a lot more than ending the pet's life. Where other owners can temper any sadness or loneliness they feel with the knowledge that they spared their pet needless suffering, the desire for self-preservation may overwhelm those feelings when owners see their pets primarily as protectors.

"Sounds pretty doggone selfish to me!" Athena huffs.

Maybe, but when it comes to criticizing others' relationships with their pets, wise owners know better than to cast the first stone. Although Jeremy's fears about what could happen to him and his kids without Noah there to protect them may strike Athena as selfish, others may feel the same way about Athena's highly maternal approach.

Neither orientation guarantees the presence or absence of love for the pet, let alone the quality of that love.

Because pets whose owners view them as protectors figure so prominently in their owners' sense of well-being, the idea of choosing to put a pet down for behavioral or bond problems can hit these people particularly hard. Recall the commonly held view that only physical illness or injury constitutes a real problem. This view allows owners who maintain it no room to euthanize a physically healthy pet, let alone a physically healthy one they depend on to maintain their own sense of well-being.

Dependent owners of animals with bond and behavioral problems commonly find themselves in a most unenviable, no-win position. If they keep the pet, they may risk public embarrassment or worse; if they give it up, they lose their primary source of protection. Here again the owners wind up facing the worst outcome without the support of the animal they'd grown accustomed to relying on the most.

For many owners, only giving up that pet to someone else could possibly hurt more.

DEPENDENT OWNERS
WHO GIVE UP THEIR PETS

If we define only physically ill or injured animals as unhealthy, the idea of giving up an otherwise healthy pet because of behavioral or bond problems poses a problem. For the owner who depends on that animal for protection of some sort, giving up the pet amounts to cutting off one's nose to spite one's face.

Additionally, conversations with owners who find themselves in this position disclose another complicating factor: Some worry about how their relationships with their pets will play out in a new home. For example, Rita reinforced certain aggressive behavior in Hugo because she wanted the dog to protect her, but he never actually harmed anyone. However, when her fears that Hugo would bite an innocent person exceeded her need for protection, she decided to give up her pet. At that point, she faced a dilemma. Theoretically, she could truthfully tell the shelter worker that Hugo had never bitten anyone. If she said that, however, she could possibly set up some innocent person for a nasty bite. On the other hand, admitting that possibility could reduce Hugo's chances for adoption.

Equally troublesome, owners who rely heavily on their pets for emotional support may find themselves feeling jealous of any new owners and also resentful of the pet for doing well in the new environment.

"But they gave it up!" Jeremy points out emphatically.

True, but remember that giving up pets for behavioral or bond reasons always presents us with the possibility that *we* screwed up, something few of us want to admit. I recall one owner who depended on her shy little cat for emotional support in all kinds of situations to which the cat responded lovingly. However, the cat also experienced almost continual behavioral and medical problems related to the stress generated by such a relationship. Eventually the cat's stress-related territorial marking and nonspecific urinary tract problems became so upsetting to the owner that she gave the animal to her sister, who lived more than a thousand miles away. From the day the cat moved into the sister's home, the cat never exhibited signs of any behavioral or medical problems. But instead of feeling happy about this, the original owner felt utterly betrayed.

In this situation, the owner considered her need for her pet so great that she couldn't fathom that the animal wouldn't suffer just as much as she did when she gave him up. When the cat not only didn't suffer, but actually thrived in the new environment, the owner felt as if the cat had deliberately deceived her. And as long as she felt this way, she couldn't acknowledge her deep, long-standing attachment to her pet and how it affected their relationship in order to work through the healing process.

The perhaps somewhat irrational but nonetheless real concern that these pets might reveal something embarrassing or unpleasant about their former owners adds to the uncertainty that already complicates giving up a pet for any reason.

DEPENDENT OWNERS AND THE LOST PET

I often think of inappropriately trained "protection" dogs as the equivalent of toddlers wandering around the house and neighborhood with loaded guns: You just never know when they're going to hurt someone. Dogs aren't the only pets who can pose a threat to their owners and others. Callie initially reinforced what she considered Marcroft's loving habit of grabbing her arm and holding it with his paws when she stroked him a certain way. As he got older, he would bite her, dig in with his front claws, and rake her arm with his hind ones when she stroked him the same way. Rather than do anything to stop this behavior, however, she defined the display as protective and tolerated it because she liked the idea of owning an "attack cat." However, like others who lose animals with aggressive tendencies, she must now live with the fear that she won't find her pet before he harms some innocent person.

This brings us back to the question of how long to keep looking for a lost pet. Owners who reinforce aggressive displays in their pets find themselves pulled in two opposite directions. Fear of what the animal might do to some innocent person compels them to continue the search for moral and legal reasons. On the other hand, their own sense of vulnerability without an animal to fulfill this protective function urges them to replace the lost pet with another one as soon as possible.

"More dilemmas!" Jeremy announces, putting down his favorite picture of Noah. "How about telling us how to deal with these feelings once we've got them?"

DEALING WITH DEPENDENCE ON A PET

Ideally, owners involved in problematic dependent relationships recognize the signs and seek to alleviate them before they lose their pets. Barring that, they must grapple with the problem of what to do after the loss occurs.

For many, the most obvious first response means getting another animal. However this poses two problems:

1. The owner may impose unfair expectations on the new pet.
2. The owner could re-create the same problematic human–animal relationship.

Nobody likes to feel afraid, and we all want to alleviate fearful feelings as quickly as possible. When faced with the fear of coping with the loss of a beloved pet we depended on for protection of some sort, the need becomes even more urgent. Nonetheless, owners who find themselves in this position should consider alternatives to getting a new pet right away. For example, instead of rushing out to adopt another dog, Jeremy asks a local dog trainer if he and the kids can observe the weekly training classes. His objectives:

- He hopes to pick up training hints that will help him with his next dog
- It allows them to be around animals
- It enables him to meet other dog lovers

In the course of these weekly meetings, not only does Jeremy come to accept the loss of his pet, he formulates a whole new concept about how he wants to relate to any future pet.

"I now realize how putting Noah in charge of me and the kids set him up to take off and get hit by that car," he explains later. "I don't want that to happen again."

But won't he feel vulnerable without an aggressive dog to protect him?

"I do feel vulnerable without a dog," he admits. "But I no longer want an aggressive one. Now I understand that a well-trained dog who respects me and the kids will be there for us if we want and need him, rather than barking and snarling and carrying on whenever he feels like it."

Meanwhile, other owners discover that the fears they projected onto their pets spring from deeper roots and seek professional counseling to deal with these fears as well as others related to the animal's loss.

Regardless of the specific path owners take to successfully negotiate this particular form of pet loss, all agree that not getting another pet until they work through the fear and other feelings associated with the loss is the most difficult, but the most important, first step.

From this we can see that the very closeness of nurturing responses, whether we bestow them on our pets or expect our pets to confer them on us, can add another stage to the healing process that we must work through when we lose an animal. As difficult as it may be to lose a pet with which we experience a nurturing relationship, even nonanimal people can appreciate the logic underlying such functional arrangements. On the other hand, when we lose a pet whom we rely on for physical companionship, others' lack of familiarity with this aspect of the human–animal bond may pose yet another hurdle in accepting the loss of a pet.

PHYSICAL COMPANIONSHIP
AND PET LOSS

Much of what makes coping with the loss of a pet so difficult arises from yet another glaring paradox. On one hand, most of us harbor beliefs that some and maybe even most people can't understand how anyone could grieve for an animal, and that these people might even go so far as to consider our grieving a moral or mental defect. On the other hand, for many of us, experiences with animals add a dimension to our lives virtually un-available to us from any other source. One client described the loss of her pet as a color completely disap-pearing from her life.

Think about that. Look around and imagine your world suddenly without any reds or blues or greens. In the case of a pet, each animal provides its own unique color, and possesses the potential to stimulate all of our five physiological senses (vision, hearing, smell, touch, taste), plus the extrasensory abilities touched on in chapter one. So it's no wonder that when we lose that pet our bodies, minds, and spirits beg us to open ourselves to a healing process, no matter how initially frightening it may seem.

Mentally run through a typical weekday and week-end with your pet, focusing on your pet's appearance, sounds, scent, the feel of its fur, feathers, or tongue, or even how it tastes (if you're one of the many owners who can't help smooching their pet occasionally, even if they'd never admit it). Now pick the strongest, most pleasant sensations from this collection, close your eyes, and just focus on them for a minute or two.

Can you feel it? For me, the most magical sensation I get from Whittington, one of my cats, occurs when he's half-asleep and senses me approaching. With his eyes still closed, he rolls over on his back to expose his tummy. When I rub it, I can feel the vibrations of his purr tickling my fingertips through the soft, silky fur, and I can see the tabby stripes edging his upper lip curl up in the tiniest of feline smiles. *Ahhhh.*

Were I hooked up to the proper equipment, I feel confident that just rubbing Whit's belly this way would register a dip in my blood pressure. I can feel how it creates all those other positive physiological effects proven in various scientific studies of the human–animal bond. So reliably does this creature entrance me that I know I can use this interaction, and even just the image of it, to calm myself in troubled times. On the other hand, if I want to make myself laugh, I walk over to Watson, my hound, and rub his head right between his eyes until he becomes so deliriously enraptured that he dozes off standing up. Even just writing about it brings a smile to my face, and I'm sure confers similarly positive physical and psychological benefits.

All the sensory input we pick up from and give to our pets, as well as how it affects our and their bodies and minds, constitutes the human–animal bond. It's something most of us consider the best part of pet ownership. Given these potent physiological and psychological benefits, how can we not feel disoriented and out of sorts when that animal dies?

NATURAL DEATH AND
THE HUMAN-ANIMAL BOND

When a pet with whom we've experienced a close, loving relationship dies, we not only lose that animal, we also lose all the sensations we shared. The effect of such a loss tends to ripple through virtually every part of our lives. For instance, Athena got into the habit of petting Julio whenever he would jump into her lap, which he routinely did anytime she sat down. Because Athena rarely sat down specifically to pet her cat but rather to read her mail, enjoy a cup of tea, talk on the phone, read a book, or watch a favorite television show, all of these events became linked in her mind with petting Julio. Consequently, when he died, she sensed a void in each and every one of these otherwise trivial daily events.

"Shortly after Julio died, I was talking to a friend on the phone and automatically lifted my hand to stroke him like I always did," Athena says, describing one of the many unnerving sensation-related incidents she experienced during this period. "When I realized he wasn't there, I was so shocked, I started to cry. Thank goodness I was talking to a friend!"

In Athena's case, Julio's protracted illness necessitated schedule changes that allowed his owner to adapt to the loss of his sensate presence gradually. Owners whose pets die of sudden illness or injury often speak of initially feeling paralyzed or even panicky because everything they do reminds them of the lost pet. This occurs because these sensations, unlike memories of specific events, permeate every aspect of our lives.

Although most of us rarely notice the routine sight, sound, odor, texture, taste, and any extrasensory perceptions our pets trigger as they meander through our lives, the sudden loss of that input may hit us like a ton of bricks. A surprising number of owners whose pets die suddenly speak of the silence caused by the lack of the pet's breathing keeping them awake at night. Others wander their homes seeking the source of the strange odor, only to discover that the "new" odor is actually the absence of the deceased animal's scent it carried when it was alive. Still others find themselves standing helplessly by the front door because they can't imagine leaving their homes without giving the pet a few farewell pats on the head. When the pet suddenly disappears from their lives, they can't remember the next step in the sequence: Do I take my car keys out before I open the door or after?

> When a pet with whom we've experienced a close, loving relationship dies, we not only lose that animal, we also lose all the sensations we shared.

Recall that these interactions with our pets become so automatic and so much a part of our lives that we don't even think about them, not unlike the unconscious act of breathing. However, when the pet dies, suddenly even the most routine task may seem overwhelmingly difficult, not unlike trying to breathe underwater. In an instant pet owners find themselves catapulted out of the intuitive sensory realm and back into the learning mode where they must think through every activity step-by-step as they restructure their lives without the animal.

Needless to say, such mental and emotional restructuring takes time and energy, and owners who choose to euthanize pets with whom they shared this kind of relationship may feel all the more grief-stricken because they can't easily blame the animal's death on circumstances beyond their control.

EUTHANASIA AND THE HUMAN–ANIMAL BOND

When Jeremy opted to euthanize Noah, even for what he and others considered the best of reasons, he ached as he watched his young children squabble over who would sit where in the living room, an issue that had never come up before because both kids so loved sitting on the floor next to the dog.

"I can't tell you how many times I wished Noah was still with us, even in the worst physical shape, just so we could all pet him again," Jeremy says.

To be sure, owners whose bonds with their pets rely on ingrained nurturing functions often find themselves faced with fulfilling that role in some other way when their pets die. However, I strongly suspect that most of us feel the loss of sensory and extrasensory input even more keenly, even to the point that the idea of losing it serves as the most common, though rarely acknowledged, reason for not euthanizing a critically ill or injured pet.

As with everything we've discussed, this aspect of human–animal interaction has a dark side, too. Owners who spend a great deal of time petting, stroking, and otherwise emotionally fussing over their pets may create behavioral and bond problems that later contribute to their decision to put the animal down. Owners of untrained dogs may unwittingly reinforce aggressive tendencies with gratuitous petting; dogs in leadership positions may bite people, including the owner, who attempts to pet the animal under circumstances the dog doesn't consider appropriate.

For example, Jeremy got into the habit of stroking Noah's head any time the dog stood near him, simply because he liked doing this and assumed his dog felt the same way. About a week before Noah died, Jeremy began petting the dog to calm him when he started barking furiously at a visitor. Instead of calming down, though, Noah turned and snapped at Jeremy's hand. Although this shocked Jeremy, it made perfectly good sense in the context of the dog-led pack he had created with his pet. Had a run-in with a car not terminated that relationship, behavioral problems almost certainly would have later.

With regard to the bond, owners who take a touchy-feely approach may create pets that expect this constant attention. This works fine as long as the owner—or someone—can fulfill this need. However, if they can't, or if the owners later define the joy they take from this exchange as somehow wrong, then they may decide to euthanize the pet.

In both situations, the owner winds up dealing with the loss of this sensory input and all of its positive benefits, in addition to the guilt that inevitably arises when we opt to euthanize rather than treat a pet for problems we know we helped create. While few owners miss a biting, snarling, clawing pet, most miss rolling on the floor with those pets and the close contact that may give rise to such negative behaviors in some animals.

Given the nature of these relationships, however, we can see how those who give up their pets may feel equally disoriented.

GIVING UP YOUR PET AND THE HUMAN–ANIMAL BOND

Again, giving up a pet lacks the certainty of losing it to death. In addition to dealing with the sensory void and guilt that stem from giving up a pet, owners who give up their pets also must contend with any fears regarding how their relationship with their former pets could play out in the pet's new environment.

For example, single owners like Rita, as well as a lot of couples, derive a great deal of pleasure from allowing their pets to sleep with them, a perfectly normal habit given all we know about the benefits of such contact. However, when Hugo developed behavioral problems that made it necessary for Rita to evict him from the bed, she found herself in a horrendous bind. She knew that she needed to make a behavioral statement about her leadership role in the relationship. But she still wanted—and needed—the dog's close physical contact because of the positive physiological and psychological benefits it conferred. Thus, even though she understood intellectually that continuing to allow Hugo to sleep with her communicated a potentially dangerous message to this particular dog, she couldn't see past her own emotional needs in order to expand her definition of a loving relationship to include the dog sleeping on the floor. Because she loved him too much to get him off the bed, naturally she loved him too much to euthanize him when what she initially maternally defined as his "neediness" evolved into downright "pushiness," and her landlord demanded she get rid of her pet.

Earlier I compared animals that serve a protective function to toddlers wandering loose with loaded guns. Animals whose aggression springs from close, physical interactions with their owners remind me more of blindfolded toddlers wandering around with loaded guns. Not only don't we know when they're going to shoot, we can't know who or what they're going to shoot at. Unfortunately, the very nature of the interactions between these types of pets and owners often leads the owners to offer less-than-full disclosure when they give up their pets. If they don't, they, too, must live with the knowledge that these animals may expose their previous habits as well as distress someone in the new environment.

"But surely not all close interactions lead to aggression," Callie volunteers hopefully, thinking about her lost cat, and bringing us to the last variation on this theme.

Losing Your Pet

Although owners who form strong physical ties with their pets may relate to the animals in such a way that it gives rise to life-threatening behavioral or bond problems, many owners involved in such relationships don't usually worry about their pets harming others. However, not unlike those who depend on their pets to protect them physically, they do speak of longing for the missing pet's emotional support. Like owners who depend on their pets for physical protection, these owners of sensory pets find themselves pulled in opposite directions, too. The highly emotional nature of these relationships makes the idea of getting a new pet unthinkable. Callie can't gush, "I'd just die without Marcroft," for eight years, and then dash out and replace him a day after he disappears. On the other hand, losing such a pet may impose such a tremendous emotional burden that the owner accustomed to such a relationship may feel incapable of coping with the loss without animal assistance.

Dealing with the Loss of Your Pet

Needless to say, anything you can do to avoid problems related to overly close physical interactions with your pet will make it easier to cope with its loss. Should problems arise, however, denying the problems creates two additional problems:

1. You can't deal with something you deny.
2. You can't get on with the rest of the healing process until you deal with these feelings.

"But how do you deal with strong feelings a lot of people don't even acknowledge as real and others think are downright crazy?" asks Callie, voicing a not-uncommon fear.

First of all, if you join just about any group of animal lovers talking openly about their experiences, you'll most likely discover someone who experiences the same feelings you did, although some will admit this more freely than others. The fact that you recognize these feelings as real puts you one major step ahead of those who don't.

Second, the nature of the human–animal bond guarantees that such feelings will occur in any close relationship we develop with a pet.

Third, whether we humans can deal with it or not, animals exist in a world where maternal, playful, and predatory behaviors exist on an exquisite stimulus-driven continuum. Regardless of how we may think we relate to our pets, they will interpret our behaviors in terms of their own species' language and culture, not ours.

Fourth, animals do relate to our physical bodies. They primarily use scent, rather than vision, to identify others, and their highly evolved olfactory apparatus enables them to determine our sex, reproductive status, and countless other details with a single whiff. For example, some scientific studies now prove what countless women who work with animals have known all along: Male animals, in particular, respond to them more aggressively during the period immediately before and during menstruation. That animals can sense so much about us isn't good or bad, but rather a normal aspect of their relationship with us that we need to take into account when we interact with them. Finally, whether or not we acknowledge the existence of this intimate communication, it will occur between us and any pet we love, it will affect us physiologically and emotionally, and it will contribute to our sense of loss when that special form of communication disappears from our lives.

Given all this, I see no good reason to feel guilty about any void created when you lose a pet with which you've experienced a strong, sensory relationship. If the people you talk to don't understand, find someone else. If you seek kindred spirits or anonymity, visit one of the virtual pet cemeteries on the Internet and pour your soul out there. If you're hesitant to talk to anyone about it, write it down so you can make it real for yourself and take a good look at your feelings.

> I see no good reason to feel guilty about any void created when you lose a pet with whom you've experienced a strong, physical relationship. If the people you talk to don't understand, find someone else.

Above all, if you feel any guilt regarding certain sensual aspects of your relationship with your lost pet, don't get another one until you work through these feelings first. Every animal deserves to be wanted for itself and its own special needs as well as for what it may contribute to the enrichment of our own lives.

The freedom we feel imposing such tender feelings upon our pets, and opening ourselves to receive equally intimate ones from them, forms the very core of the human–animal bond. As we'll see in the next chapter, fearing to take that risk lest we exceed our own or someone else's definition of propriety may leave us with a far greater sense of regret when we lose a pet.

CHAPTER SEVEN

THE MASCULINE RESERVE

Pet Loss and Loss Logic

One runs the risk of weeping a little, if one lets himself be tamed. . . .
— ANTOINE DE SAINT-EXÚPERY
The Little Prince

"I'LL CLEAR the table while you folks talk," Gil Osgoode suddenly tells his wife, Barbie, when the postdinner conversation turns to the death of her brother Sean Rubin's cat. But even as he scrapes the plates and fills the dishwasher, Gil can't help eavesdropping on the conversation.

"I don't know what I would have done without Gil when Bristol died," Barbie Osgoode confesses to Sean and his partner, Ted Ranclift. "Bristol was an old dog and we knew it was coming, but that didn't keep me from going to pieces. Then when Chloe disappeared a year later, well, thank God Gil was there for me then, too!"

215

"But you go to pieces pretty easily," Sean reminds her. "When I put Figgy to sleep, sure I felt bad, but I knew I was doing the right thing."

"Sean didn't go to pieces when Figgy died," Ted adds to the discussion about the euthanasia of Sean's cat. "But then he lost it completely when one of his students gave up her cat just because it was clawing the furniture."

Gil Osgoode silently listens, secretly envying their ability to discuss their feelings so openly. How can he possibly explain to them how the loss of his two dogs still haunts him years later?

~~~

IF WE view the more feminine, intuitive, and nurturing component of our psyches as coming from the heart, then we may assign the more logical and reserved qualities we all possess—but which our culture attributes more often to males—to the brain. Like our nurturing qualities, though, the degree to which we rely on these intellectual qualities when faced with the loss of a pet depends far more on our mind-set than our gender.

I deliberately use the word "reserve" in conjunction with these characteristics because it sums up the confusion that so often attends our view of this mind-set. When used as a verb, reserve can mean:

- To hold back for a future or special use
- To keep or hold secure for one's own use

When used as an adjective, the word picks up these additional meanings:

- The keeping of one's thoughts and feelings to oneself
- Self-restraint in expression; reticence; discretion
- Lack of enthusiasm; skepticism

"Reserve" gains even more meanings in the world of animal behavior. Traditionally, animals with reserved temperaments display a combination of self-restraint and self-confidence that render them highly adaptable and easy to train. However, as the focus has shifted more and more toward breeding animals for looks rather than function, some breeders now apply this same term to shy and timid animals, two characteristics completely at odds with the original meaning.

All of these contradictory definitions are like Alice's Wonderland pronouncement that "Words mean what I want them to mean." However, these same contradictions also sum up exactly the dilemmas we encounter when we seek to respond in a certain way to the loss of a pet. Do we hold back our feelings so we can respond with what we consider maximum reason and logic at a difficult time? Or do we hold back our feelings because we fear the consequences of expressing them?

We can put some order into this chaos of conflicting definitions and responses if we view this "reserved" orientation as arising from one of two familiar sources: intellect or emotion.

Although conventional wisdom portrays this orientation as unemotional, three emotions may actually fuel this supposedly unemotional response:

- Misplaced concern for others
- Fear
- True reserve

Gil tells himself that he didn't openly express his grief over the loss of his pets because he didn't want to upset Barbie. However, he also didn't express his feelings because their magnitude shocked him, and because he typically evaluates situations objectively rather than emotionally.

Finally, because we often link nurturing and sensual feelings to a more anthropomorphic view of animals, a temptation exists to link more intellectual feelings with a view with animals as possessions. While perhaps true in some cases, this in no way means that everyone who takes an intellectual approach cares less about the loss of his or her pet. Indeed, some very reserved people care tremendously. Put another way, the inability or unwillingness to express our feelings doesn't mean that those feelings don't exist.

> The inability or unwillingness to express our feelings doesn't mean that those feelings don't exist.

Let's look at the four different kinds of pet loss through the eyes of those who tend to view the world through a more logical lens, always bearing in mind that we all may adopt this approach if we believe it better suits our needs.

ANALYZING PET LOSS

Our society tends to hold in higher esteem those who can analyze a traumatic event coolly and logically than those who respond emotionally. When Barbie fell apart after Bristol died, she automatically viewed her response as inferior to Gil's.

"I felt so foolish about the way I was crying and carrying on compared to Gil's objectivity that I worked really hard at making my peace with the loss," she says.

In this situation, what Barbie viewed as her husband's calm handling of a traumatic loss stimulates her to actively embrace the healing process. However, sometimes the social acceptability of the logical approach leads some people to use it as a delaying technique rather than a coping technique.

"But isn't delaying the same as denying?" Ted wants to know.

Owners who take a more intellectual approach to pet loss can and do experience the denial stage of the healing process, but their logical orientation makes it more difficult for them to deny loss when it occurs. Instead, they seek to bury the fears elicited by the various stages of the healing process beneath a collection of what they consider logical facts. If such facts actually address the owner's true fears, then this process facilitates the healing process. On the other hand, for pet owners like Gil who accumulate information to avoid dealing with their feelings about the pet's loss, this approach will prolong the healing process.

INTELLECTUALIZING NATURAL DEATH

From the moment it became apparent that Bristol, the Osgoodes' old golden retriever, could die any day, Gil began running through all of the probabilities.

"Gil spent a lot of time talking to Bristol's veterinarians about everything that could possibly happen to Bristol and our options with each one, so we'd be sure to do the right thing," Barbie recounts later. "After Bristol died, he looked into all our options about what to do with the body, then explored all the pros and cons of getting another pet."

Initially, Gil's willingness to do this served the couple and their pet well. Gil gained the comfort that comes from doing something concrete and meaningful at a critical time; his thoughtful evaluation helped stabilize Barbie's careening emotions; and Bristol's care always reflected Gil's careful consideration of the dog's well-being as well as his and Barbie's.

Both before and after the fact, however, Gil also used this busywork to avoid coping with the impending and then actual loss of his pet. Gil erroneously equated his ability to analyze a crisis situation objectively with coping; as long as he kept analyzing it, he fooled himself into thinking he was dealing with the loss.

The shock of losing a pet to sudden illness or injury often short-circuits most of the intellectual responses we can muster when faced with more chronic conditions. Still, some who feel more comfortable with this approach automatically will use it even though it may seem curiously out of place. One man whose cat was killed by a car discussed every conceivable aspect of burial and cremation with me for over two hours. When another emergency demanded my attention, he kept other staff members similarly engaged for an hour more. Other owners will go over the bill for any medical services for a deceased pet with a fine-tooth comb, seeking an explanation for every item even though they never questioned any charges on previous visits.

Owners whose pets die prematurely as the result of behavioral or bond problems find the going even rougher because these problems don't lend themselves nearly so well to analysis for the following reasons:

- They lack the social validity of medical problems
- They lack the specific, often extensive, databases available for most medical problems
- We can't avoid acknowledging our own contribution to them as easily as we can when a disease or out-of-the-blue accident befalls our pet

Consequently, owners who desire to adopt a rational and analytical approach find themselves with few acceptable facts to consider. Instead, they may find themselves rerunning the pet's life, focusing on its behavior and/or their relationship with it over and over again. Ostensibly, they say they do this to avoid making the same mistake again. However, if such analysis leads them to think thoughts that begin with "If only" or "I should have," guilt rather than a desire to accept the loss most likely fuels the analysis.

INTELLECTUALIZING EUTHANASIA

Odd as it may seem, most owners have thought more, and possess more knowledge about, euthanasia than any life-threatening disease or injury that may befall their pets.

"Get serious!" laughs Barbie. "I never gave it a thought and never want to!"

Many owners may share Barbie's aversion to the topic, but the fact remains that both state and federal governments grapple with the legal and moral dilemmas posed by physician-assisted suicide in humans, and reports about this subject crop up in the media every day. Moreover, I strongly suspect that this trend in human medicine paralleled the rise in pet ownership in this country as well as the shift to our current, more intimate view of animals. You needn't practice veterinary medicine for more than a few weeks to hear some owner exclaim, "I hope the end comes as peacefully for me when my time's up!" following his or her pet's euthanasia.

Because of all this and in spite of any personal aversions to the idea, in the larger scheme of things most of us know and have thought more about euthanasia than about our pets getting hit by cars or succumbing to a life-threatening virus. Thus, when faced with this choice regarding a pet, those who lean toward more logical reactions can summon more data to fuel the process.

Consider what happened to Barbie's brother, Sean, who considers himself a "quality of lifer." He has no desire to die in a hospital hooked up to machines, and he has prepared the necessary legal documents to guarantee that this will never happen to him. When Figgy, the feline light of his life, succumbs to heart problems, Sean's thoughts about his own end immediately come into play.

"I'm not going to let Figgy die in a cage in a vet clinic or languish here at home, any more than I want to die in a hospital or languish at home myself," he tells Ted. "She and I had a good life together and it's time to let her go."

Sean then supports his view by describing the process of euthanasia to prove to his companion that it's nothing to fear.

After Figgy dies, Sean tells Ted and others the same thing, only in the past tense. Sean then describes the mechanics surrounding Figgy's final moments and reiterates the principles underlying his own "right to die" view. Many who discuss Figgy's death with Sean come away from the experience feeling more educated than comforted by the experience.

"I know Sean teaches accounting at the college and is terribly logical, but he was so clinical about euthanizing Figgy that it didn't seem natural," Barbie remarks later.

Regardless how bizarre this or any other response to the loss of a pet may appear, always bear in mind that the people who adopt this method do so because they believe it works for them. Like Gil, Sean attempted to use logic to make order out of chaos. As long as he could define everything that happened to Figgy logically, he believed he could control his reaction to Figgy's loss.

In my experience, euthanizing a pet elicits such conflicting emotions that those who feel uncomfortable expressing them under the best of conditions may fear losing control. Under those circumstances, these owners may feel incredibly driven to control the aspects of the process that are within their control to help alleviate the sense of impending emotional chaos.

I encountered a prime example of this behavior one hot August day when an owner asked me to come to her house to euthanize an old dog I'd never seen before. Not knowing what to expect, I asked my technician, Lori, to accompany me. Let me preface what happened next by saying that I'm about five feet, three inches tall and weigh 108 pounds; Lori is three inches taller, but doesn't weigh much more.

When we arrived at the owner's decrepit farmhouse, she greeted us with, "My husband ain't home. The dog's in there."

We followed her into a boiling hot, dimly lit, fetid pantry where a very nasty, obese yellow lab lay wedged into a narrow gap between a washer and dryer on a filthy sheet. After some consideration, I muzzled the dog from behind, with one foot literally inside the dryer to gain enough room to straddle his broad body. Then I leaped over the angrily growling creature and euthanized him while Lori steadied him from the precarious position I had previously occupied.

By then, dirt and sweat covered both of us and visions of a shower filled my mind.

"My husband's dug a hole out back. Put the dog in it." Only the lack of expression in the woman's eyes exceeded that in her voice.

It took an eternity for Lori and I to unwedge, then drag, the hundred-plus pounds of doornail-dead dogweight to a hole the husband had dug a quarter-mile from the house. Of course, we cursed the man for deserting the old dog every sweaty, bug-infested inch of the way.

When we reached the hole, however, it immediately became apparent that, in his own way, the man had cared very much about his pet. A six-foot-long, three-foot-wide, and about six-foot-deep opening gaped up at us, its perfectly chiseled sides and immaculately clean bottom attesting to hours spent shoveling in the inhospitable, rocky New Hampshire soil: a final labor of love, no doubt with a heavy dose of guilt for deserting his pet thrown in, if ever I saw one.

With some effort we lowered the dog into the grave as respectfully as we could without tumbling into the hole after it. When we finished, we staggered back to the house.

"Where's ma sheet?" asked the woman flatly. "You din't put ma good sheet in the hole with the dog, didja?"

When I admitted that we had, she replied, "Well then, go git it."

Realizing how death can cause pet owners to react irrationally, and having noticed an impressive assortment of shotguns leaning in various corners of the house, Lori and I staggered back to the burial site. There we spent a good five minutes trying to figure out which one of us should jump into the hole to retrieve the sheet. I thought I should because of my senior status, but Lori pointed out that whoever went into the hole would need the other to help pull her out. Since she was taller, it would be easier for me to grab her. More analytical minds might find such logic faulty, but this sounded totally reasonable to my dirty, sweaty, bug-bitten, exhausted, and increasingly more frantic ears.

Lori leaped into the hole, tugged and pulled for another eternity until she finally dislodged the urine-soaked, filthy sheet from under the dog's body, and flung it up to me. Then I lay prone on the edge of the opening clutching her hands and, after a few false starts, finally hauled her out of there. We returned to the house where I handed the sheet to, and accepted payment from, a woman who never once showed an iota of emotion the entire time.

If more taciturn owners who euthanize their pets for socially acceptable medical reasons want to distance themselves from their pets' death, those who put their pets down for behavioral or bond problems may tend to do this even more. Now that I've switched from a medical to a bond and behavioral practice, I'll occasionally encounter an owner who appears to take in every word I say and asks a lot of intelligent questions, but who also displays a certain detachment from the process. The first questions usually center around quick-fix cures. If that option proves unworkable for some reason, these folks switch into data-collection mode. Then, after what they consider a suitable amount of time, they say something like, "So you're saying that there's nothing you can do to solve Puffy's problem?"

> *Regardless how bizarre any response to the loss of a pet may appear, always bear in mind that the people who adopt it do so because they believe it works for them.*

Of course, I never said any such thing. I gave them several solutions, but all would require more commitment than they wanted to invest in that particular animal. When I point this out, they simply don't hear it. I often learn later that they had the animal euthanized "because Dr. Milani said there was no hope for her."

Other trainers and behaviorists also describe owners who reduce the whole process to numbers. These owners' definition of "doing enough" involves spending a certain amount of money; some of them even give the impression that they'd prefer to pay the fee and forget the rest of it. (One woman spent the entire consultation looking at her watch or at the door. She never heard a word I said.) Accepting that these owners might project the responsibility for the pet's death on me remains one of the saddest lessons I learned when I first began working with animals and owners with serious behavioral and/or bond problems. In reality, most owners who have already decided to euthanize the animal don't want to change their minds; they just want someone to provide them with a reason, no matter how tenuous or inappropriate, to rationalize their decision. If they can also logically project the responsibility for the animal's death away from themselves and onto someone else, all the better.

INTELLECTUALIZING GIVING UP A PET

When Sean's student Bethany Purdy gave up her cat, she considered it her only reasonable option.

"Nutmeg was ruining my furniture, I didn't have the time and money to correct the problem, and I don't believe in declawing," she explains. "I really liked the cat, but . . ."

As a full-time student working a part-time job and living a hand-to-mouth existence, Bethany essentially reduced her cat, his behavior, and their relationship to a profit-and-loss statement. On the profit side, she valued the benefits of Nutmeg's company; on the loss side she tallied up his ruining her furniture, her limited finances and time, and any other problems she attributed to him. Comparing the two, she decided the losses outweighed the benefits, and elected to give him up.

Once she did, though, she continued to analyze his behavior and rationalize her own.

"This article says you can prevent clawing using double-sided tape, but I know it wouldn't have worked with Nutmeg." Bethany waves a cat magazine in a friend's direction as she elucidates. "I've read everything I could find on the subject and I know that *nothing* would've stopped that cat from clawing. Besides, that tape is way too expensive. I never could've afforded it. I'm glad I gave him up because I'm sure he's now in a home where he can claw whatever he likes because people who adopt cats expect them to do that."

Of course, unless Bethany placed Nutmeg in a new home herself, she can't say that for sure. However, if pressed, she'll come up with all kinds of reasons—which seem logical to her—for this rosy view.

Once again we see how these owners may use this approach to protect themselves from the harsh reality of their situation. In terms of the given-up pet, all owners want to believe that they gave the animal up for the very best reasons and that it went to the very best home. And while Bethany might scoff at a more maternal owner's fantasies of Spot or Fluff living in a mansion with doting owners to fulfill every animal need, she, too, uses her more "realistic" musings to fill the void.

The unknown further complicates Bethany's situation by providing her with infinite probabilities to ponder. While more maternal pet owners may endure agonies comparable to those associated with giving up a child, that perception remains consistent, regardless of any real or imagined circumstances surrounding the pet's fate. However, every time Bethany sees a cat roaming the streets, in someone's yard, in an apartment or condo, she analyzes those different settings as they might affect Nutmeg.

INTELLECTUALIZING THE LOST PET

When Chloe, the Osgoodes' spaniel, disappears from their summer home the day after they arrive, Gil poses the logical first question: "Where did she go?" At that point, he assumes the dog wandered off and got lost in the unfamiliar surroundings, and he pours all of his effort into correlating everything he knows about his dog with everything he knows about the area. Using this data, he then formulates a systematic search plan.

When he fails to locate his dog, Gil then considers all of the acceptable, if more remote, probabilities regarding her whereabouts.

"Come look at this," he calls to Barbie as he pores over a map of the region. "As the crow flies, the main highway's only ten miles away and there's a little town where a secondary road intersects with it. I think I'll drive over there and see if anyone's seen Chloe."

When Gil exhausts these probabilities, he asks himself, "Why did this happen?" During this period, he analyzes everything he and Barbie did or didn't do with or for Chloe from the first day they got her until she disappeared.

"I want to be sure we don't make the same mistakes again," he explains as he reviews all of Chloe's medical and training records.

The lack of finality that surrounds the disappearance of a pet creates an unfillable vacuum for those who take such an analytical approach. Unless a pet happens to disappear in a confined space, we can postulate an infinite number of fates for it. Gil imagines a family picking up Chloe. That image immediately gives rise to those of all the opportunities for family activities in the area around the Osgoodes' summer home: a state and a national park, beaches, an amusement park, campgrounds, and a county and several local fairs. Each option he explores opens up new possibilities for further exploration. The family who picked up Chloe might have been part of the group touring all of the state parks, or maybe they'd participated in the fiddlers' contest, stock car races, or the Boy Scout Jamboree held at the county fairgrounds.

The list never ends.

"Don't tell me what I already know," Gil declares gloomily. "Tell me how to get out of this mess."

DEINTELLECTUALIZING LOSS

Not surprisingly, recognizing that the problem exists lets us take that critical first step toward finding a solution. However, the very nature of the intellectual approach makes it easy to avoid this realization for two reasons. First, society has arbitrarily elevated this response over the more emotional option. Second, people who habitually intellectualize situations always can marshal sound and logical reasons why they should continue in this vein. Gil comes up with two that go right to the heart of the problem:

1. The people he cares about want him to remain in control.

2. He'll need to find something else to replace all those reasonable thought processes.

"What if I tell Barbie that inside I'm not at all cool and logical about what happened to the dogs?" Gil retorts somewhat defiantly. "Then what? Does she go to pieces while I turn into a blubbering idiot?"

Hardly. But before Gil can stop intellectualizing the loss of his pets and begin the healing process, he needs to dismantle the logical framework that enables him to repress his feelings.

I'M DOING IT FOR YOU, BABE

Like all domestic animals, except cats, we humans inherently adhere to a more social structure. Because of this, any intimate collection of two or more people will have a leader. Although that person may not display any obvious signs of leadership most of the time, when crises occur, the others in the group automatically turn to him or her for guidance and reassurance. Typically, true leaders don't use force or display negative emotions in their leadership role. Unfortunately, however, a lot of people mistakenly assume that strong leaders don't display any emotions at all. Putting these two points together, we wind up living in a society that elevates an unemotional intellectual response above an emotional one in times of crises. People who tend to face crises stoically often cite other people's dependence on their "strength" as the logical reason they can't give in to their emotions.

THE PSEUDO-LEADER
OF THE MOURNING PACK

When Bristol died and Chloe disappeared, Gil automatically assumed his cool, analytical approach "for Barbie's sake." He also did this for his own sake, even if he didn't admit it to himself at the time, but Barbie certainly appreciated the way he handled the situation. Consequently, Gil could conceivably make a good case for his wife feeling this threatened, or even more threatened, if he abandons his stance. I still vividly recall how vulnerable and even betrayed I felt the first time I saw my dad cry. I was about ten and clinging to his hand as a dour Lutheran minister flung heavy clumps of dirt onto the lid of my grandmother's casket, where they broke apart and ricocheted off the sides of her grave. Dad was supposed to be strong and take care of *me!* How dare he break down like, like some *woman?* While my view definitely reflected the sexist thinking in place at that time, more openly emotional pet owners speak of similar feelings when the person of either sex who assumes the role of the cool, calm voice of reason gives in to emotion.

At the same time, though, most of us older, more emotional folks who find ourselves depending on the Gils of the world to stabilize us eventually come to resent their behavior.

"I totally agree," Barbie confesses with some embarrassment. "At first, Gil's coolness comforted me, but then it started to bug me. Why should I feel guilty about crying over two dogs I loved a lot? In a way I think his reaction helped me more than it helped him because it made me determined to make my peace with losing Bristol and Chloe to prove to him that I wasn't the baby he thought I was."

Bottling up feelings and taking an intellectual approach to pet loss while claiming that we do it for others rather than ourselves is an example of paternalism, what some ethicists even refer to as crass paternalism. People who act paternalistically essentially treat others like children, regardless of their actual age. Although this seems like a perfectly natural approach to take toward children, most adults grow tired of such treatment after a while. And even in the case of children, unyielding paternalism may do more harm than good.

"Don't you think you should put on a brave front for your kids?" Gil asks incredulously.

As we'll see in the next chapter, adults easily can find themselves projecting their own fears onto children rather than responding to a pet's loss in a manner that meets the child's needs. Put another way: Holding back our feelings to protect others doesn't work if we do so to avoid those feelings rather than doing so because we know for sure that it's the kind of support those others need.

People who adopt a paternalistic approach for the benefit of others also essentially wind up lying to their loved ones. When Bristol died, Barbie initially interpreted Gil's cool response as evidence of a solid reserve of calm energy she could count on to see her through this awful event, an image he did nothing to dispel. But in reality, Gil adopted this approach as a socially acceptable mechanism to suppress his considerable emotions regarding the loss of his pets lest they overwhelm him. However, it takes a lot of time and energy to keep a lie going. As Barbie grew to resent Gil's paternalistic attitude, even as she worked her way through the healing process, she began to notice flaws in his approach.

> "At first, Gil's coolness comforted me, but then it started to bug me. Why should I feel guilty about crying over two dogs I loved a lot?"

"After a while, I found that I could easily talk about the dogs and even make jokes about the things that they and we did," she says. "When I did that, though, Gil would become very upset. That's when I realized that, for as much as he wanted me to believe that he'd handled the loss, he really hadn't at all."

Other owners, like Sean, who intellectualize euthanasia or, like Bethany, who intellectualize giving up their pets, often position themselves as experts in their respective areas, not unlike the way that Gil became an expert on natural death and lost pets. A common approach people take involves seeking legislation or other changes to protect other owners and animals from any of the real or imagined causes of their pet's loss. Thus, some owners may lobby for laws requiring seat belts for cats or specific forms of pet identification, while others may focus all their efforts on getting the town to fill the abandoned quarry where their pet drowned or raising funds for an enclosed dog park, safe from cars, poisons, or any other evil like the one that befell their free-roaming pets.

"You don't see those as good things to do?" Sean wants to know.

I do see many of these solicited changes as beneficial for both owners and pets. However, these won't benefit the person who seeks to evade the loss-related feelings that are a natural part of the healing process. No matter how beneficial the change the owner convinces any state or local governments to make, it won't help that person deal with the loss of his or her own pet.

"So how do we know if we're doing things because we truly care about others, or just to run away from our own feelings?" Gil asks the obvious question while Sean nods in agreement.

THE TRUE LEADER OF
THE MOURNING PACK

Even though so much of science and life in general seems process-oriented, working with pets and their owners leads me to recommend a purpose-orientation to pet loss. When we feel like we're spinning our wheels when it comes to accepting the loss of a beloved pet, we might ask: "What is the purpose of all this?" If we can truthfully answer, "To help me accept the loss of my pet," then we're on the right track, regardless of what others may think of any path we follow to achieve that goal.

On the other hand, consider the following answers to that same question given by the three individuals struggling with pet loss in this chapter:

> GIL: I'm doing it for Barbie.
>
> SEAN: I'm doing it to demystify euthanasia for other pet owners.
>
> BETHANY: I'm doing it so that others don't have to give up their cats like I did.

Because these owners use logic to protect themselves from their own feelings *and* place themselves in an expert position above others, they don't serve as very good role models when it comes to accepting the loss of a pet.

Which brings me back to the story of my dad. The whole time Dad cried as we stood next to my grandmother's grave, he never let go of my hand. Maybe he clung to me for support during his moment of weakness, but once I got over my shock at his behavior, all I remembered was his strength. In that moment, yes, I suppose my dad did suffer a demotion and became merely human in my eyes. On the other hand—far more critical in helping me handle my own feelings about my grandmother's death—he became *approachable*, the hallmark of a true leader.

"I think you hit the nail square on the head there," pipes up Ted. "If someone takes a cool, calm, and collected approach because it works for them, then they should be open to others' comments about the dead or lost pet. What bothered me most after Sean put Figgy to sleep was how difficult it was to talk to him about her. Every time I tried, he either started giving me all his facts or he shut me out completely."

"That's what Gil did, too," Barbie adds. "He held things in for so long, it seemed like he'd either explode or become completely numb to all caring emotions."

This bring us to Gil's second big fear: If he gives up his more logical approach, will he go spinning out of control?

THE EMOTIONAL SIDE OF LOGIC

I received my veterinary education at a time when men far outnumbered women in the profession. Given my interest in human as well as animal behavior, I spent four years in what amounted to a living–learning male laboratory. For the first time, I realized exactly how much courage it took for my dad to cry in public. Most men in those days acted as if openly expressing emotions defined as "feminine" by years of cultural conditioning would open a Pandora's box, unleashing monthly menstrual cycles, menopause, and a plague of other "female problems" on them.

Fortunately, those rigid views disintegrated over time along with other gender-based stigmas. Today, men seem to cry a lot more easily, especially those in the public eye.

However, in spite of what the androgynous touchy-feely literature may claim, most of us can't just sweep all those years of conditioning under the rug. Letting it all hang out still doesn't come easily to anyone who sees an openly emotional response as inferior to a reserved one, regardless of gender. The fear of losing control simply looms much too large.

RECOGNIZING THE FEAR

In our discussion of the different human responses to pet loss, time and time again we encounter fear undermining the healing process. Two primary fears plague the logical mind at this time:

1. What will rush in to fill the void that obviously will occur when we stop intellectualizing?

2. Can we handle it?

Gil invested two years of his life responding in what he considered a mature, logical manner to Bristol's death and Chloe's disappearance. Can we blame him for worrying about what will happen if he stops doing this?

"What if I completely lose it?" Gil voices his most immediate concern as he and Sean play golf one Sunday afternoon. "Or what if I don't feel anything at all?"

"I don't know what will happen if you don't feel anything, but I can tell you what will happen if you completely lose it," Sean replies as he studies the line of his putt, avoiding eye contact with his brother-in-law. "You'll survive and you'll feel a lot better about your pets and yourself, too."

"Is that what happened when you flipped out over your student giving up her cat?" Gil asks, recalling Ted's description of something Gil had previously dismissed as a fluke in Sean's normally controlled behavior.

"Yep," Sean concedes as he sinks his putt. "Bethany came into the classroom and started talking about giving up her cat, and I lost it completely. Started screaming at her about how thoughtless and irresponsible she was and a lot of other horrible things, too. She was so surprised and hurt, she started to cry, and I was so embarrassed, I ran out of the room and locked myself in my office for the rest of the day."

"And what did you do there?" asks Gil, staring at the hills surrounding the golf course.

"I cried."

UNCORKING PENT-UP FEELINGS

For some of us, the internal tension created by the failure to accept a loss eventually builds to crisis proportions until some often insignificant or even unrelated event causes us to spew out those pent-up feelings. This occurs sufficiently often that some mental health professionals give it its own name: uncorking. Within the human–animal arena, uncorking takes two forms:

1. Some later event may cause the more controlled owner to suddenly deal with his or her repressed feelings regarding the pet's loss.

2. The pet's loss itself may serve to unleash previously unexpressed emotions regarding other losses that the person has suffered in the past.

Most of us can appreciate how Bethany's innocent remarks about giving up Nutmeg could precipitate Sean's sudden explosion. However, many times the precipitating event appears so unrelated, it cracks open the door to those repressed feelings before we even realize what's going on. That's what happened to Gil.

Shortly before Bristol died, Gil stopped golfing with Sean every weekend. At first he told himself and others that his pet's deteriorating condition and Barbie's distress left no time for games. Immediately after Bristol died, he continued to use his wife as his excuse. Just about the time it became obvious to everyone that Barbie had accepted the loss of the old dog, Chloe disappeared, and Gil started the process all over again.

When Gil unexpectedly invited Sean to resume their weekly game, the request so surprised the younger man that he couldn't help asking Gil what prompted the change in heart, especially after he confessed to Gil how he went to pieces about Figgy.

"A few weeks ago, while Barbie's bridge club was meeting at the house, I came over here for a walk," Gil replied, gesturing at the footpath that meandered through the woods rimming the golf course. "As I was walking, it suddenly hit me that Bristol and I had walked that path almost every day for thirteen years. That's why I quit playing golf and jogging."

"I don't understand." Sean discreetly studied his golf ball rather than his obviously agitated friend.

"Every day Bristol and I would meet other walkers, joggers, and cyclists on that path," Gil said, struggling to keep his emotions from blocking his words. "A lot of them stopped and talked to me because Bristol always greeted them so cheerfully. After he died, how could I walk there? How could I face all those people I knew would ask, 'Where's your dog?' How could I play golf someplace that reminded me of him so much?"

"So you just blocked it all out instead?" Sean carefully replaced his putter in his golf bag.

"Yeah. At first I'd golf and jog when we went to our summer place, but then when Chloe disappeared, I quit that, too."

"But your golfing and jogging didn't have anything to do with Bristol's death or Chloe's disappearance," Sean reminded his brother-in-law.

"I know that, but I just couldn't deal with all the memories. They were both such damn good dogs. It seemed safest to avoid the situation altogether."

"So what got you out walking and golfing again?"

"My doctor."

"Your doctor?" Sean couldn't keep the surprise out of his voice. "What does your doctor have to do with Bristol and Chloe?"

"I've gained weight and my blood pressure and cholesterol are both up," Gil explained. "The doctor strongly recommended that I get more exercise. When he said that, I felt like a sleepwalker waking up. I remembered that I used to exercise a lot and didn't drink those four bottles of beer every night, but I couldn't remember why. But even when he said that and Barbie suggested I start walking again, it wasn't until I was actually on that path that I realized how I'd completely changed my life to avoid dealing with the loss of my dogs."

"So how'd it go?"

"The first couple walks were pretty tough, but I made it. Yesterday, I even found myself thinking it would be fun to have a dog with me again."

In this situation, Gil experienced a moment of revelation that toppled the intellectual barrier he had erected to protect himself from his emotions. However, unlike Sean and more like a carefully removed cork from vintage wine, his emotions didn't explode with that knowledge. Rather than experiencing some dramatic conversion, he applied the same logical analysis to this new insight that had marked his avoidance of his pet's loss. Once he did, he recognized the negative impact his former approach had on his physical and mental health, and he set about making meaningful changes.

In these situations, uncorking serves to help owners cope with the loss of a pet. However, because the magic of the human–animal bond works both ways, sometimes the death of a pet serves to uncork pent-up feelings about other losses, too.

WHEN PET LOSS CAUSES
EMOTIONAL UNCORKING

On more than a few occasions over the years, I've heard people worry or complain about family members who grieved more over the loss of a family pet than they did over a lost human loved one. A former law enforcement officer shared one particularly poignant story that demonstrates why this phenomenon may occur.

The case involved the murder of a young wife and mother whose husband became the primary suspect because he displayed so little emotion at the time. In spite of the fact that no one ever discovered any evidence linking him to the death, his lack of response so violated others' definitions of how he should respond to such tragedy that most of the small-town residents branded him guilty.

About a year later as he backed out of his driveway, the man accidentally ran over his dog and killed it. When he realized what he'd done, he immediately broke down sobbing.

"What kind of a moral degenerate would show no emotion when his wife died and then cry like a baby over an animal?" the local residents buzzed angrily.

However, given what we know about the human–animal bond and the uncorking phenomenon, the man's response makes perfectly good sense. At the time of his wife's murder, he put all of his emotions on hold, conceivably telling himself that his young children and his wife's elderly parents would need him to counteract their own considerable emotions at that time. When the community attributed his lack of emotion to guilt, he found himself in a no-win situation. When he didn't grieve, everyone considered him guilty; but if he allowed himself to do so, they'd see him as doing it just to prove his innocence rather than because he truly cared about his wife.

When he ran over his dog, though, the volcano erupted. I don't know this for sure, but like any pet owner I can easily imagine that dog as the only living being with which the man could relate honestly during this horrendous period in his life. In this particular case, the dog might also have been the only being the man felt truly believed in and trusted him. Thus his dog's death suddenly wrenched the scab off the wound of his unresolved feelings about his wife's murder, finally reducing him to tears.

Most instances of pet loss that contribute to the uncorking of repressed emotions about other losses aren't quite as dramatic, but the principle remains the same. Recall that by custom, tradition, and convention we automatically turn to the strong, silent types in times of crisis. Even if they don't feel strong at those times, they feel obligated to meet our expectations. When the pet dies, however, the logical mind allows them freedom to show emotion by saying, "Hey, it's not a person, you know. It's just a cat. Go ahead and break down. The others can take care of themselves."

When I consider the role animals play in the uncorking phenomenon and the blessed relief this may bring those who fear undertaking the healing process, it surely ranks as one of the greatest gifts of the human–animal bond.

PRESENCE AND THE HUMAN–ANIMAL BOND

Most of us readily can recognize how our more maternal and sensual natures become incorporated into the human–animal bond. However, because of societal changes that have made these feelings more acceptable, it's become much easier to view the reserved temperament as one we should discard. However, I believe doing so would seriously undermine the power and strength of the bond.

"You think people should act aloof about their pets' loss?" asks Barbie in surprise.

Not at all. I'm thinking more in terms of reserve as it originally applied to animals. I don't know exactly how the true meaning of the word disappeared or where it went, but at this point so many conflicting, mostly negative connotations surround it, I would like to replace it with another: *presence*. Presence, too, bears the burden of multiple definitions, but I believe that the ones given by my somewhat dated copy of the *American Heritage Dictionary of the English Language* (Houghton Mifflin, 1978) provide a far more valid description of what I consider an owner with true reserve:

1. Being present.
2. Immediate proximity in time or space.
3. The area immediately surrounding a great personage, especially a sovereign granting an audience.
4. A person's manner of carrying himself; bearing.
5. A supernatural influence felt to be nearby.

Owners with true reserve, or presence, don't hide behind their intellect. When the going gets rough, and it seldom gets any rougher than when they're facing the loss of their pet, others can count on them to be there. At the same time, however, they create their own special aura that both animals and other people can sense. They exude trust and confidence in themselves and others.

This brings us to definition four. In chapter six I mentioned how physiology can drive behavior and vice versa. My more feminine physiology leads me to behave in a more nurturing and sensory way, but my nurturing and sensory behavior also feminizes my physiology. Within the animal arena, we can see evidence of behavioral responses driving physiology, too. Many dogs—males and females, neutered and intact—thrust into the leadership position in a human–canine pack will lift their legs when they mark their territories, a behavior we physiologically only associate with intact males. Similarly, although we traditionally only associate urine spraying with unneutered male cats, cats of either sex regardless of their reproductive status may display this behavior if environmental circumstances drive them to respond in that more typically male manner.

> *Owners with true reserve, or presence, don't hide behind their intellect. When the going gets rough, and it seldom gets any rougher than when you're facing the loss of the pet, others can count on them to be there.*

When it comes to true reserve and presence in both humans and animals, I'm not speaking of some outward show of power in response to some real or imagined threat. Animals with true reserve or presence rarely, if ever, feel the need to mark their territories or fight, any more than people with that quality do. Instead, their bearing communicates their strength.

A clue to where that bearing comes from lies in the realm of a medical and sports technique called visualizing. In medicine, cancer patients mentally picture themselves wiping out rampaging cells or enhancing their immune response, while athletes envision themselves performing superbly. I, too, use visualizing to help owners get over various loss-related fears, and I'll specifically discuss its use in such a situation in chapter ten. For now, I want to focus on one particular aspect of visualizing that works for my clients: I ask them to imagine the worst- rather than the best-possible scenarios.

"You're joking!" exclaims Barbie. "Why would anyone want to put themselves through that?"

To develop that special aura and bearing that comes with presence, I ask my clients to picture the worst experience with their pets so vividly that they can feel it in their churning guts, their pounding hearts, and their racing pulses. Then I remind them that, thanks to the human–animal bond and their pets' amazing sensory perception, the animal will sense all that fear almost the instant they do.

Over the years I've been blessed with some extraordinary clients and I remain in awe of the effort they make to deal with their various fears to avoid inadvertently communicating them to their pets. Once people vanquish the fear, a most wonderful transformation occurs. Their entire demeanor changes. In addition to emitting an aura that draws others to them, their carriage, posture, and the way in which they move—their bearing—alters completely. The animal immediately picks up on that change, too, and a very special kind of bond forms. It is a bond that I think embodies the supernatural essence of presence.

When visualizing works, it works because a proper balance exists between the heart and the mind, our emotions and our intellect. Although our more intuitive, emotional, and maternal natures may provide the love and desire necessary to face the fears associated with the loss of a pet, our confidence in ourselves and our ability to make it through the healing process—our intellectual natures—contribute to the presence of mind to validate those emotions.

Once again, we've come full circle. In spite of all the conflicting definitions we might assign to different aspects of intellectualizing, and despite how paradoxical we may see it from our nurturing and sensual selves, the two actually work together, often inextricably. When it comes to coping with the loss of a pet, the key remains to recognize whether any balance we strike enhances rather than undermines the healing process.

Now that we understand the fundamental qualities that most commonly color our responses to the loss of a pet, we need to look at two specific groups of people: children and those with special needs. In the next chapter we'll see how, even as we say we seek to protect children from the harsh realities of pet death and loss, we must take care to ensure that the methods we choose to do this don't serve our own needs far better than theirs.

CHAPTER EIGHT

THE LOSS *of* INNOCENCE

Children and Pet Loss

Feel the dignity of a child.
Do not feel superior to him, for you are not.
—ROBERT HENRI
The Art Spirit

ANYONE WHO happens to drive into the Kinder Brook Animal Hospital parking lot and see the dead cat laid out on a tablecloth on the tailgate of the Ford station wagon might wonder what the two adults and three children staring at it hope to accomplish. But Barry and Jeanne Hearne, the two adults in the group, harbor no such doubts.

"We want to deal with Mahitable's death right away for the children's sake," Barry announces gravely. "They all loved her and her death makes us all very sad."

While Jeanne nods in agreement and dabs her eyes, five-year-old Jessica barely stifles a giggly "Blech!" when a fly alights on Mahitable's face and marches across her eye. Ten-year-old Megan solemnly reads a lengthy poem she composed just for the occasion. Fifteen-year-old Jared stares straight ahead.

After the funeral ends, the parents wrap up Mahitable's body and put it into a cardboard box.

"It's so important for children to have a sense of closure at these times," Jeanne murmurs confidently.

At that moment Jared leaps into the car and slams the door closed with such force, the entire vehicle shakes with the impact.

EVEN THOUGH parents or guardians often express a great deal of concern about how children will respond to the loss of a pet, their own reactions to the loss plus today's often hectic lifestyles have the potential to undermine their handling of the situation.

"I read an article on children and loss that said rituals are very important to kids because they help them find closure," Jeanne says, describing many parents' feelings at these times.

Within the culture of loss, "closure" has become the buzzword of the day. Many people typically, and rightfully, use it to mean acceptance, the final stage of the healing process. Unfortunately, in our quick-fix society, the word has also taken on a quick-fix connotation. Thus, harried two-income parents like the Hearnes may mentally pencil "closure" into the quality time slot they allot to cope with the loss of the family pet, unmindful that their children might not reach that state for weeks or even longer. Parents who do this, however, often do it for legitimate reasons:

- They want to acknowledge the loss of the pet
- They want to get on with their own healing

"Why don't parents just combine acknowledging the loss of the pet to the child with working through the healing process at the same time?" asks Pete Wyman, a single parent whose twelve-year-old son, Chip, rides the school bus with Megan Hearne.

Ideally, adults should. However, kids don't all react the same way to loss any more than adults do. Sometimes, in an effort to ensure that they do the best by the youngsters, adults will try to put their own feelings on hold until after they believe the kids can handle the loss. Other parents feel an instinctive need to put on a calm front for their children in times of distress. All parents do this, but single and other nontraditional parents who believe their children are more vulnerable may feel this need the most strongly.

"I understand what you mean," Pete says, nodding his head slowly. "I felt as bad as Chip did when the vet diagnosed a terminal cancer in our dog, Louie, two months after Chip's mom left, but I told myself I just couldn't go to pieces no matter how much I wanted to."

Other times adults become so involved in helping youngsters cope, they fail to set aside sufficient time to address their own needs. Once they believe that the kids accept the pet's loss, then they may break down completely.

In addition to taking into account any child's age and development, adults need to keep three other rules in mind that they may find difficult to implement at such a difficult time:

- Assume responsibility for the animal
- Don't lie
- Provide age- and experience-appropriate information

As soon as adults violate any of these rules, their ability to help the child negotiate the healing process diminishes accordingly. Not surprisingly, though, adults who experience difficulty accepting responsibility for the pet under the best of circumstances often flounder helplessly when the human–animal relationship ends.

WHOSE PET IS IT?

I've mentioned in previous chapters that getting a pet for any reason other than wanting that particular pet for itself can result in a relationship that complicates the healing process if you lose that pet. Among a list of inappropriate reasons, getting pets for kids ranks as one of the most common but also the most problematic because:

- Parents may consciously or subconsciously make the child feel responsible for the pet
- The child may share a much different bond with the pet than the parent

To understand how children respond to loss, we need to recognize how these realities may affect the child's relationship with the animal.

CHILDREN AS PET PARENTS

Few veterinarians can help cringing when parents arrive with a new pet and a youngster in tow, proclaiming, "This is Tiffany and her new kitty, Barney." While such a pronouncement sets off alarms regardless of the child's age, these clang most loudly when the child is very young—physically or developmentally. Tiffany might possess an extensive vocabulary for a four-year-old and read books far above her age level—including every book on responsible pet ownership her parents bought her. However, while even very young children can grasp the basics of pet ownership, dealing with all the mental and emotional turmoil that attends the loss of a pet can tax far more mature minds. The Hearnes got Mahitable for Megan's sixth birthday because the child begged and pleaded for a kitten. Barry and Jeanne personally felt no desire to add a pet to their hectic household, but they agreed, uttering the usual parental rationalizations:

"Megan's old enough now to take care of a pet herself."

or

"Every child should have a pet."

or

"We had pets when we were kids and we want our kids to have that same experience."

Parents in this position who didn't own pets as children often will use that fact as the reason for getting their kids a pet: "My mom never let me have a dog when I was a kid and I really wanted one. I'm not going to do that to my kids."

While telling Megan that Mahitable belongs to her may boost the child's self-esteem, it only works if her parents only delegate responsibility for the aspects of pet ownership that Megan can successfully handle. If they expect her to accept responsibility for everything related to the pet, she may become overwhelmed and, much worse, overwhelmed with guilt if something bad happens to the animal. Perhaps the absolute worst example of this I ever encountered involved parents who insisted that their horrified children observe the euthanasia of their dog who had succumbed to heartworm disease "because you kids didn't give him his pills like you were supposed to." That dreadful example brings us to the second reason parents shouldn't get pets for their kids unless they also truly want one.

DIFFERENT BONDS FOR DIFFERENT FOLKS

In the example I just mentioned, the parents obviously shared little or no bond with the family dog. If they had, they would have treated its treatable heartworm disease. Unfortunately, parents or guardians who experience no bond or only a minimal one with the family pet often fail to recognize the nature and magnitude of the bond that their children experience. Barry views Mahitable's death as a sad but understandable fact of life for owners of a free-roaming cat. Although he loves his children and wants to support them any way he can, he functions more as an actor, making the proper responses and participating in any pet death-related rituals his wife or the kids suggest.

> *While even very young children can grasp the basics of pet ownership, dealing with all the mental and emotional turmoil that attends the loss of a pet can tax far more mature minds.*

When Megan woke up sobbing the night after Mahitable's funeral and Jared refused to talk to him, Barry floundered in confusion.

"I had no idea how much that cat meant to them," he confesses. "I felt like I really let them down when they needed me the most."

Adults who raise animals for show or food often express similar dismay when a child becomes emotionally attached to a creature they view more as an object. It never dawns on them that someone could grow attached to the runt of the litter, or value a lamb or calf as anything other than a source of meat. Children who develop strong attachments to pocket pets such as hamsters, gerbils, and guinea pigs, or exotics such as snakes, turtles, and iguanas also may react to the animal's loss in ways that leave the parent completely perplexed.

At the opposite end of this spectrum, we see parents who automatically expect their child to develop a strong bond with the pet though the child may feel nothing at all. Whereas the Victorians got their daughters kittens to teach them cleanliness and maternal skills, and their sons puppies to teach them fidelity and courage, some modern parents view getting a pet "for the kids" as some sort of universal parental obligation, kind of like attending every softball game or band concert. When they discover the lop-eared bunny sitting in filth without food or water because Junior forgot to feed and clean it, or that the once cuddly pup now terrorizes the neighborhood for want of training, they can't believe it.

Even animal-neutral or antagonistic parents may beget animal-loving offspring. Nonetheless, parents have a moral responsibility not to bring any animal into their households unless they're personally willing to accept total responsibility for that animal's well-being. This may mean helping Junior develop the necessary nurturing skills to properly care for his bunny, hamster, or dog. Or it may mean that the parent assumes full responsibility for the animal's care if the child can't or won't. It's one thing to allow a child who won't pick up his room to live with his mess; it's quite another to allow a pet to suffer with the idea that the child might eventually feel guilty enough to care for it. If parents can't do this, they should accept the responsibility of terminating the relationship.

"You mean put the bunny down?" gasps Junior's mother.

Yes, if no good home for the animal can be found.

Additionally—and this is the last thing parents who hope to divorce themselves from their children's pet experiences want to hear—adults who haven't developed as strong a bond with the pet as their children have must accept one final responsibility: They owe it to their kids to help them through the healing process. Parents whose kids care less or not at all about the pet owe it to members of the animal kingdom as well as society not to allow those children to own a pet until they can do so responsibly.

Once we assume the responsibility for adding a pet to our household and recognize that our children may relate to the animal differently than we do, we need to face any fears or misconceptions we might harbor about how kids cope, or avoid coping, with the loss of a pet. Lying to anyone about anything always spins a tangled web, but lying to kids about a dead, given-up, or lost pet may create a particularly sticky situation.

HONESTY—THE BEST POLICY

Evolution has imbued parents, and especially mammalian mothers, with a fierce desire to protect their offspring. Within the human species this may include protecting them from perceived mental, emotional, and physical harm. Although this can serve a survival function for the young, such protection only works if it springs from solid knowledge rather than fear on the adult's part. If the Hearnes tell their children that Mahitable died because the veterinarian couldn't treat her injuries rather than that they opted to euthanize her, they set into motion a healing process based on a monstrous lie, a choice that may cost them dearly.

THE HIGH COST OF LYING

Adults who lie to children do so hoping their children will never discover the truth, or that the children will only discover the truth under circumstances that won't harm the adult–child relationship. However, recall how the loss of a pet can affect adults. In one study of dog-owning adults, 58 percent ranked the death of their dog as one of the worst experiences of their lives. Given the impact of such a loss, adults might easily forget any comforting lies they told their children as they attempted to cope with the loss themselves.

In my experience, this kind of well-intended lying happens a lot, with one adult inadvertently mentioning some detail about the animal's loss that conflicts with the explanation the other adult gave the child. Even if adults manage to censor any references to the pet's loss in family conversations, they may accidentally reveal their lies in some other way.

"Putting that cat to sleep was the hardest decision I ever made in my life," Jeanne tells a friend at a neighborhood barbecue a month after Mahitable's death, unmindful of Jared's and Megan's presence in a group of children nearby.

Once they unwittingly expose their lie, the adults must deal with the distrust exposure generates. The children, who have already asked their parents many questions about various aspects of the pet's loss, may suddenly clam up on the subject. Other children become belligerent: "You killed my pet!" Still others feel even sadder about the pet's death than they did before.

And why shouldn't they? Now, in addition to coming to grips with the pet's loss, they must deal with the fact that their parents or some other trusted adult lied to them. This double whammy leaves them in the unenviable position of facing one of life's most difficult situations minus the support of an adult they believed they could trust, to say nothing of all the doubts the lie raises about that adult's trustworthiness in other areas. As if this weren't bad enough, because learning the truth often causes children to reconsider the pet's loss in a whole new light, they find themselves back at square one of the healing process.

Ironically, adults who lie about what happened to the pet invariably say they did it for the child's own good. In reality, though, fear rather than love or concern drives them, and that fear arises from two sources:

1. They don't trust the child's ability to handle the loss.

2. They fear the child will blame them for the pet's loss.

If the majority of pet owners rate the loss of a pet as one of the worst experiences in their lives, then their parental instincts might cause them to assume that their kids will fare even worse. However, children maintain their own special views of loss, and projecting adult fears about coping onto them may not serve them well. I recall one woman who arrived at the clinic with her severely injured Dalmatian and her ten-year-old son. Initially, both mother and son hovered worriedly around the table as I examined the dog and shared my findings. Soon, however, the mother asked the

> *In one study of dog-owning adults, 58 percent ranked the death of their dog as one of the worst experiences of their lives.*

boy to go wait for her outside. Once he left, she told me she wanted me to euthanize the dog.

"For a lot of reasons, I just can't afford to treat him. But," she continued, "I want you to tell my son you're going to do everything you can to save the dog."

The woman correctly interpreted my flabbergasted expression because she rushed on.

"My son goes in for major surgery tomorrow and I don't want anything to upset him," she explained. "When he's feeling better, I'll tell him the dog died."

Granted I could understand her desire not to upset the boy, but the idea of her asking me to lie to him, to say nothing of allowing him to believe that the dog died under my care, troubled me greatly.

I started to protest, but she gave me an anguished look and begged, "Please?"

Even as I walked toward the small figure hunched down on the curb in the parking lot, I still had no idea what I'd say to him. Luckily for me, though, he spoke first.

"My mom sent you out here to tell me Spot will be all right, but he's going to die isn't he?" he asked with a surprising amount of determination for one so young.

Any temptation I felt to lie to him faded when he locked his clear young eyes with mine. Instead, I merely nodded.

"Well, I don't want him to suffer. I don't care what my mom says. Will you put him to sleep for me?"

Cool professional that I am, I burst into tears, hugged him, and promised him I would. Then we discussed what the process involved, he asked the usual questions, and I answered them truthfully.

"You and Mom put Spot to sleep. I'll wait in the car," he finally decided after careful consideration.

Then as I started to leave, he said something I'll never forget.

"Thanks for not lying to me just because I'm a kid."

In addition to any parental instincts and projected fears about death complicating the healing process for kids, adult lies told to avoid being blamed for the loss of the pet can do a lot of damage. Whereas adults most commonly doubt a child's ability to cope with death from natural causes, they more typically fear censure when they opt to euthanize or give up a pet. This makes sense because the latter two involve conscious choices on the adult's part. Once my client decided to euthanize Spot and her son forced her to admit this, she couldn't tell him that she played no part in the animal's death. Similarly, when Pete takes a stray cat to the local shelter rather than keeping it as Chip begs him to, Pete can't escape the responsibility for this act, either.

Lying to kids to avoid blame serves no useful purpose for one glaringly obvious reason: As adults we are legally and morally responsible for anything that happens to the animals in our charge. Tragic avoidable and unavoidable injuries and ailments will take our pets' lives or cause us to give them up. Equally tragic avoidable and unavoidable circumstances will cause our pets to disappear. How much blame we must bear depends on how much guilt we feel about the circumstances surrounding the pet's loss, not on how much others know about what we did or did not contribute to the problem. Consequently, lying to avoid blame only increases the magnitude of our questionable behavior, thereby increasing our reasons to feel guilty. Because we know how guilt can block or destroy the healing process, neither those adults who take this approach nor the children on the receiving end of it benefit.

If this discussion about the evils of lying has made you vow to tell your children everything should you ever lose a pet, not so fast. That approach poses some problems, too.

TRUTH AND BALANCE

When I told my friends in the animal care community that I planned to write a chapter about children and pet loss, virtually everyone made the same request: "Will you *please* say something about those parents who insist on treating their kids like adults?" When I pressed for more details, I heard horror stories from veterinarians and vet techs that paralleled my own experience, such as:

- The parents who parroted the veterinarian's description of a complex, terminal medical condition almost verbatim to a three-year-old, then asked the child, "What do you think we should do, Amber?"

- The parents who presented a severely ill animal in great pain at 8 A.M. fully intending to euthanize it, but who then refused to grant permission for this procedure until they discussed it with their children, who wouldn't get home from school until 3 P.M.

Regardless how unthinking and even ridiculous and inhumane these parental approaches may appear to an outsider, most of these parents will say unequivocally that they did it with their kids' best interest in mind. However, as we'll see, helping kids means giving them information that makes sense to them. When Amber's mother rambles on and on to her daughter about how Kitty's blood tests reveal that he suffers from adrenal insufficiency complicated by hyperthyroidism and pulmonary edema secondary to a progressive cardiomyopathy, she sends one of two quite different messages.

1. The parent hopes to make sense of the damning data by repeating it aloud within a socially acceptable context.

2. The parent hopes to project the responsibility for making the necessary decisions regarding the critically ill or injured animal onto the child.

Virtually no animal healthcare professional I talked to believed that these children possessed the capacity to comprehend what their parents were saying.

"They might get bits and pieces of it," conceded one particularly astute observer, "but they don't get all of it. Certainly not enough to make an informed decision even if they had the legal right to make one. Some of them are just too darned young, but practically all of them expect their folks to make the final decision, so there's not that big a need for them to understand the details."

This brings us back to balance. Children certainly want and need to be included in the circumstances surrounding the loss of a pet, regardless of how it happens. However, adults should balance the child's right and need to know with a desire to provide that information in a manner that meets that particular child's needs.

"So how do we know what a particular child needs?" asks Pete. "Chip seems so mature for his age, it's hard not to think that he can cope with just about anything. Of course," he admits after some momentary reflection, "I just might want to believe that because he's a latchkey kid."

Because we may need to sort through a whole raft of highly variable lifestyle factors that influence how children respond to particular instances of pet loss, it helps to understand the basic traits that characterize the different stages of child development so we can best assist children through the healing process.

CHILD-SPECIFIC NEEDS

It's an understatement to say that it may require a fair amount of knowledge and effort to shepherd kids through the healing process, particularly if you have more than one child. How children respond to loss may vary greatly, but in general their responses fall into one of three categories, which also parallel their age and development:

- Multidimensional
- Concrete
- Breakaway

Very roughly, the multidimensional phase ends around age seven to eight, the concrete phase lasts through the preteens, and the breakaway period begins during the teenage years.

My reluctance to apply more specific ages to these phases springs directly from my knowledge of animal behavior and experience with kids facing the loss of their pets. In higher primates, it takes about a third of the lifespan for animals to learn all they need to know to survive in their complex social environments. Given both the increased lifespan and even greater complexity of many peoples' lives, it seems reasonable to expect that it will take longer for children to master the necessary skills to survive in that environment. The Hearnes want all of their children to excel, and their lives bulge with all kinds of school activities, private lessons, and other parental attempts to give Jessica, Megan, and Jared every possible advantage. Barry and Jeanne fully expect to extend this parental support through college and even beyond in an ongoing attempt to help their children get ahead. In such an environment, then, we can understand how a child might not become an adult until well into his or her twenties rather than the legally defined eighteen or even twenty-one.

On the other hand, children raised in harsher environments must often grow up much sooner. In extremely harsh environments, such as in those torn by violence, physiological maturity may come much, much earlier, with children becoming sexually mature as early as nine years of age. Although this may appall parents raising their young in more sheltered settings, it makes extremely good evolutionary sense. Biologically, the goal remains to get our genes circulating in the species gene pool. Children living in areas where gang or military warfare could snuff out their lives in an instant don't have the luxury to amass all the social and other skills that make for good parents. If they want to contribute to the gene pool at all, they need to do it as quickly as possible and hope for the best.

Between these two extremes, we find a growing population of kids like Chip Wyman, latchkey kids who go home to residences where the family dog or cat more likely greets them than any parent, or those legions who go from school to a sitter's, relative's, or neighbor's home where they remain until their parents pick them up after work.

Our hearts may go out to these particular children, but any child may encounter problems when faced with the loss of a pet, and each lifestyle carries advantages and disadvantages that warrant attention. True, the Hearne children's many activities might distract them from the loss of their pet, as may Chip's many chores at home. On the other hand, Jessica's, Megan's, and Jared's many activities may not allow them the time alone they need to work through their feelings—time that Chip may have to the point that it becomes detrimental. Given that background, let's examine our youngest group of mourners to see how their multidimensional view of animals may affect their response to the loss of a pet.

POOH, MAHITABLE, AND ME

Like many young children, five-year-old Jessica Hearne doesn't differentiate between toy and real animals or those she sees in cartoons or reads about in books. When she wheeled her baby carriage around the yard, her stuffed Winnie the Pooh and Mahitable shared space with her favorite doll, and she kept up a running string of chatter with her charges and any other live animals or toys they encountered on their journey.

"Look, Pooh. I bet Ms. Bee on that flower is going to make honey," she'd announce sagely, proud of herself for remembering that all worker bees are females. "You better fly up into a tree, Robby Robin," she then warns the red-breasted bird bathing in a nearby puddle. "Mahitable's with me today. But you wouldn't hurt him, would you, kitty? If you did, Dolly and the Pooh Bear won't play with you."

If a young child doesn't differentiate toys from live animals, it naturally follows that the lines between dead and alive may become rather blurred, too. While this appears to cause children few problems, adults observing their young charges may not fare as well.

DEATH AND THE VERY YOUNG CHILD

Jessica's attention wandered at Mahitable's carefully orchestrated funeral because the lifeless form lying on the tailgate wasn't *her* Mahitable. Her Mahitable possessed (for want of a better word) a spiritual dimension that allowed Jessica to attribute all kinds of wonderful characteristics to her. Her Mahitable not only listened to her, but the cat talked to Jessica, too. Although the lifeless, glassy-eyed body looked like Mahitable, any resemblance ended there.

How do very young children view pet funerals? The same way they view human funerals, weddings, and other rituals: as adult creations they choose to emulate primarily for their entertainment and educational value. The week after Mahitable's funeral and burial under the towering blue spruce, Jessica systematically held funerals and burial services for a wide collection of objects, including her favorite doll and a live beetle. When her disgusted older sister showed her the difference between a live beetle and a dead one ("See? The dead ones don't move"), Jessica then combed the house and yard for only those subjects meeting this new criteria.

> *How do very young children view pet funerals? The same way they view human funerals, weddings, and other rituals: as adult creations they choose to emulate primarily for their entertainmnt and educational value.*

To adult observers, Jessica's rituals possess a certain charm, but they also serve a valuable function for the child. Via her experiments, Jessica begins to hammer out her definition of dead versus alive, a task we know still boggles the minds of experts in many fields. Additionally, bond studies link children's concern and respect for animals to their concern for humans. Consequently, whether Jessica holds mock funerals for Pooh Bear or real ones for the dead moth she finds under the lamppost, all carry equal weight with her.

However, while Jessica may bury her Pooh Bear in a very serious mock funeral, when her father and older brother start playing touch football and use the bear as a ball, the little girl screams in obvious distress, "Don't hurt my bear!"

"Don't be such a baby!" scoffs Jared. "It's just a toy and we're just playing a game, just like you did when you buried him."

But Pooh isn't just a toy and his funeral wasn't just a game, not to Jessica and not to many children her age.

From this we can see that, although it may appear that young children don't benefit the same way from the rituals with which their parents and other adults might wish to surround the pet's death, they do benefit in the long run because these experiences provide them with the raw materials to begin fashioning workable definitions of life and death.

On the other hand, while young children need some information to fuel their early forays into the world of death, they don't need to know *everything*. An old truism in education maintains that the mind can only absorb what the rear end can endure, and this definitely holds true for kids. For a lot of young children, all the events surrounding the loss of a pet function like a handful of seeds randomly broadcast in their fertile but inexperienced young minds. For a while, some may appear totally oblivious to what happened. Initially, Jessica only wants to know what happened to Mahitable and the answer, "She got hit by a car" satisfies her. Over time, though, she asks for more details.

"Would Mahitable have looked like that if Daddy hadn't found her in the road?" she asks as the Hearnes' station wagon whips past a particularly flattened piece of road kill on the interstate two months after the cat's death.

Older folks hit with these out-of-the-blue references to the dead animal may recoil in shock. Like many people, the Hearnes find Jessica's inquiry at least troubling because it forces them to think about a sad event they'd rather forget. Additionally, they find that the guileless young child's fascination with "yucky stuff" borders on ghoulish when she applies it to a pet they loved and lost. However, Jessica doesn't see it that way at all. When Mahitable died, the event presented her with a lot of facts, impressions, and sensations in a relatively short period of time that she couldn't relate to other experiences in her young life. Consequently, she makes those connections after the fact with the ultimate goal of making sense of those aspects of the event that remained the most vivid in her mind. Thus, when asked what she remembers most about Mahitable's death, one day she immediately pipes up, "That fly walking across her eye! Blech!" but the next day, she murmurs tearfully, "That I lost my very best playmate."

When pets die as a result of bond or behavioral problems, adults must walk a very thin line. For one thing, a strong temptation to turn some forms of pet death into object lessons may assail us, if for no other reason than to salvage something beneficial from a bad situation: "Mahitable got hit by a car and died because she ran into the street without looking." or "Tuffy didn't listen to me when I told him not to get into stuff under the kitchen sink."

However, we already know that our own complicity often makes death that results from behavioral or bond problems particularly troublesome: Our pets looked up to us and expected us to train and relate to them in a way that would keep them safe, and we failed them. Because kids, and especially young ones, often view us the same way, foisting the full responsibility for the pet's death onto the animal may make the child feel vulnerable about his or her own welfare.

To further complicate matters, although the majority of kids never experience a life-threatening illness or injury, what child of any age hasn't misbehaved? Thus, when a parent opts to tolerate rather than deal with such behavior in a pet and doing so costs that animal its life, some children may rightfully wonder what their folks are setting them up for. Consequently, and particularly in the case of young children who see themselves on the same plane with their pets and take what others say quite literally, adults must carefully present the animal's death in a manner that won't cause children to worry needlessly about their own safety.

Children's tendency to assume that adults' behavior toward animals will translate to the way adults treat them can also be problematic when parents treat pets as expendable. A surprising number of parents will adopt animals when they move into summer homes, often for the express purpose of allowing their children to witness the "miracle of birth." At the end of the summer, many simply abandon the pets and any animal offspring because they consider euthanizing a healthy animal "cruel." I couldn't help thinking of these people when, as part of a rabies-control team, I toured the beaches of one small New Hampshire coastal town in sub-zero temperatures one particularly brutal winter. Unable to fend for themselves, numerous cats froze or starved to death when they sought shelter in crawl spaces under the familiar cottages, which then became sealed with an impenetrable layer of snow and ice following a freak storm.

Parents who indulge in such activities may tell themselves that they're teaching their children the miracle of life, but in reality they teach them just the opposite: that life is cheap and animals rank as little more than throwaways to discard when one gets tired of them. Because so many children, especially very young ones, see animals on a par with themselves, such parental behavior becomes even more reprehensible.

Given that young children who take a more multidimensional view toward life and death don't see death the same way older children and their parents do, does it come as any surprise that they don't relate to euthanasia the same way older folks do, either?

EUTHANASIA AND THE VERY YOUNG CHILD

Were it not so sad, observing parents trying to incorporate young children into the euthanasia decision-making process would be almost comic. If the situation allows them enough time, adults may attempt to prepare the child in advance. However, that preparation usually involves little more than coaching and results in exchanges at the veterinary clinic such as this:

> MOM: Jessica, do you know why we must put Mahitable to sleep?
>
> JESSICA: Yes, Mommy, she really hurts a lot.
>
> MOM: So you think it's the best thing to do?

JESSICA: Yes, because then she'll go to cat heaven and won't hurt anymore.

Adults who don't lay any groundwork prior to broaching the subject may face a wide variety of responses ranging from a barrage of questions—many of which hardly relate to the subject—to total disinterest. Unfortunately, because we adults so dread making the decision to euthanize a pet, a youngster's failure to take this event as seriously as we do may cause us to respond angrily. The owner who screamed at her six-year-old, "Stop playing with that toy! I need you to help me decide whether to put Fluffy to sleep!" sadly comes to mind here.

Euthanizing pets with behavioral and/or bond problems opens Pandora's box for the reason I mentioned earlier: What child hasn't done something he or she later regretted? For as long as Jessica could remember, her Aunt Mary allowed her dog, Ralphie, to snitch cookies from a plate on the kitchen counter. On several occasions, the Hearne children witnessed the canine raids and took advantage of the situation to help themselves to a few cookies, too. When Aunt Mary later announces that she'd put Ralphie to sleep because "That dog was such a nuisance!" all three of the children cringe, but Megan and Jessica take this declaration much more literally than Jared.

"Didja hear that?" Megan hisses to Jessica. "She killed the dog because he snitched cookies! Don't tell her what we did!"

The younger child now finds herself in an awkward position. She wants and needs to ask questions to understand what happened to the dog, but her sister makes it quite clear that she'll fare no better than Ralphie if Aunt Mary finds out about Jessica's own misbehavior. Aunt Mary's remark not only undermines Jessica's trust in her, but it could diminish the child's trust in other adults as well. Jessica knows her mom adores Aunt Mary and that the two women confide everything in each other. How can she possibly ask her mom if she or Jessica's dad would kill her if they knew she snitched cookies with Ralphie?

Because parents often will euthanize pets that display aggression because they fear for their children's safety, these problems deserve special mention. First, even though you feel 100 percent sure that you euthanized or otherwise got rid of the pet for the kids, *do not* say that to the children or anyone who might tell them.

"I thought you said we were supposed to tell them the truth," Pete reminds me.

You should, but that means the whole truth. The whole truth is that improper selection and training of the pet created problems the owners elected not to resolve when the problems progressed to a point where they threatened the well-being of the children. Also, telling a child, "We got rid of Skeezix because of you," amounts to blaming the child for the animal's loss or death. Although this may help soothe any parental guilt, it merely transfers that guilt to an innocent child. In fact, I recall one tragic case in which the father actually yelled at the child bitten by the family's untrained German shepherd dog, "If we have to get rid of the dog for biting, it will be because of you!" For weeks after this, the boy experienced sleep disturbances and finally admitted to his mom that he was scared to death that his parents were going to send him away rather than get rid of the dog. Needless to say, the dog's behavior exposed a lot of flaws in the family's relationships, too.

Another client worked diligently to correct her seventy-pound dog's aggressive behavior, but trying to accomplish this in the midst of a hectic life that included a four-year-old daughter and an eight-year-old son eventually wore her down. The day after the parents euthanized aggressive Albert, the little girl started carrying a toy dog wrapped in a doll blanket and wearing the deceased dog's collar around the house. When her brother, who had cried himself to sleep the previous night, appeared, the little girl held out the toy.

"Here," she offered. "Do you want to hold Albert?"

The mother froze, not sure how her son would react. The boy hesitated for an instant, then replied, "Sure," and walked off cuddling the toy.

When the mother asked me about this behavior, it reminded me of similar cases. So often we adults harbor this media-reinforced image of a big dog lovingly taking care of our children. Ironically, though, if you ask young children what they see in those images, they see exactly the opposite: a big, strong dog who obeys *their* every command. Put another way, a lot of kids want to nurture rather than be protected by their pets.

In addition to wanting to nurture rather than feel dependent on an animal for their own well-being, children don't like feeling intimidated by the family pet, either. Albert became an obstacle in the kids' lives when his pushy personality made them feel more vulnerable than secure. This, in turn, led to ambivalent feelings toward the pet that they needed to work through when he died. At that time they replaced him with an Albert they could cuddle, a pet they could trust.

Once again balance remains the key when dealing with potentially dangerous pets. We owe it to kids to keep them safe from harm, and that means following these basic rules:

- Select the most stable, child-safe pet possible
- Properly train that animal to ensure its continued safety
- Undertake any training in a manner that ensures the safety of the child
- End the relationship with the animal if you can't properly train it
- *Do not* blame the child if problems arise with the pet

Although some parents may see giving up or losing a pet as a lesser evil than death, young children bring their own special views to these forms of pet loss, too.

The Very Young Child and the Given-Up or Lost Pet

If young children can make a connection between adults putting them down for a nap and waking up as ashes in an urn next to Fuzzy's remains on the bookshelf, imagine what might run through their minds when adults give up their pets or the animals disappear. I lump these two forms of loss together because, unless parents make specific arrangements that permit children to see the pet again, young kids tend to respond to both the same way. In fact, at this age, they may not differentiate these forms of loss from death or euthanasia, either.

How much young children differentiate and how they respond once again depends on the amount of guidance and the example older folks set. Ideally, the adults in the household will serve as the primary source of information, and dole it out in an age-appropriate manner that fulfills the child's rather than the parents' needs. When that doesn't happen, young children will turn to older siblings, friends, television, or whatever or whoever they think can help answer their questions.

And believe me, they *will* ask questions about the missing pet. However, kids in this age group may find articulating their questions tough. When Jessica asks her father, "Do cats go to heaven?" the thought itself pleases her as much as the answer. Consequently, a brief but true answer followed by a related question—"I don't think they do, but your mother does. What do you think?"— may fill her needs far better than a long discourse on the subject. She can continue the discussion if she desires, but she needn't digest more information than she wants.

Admittedly, this runs contrary to giving the child the complete picture, an approach often favored, paradoxically, by those who dread discussing the lost pet with their kids. However, most youngsters find this very confusing, like having someone dump the pieces of a 250-piece puzzle on the table in front of them. Most much prefer to get a little reliable information, ponder it, fit it into the emerging scheme of things, then go back for another piece of the puzzle.

"But the older kids want more information!" Barry protests.

Yes, they do, as we shall see. On the other hand, parents should resist the urge to call a family conference to formally discuss the pet's loss if they're not prepared to accept a variety of responses to it, including the child who chooses to wander in and out of the discussion while another refuses to participate at all.

"Then why bother holding it?" Barry retorts somewhat irritably.

Because it is important for children to know that their parents or other adults are willing to discuss the animal's loss. Setting aside a specific time for this lets them know that and provides a more focused setting for any discussion. However, because the goal remains to meet the children's needs, parents should allow for a certain amount of flexibility. Even though Jessica may bounce in and out of the family sessions, she still benefits from having them.

"Mommy says that Mahitable went to cat heaven, but that some nice people who live in the country took Mr. McMurtry's cat to live with them," she explains to her dolly. "We won't see Mahitable any more because she's living with angels, but maybe someday we'll see Mr. McMurtry's cat on the farm!"

Although perhaps not as common an occurrence in this age of nontraditional families, some young children go through a phase when they wonder if they were adopted. Here again, a paradox emerges: Do these children worry that their parents aren't their real parents? Or do they worry that one set of parents already gave them up and this second set might, too? Given the number of young children who compare their own behavior to that of their pets, I suspect the first question worries kids the most. In the previous section, I mentioned the little boy who feared his parents would abandon him to an orphanage, a concept you would think would never enter the mind of an upper middle-class child like him. However, this belief progressed logically from his parents' early discussions

> *Parents should resist the urge to call a family conference to formally discuss the pet loss if they're not prepared to accept a variety of responses to it.*

about finding a new home for the dog after he bit the child the first time. Later, when the father blamed the boy for the dog's behavior, visions of his father finding a new home for him rather than the biting dog filled the boy's mind.

No matter what we adults may want to believe, young children *will* view who we give up a pet to and how, as well as how long we search for a lost pet, as indicative of how much effort we would make in their own behalf. If we make only minimal attempts, we communicate that we place little value on relationships. If the child isn't particularly attached to the pet, we can probably get away with it. However, if children experience strong bonds with animals that they consider on a par with those formed with parents or siblings, and the parents treat giving up or losing the pet casually, youngsters may believe that their folks feel the same way about them.

But don't let this talk of complications tempt you to whisk your child's pet away in the child's absence and plead ignorance. That leaves the child with nothing but his or her fears. We owe it to children to make ourselves available to answer any and all questions in a way that is meaningful to them, regardless whether we take the pet to a shelter, lose it at a rest stop, or attend its natural death or euthanasia.

Given all the curveballs the many dimensions of the young child's world may throw into the healing process, the concrete phase seems almost relaxing—until the kids in this phase start asking serious questions!

BUT YOU *SAID!*

As children grow older, they begin to learn that not everyone shares their multidimensional view of life. Not only that, they discover that adults maintain some very specific ideas about what constitutes reality, and many of these ideas begin to take hold in the growing child's mind. Whereas younger children often ask questions as much for the joy of asking them as for getting what adults consider any meaningful answers, older children may become deadly earnest about their quest for knowledge. Moreover, they typically take what we tell them quite literally.

"Tell me about it!" groans Pete. "When Chip first went into this phase, every other sentence out of his mouth was, 'But you *said.*' He had no concept of relativity at all!"

Kids at this stage can be frustrating to their busy parents and other adults, but you can't help but admire the enormous task they accomplish in a such short time. Through their often maddening questions and demands for concrete answers, these children make the transition from a multidimensional world where humans, animals, and toys all rank equally, to one in which animate or inanimate serves as the major differentiating factor. Within that system, the child also somehow makes sense of a wide range of often arbitrary and conflicting adult "facts."

"Megan, please don't bother Daddy while he's putting out bait to catch the mice," Jeanne tells her daughter.

Where younger Jessica might ask her Mom to define "bait," Megan interprets her mother's remark quite differently.

"How come it's all right for Daddy to kill mice?" she asks. "You told me to be kind to *all* animals."

Depending on their personal orientation toward rodents, some adults might laud Megan's question as indicative of her mature sensitivity about animal rights; others might condemn the child for her lack of maturity regarding the realities of life. Any adult who gets backed into a corner by one of these youthful seekers of concrete facts quickly discovers that many of them won't give up until you satisfy their curiosity, and do so in a manner that makes sense to them. To complicate matters further for adults—who live in a gray-shaded world, rather than one marked by the crisp black-and-white certainty these children desire—children at this stage will expect what we tell them to hold true, for the situation in question as well as for similar ones. What's more, and no matter how the child has been raised, many boys in this phase will respond differently from girls: Boys will already lean in a less emotional direction.

"I know about that, too!" Pete exclaims. "When I put Louie to sleep, I practically had to beg Chip to let out his feelings even though I knew how much he loved the dog."

However, even as Pete anguished over Chip's lack of response and any detrimental effects it might have on the healing process, he also felt obligated to put up a brave front for his son during this difficult time. Because one way to figure out the rules of any game involves watching the experienced players, can we blame Chip for learning more from what his dad does than what he says?

As we explore how children in the concrete stage respond to the various forms of pet loss, bear in mind that not all kids will fit a particular developmental mold all of the time. They may respond in what we consider a very immature manner to one kind of loss, but stun us with their mature handling of another. Also, as kids get older, their peers and other adults (including celebrities and others in the media) play a more important role in their lives. Daycare providers and teachers often appreciate it when parents tell them about the loss of a pet in the family. Not only does such information enable them to help that particular child, but it provides educators with an excellent opportunity to discuss pet loss with other children. This serves two beneficial purposes:

1. Because we know that many children first deal with the loss of a loved one in the form of a family pet, teachers can provide age-appropriate information about the subject that may help other children deal with losses they encounter later.

2. The extra attention bestowed on the child who suffered the loss will make him or her feel like a vital part of the group at this difficult time.

Many parents have told me that their children's open discussion of pet loss at school made it easier for the entire family to cope. Additionally, I've heard parents express surprise and delight when they attended a school event and their more reserved children proudly showed them a collection of stories or pictures, all about the lost pet; until then, they'd feared that the youngsters had denied the loss completely. I cherish one particularly loving memory of a mother who described sitting on a teeny chair at a tiny table with her young son, tears streaming down both of their faces and his arm protectively around her, reading story after story about their beloved cat who had been hit by a car.

Even though I said it before in reference to all kids, I can't overemphasize the need to resist any urge to lie to kids in this stage. We might get away with lying to younger kids simply because they may either misunderstand or disregard much of what we try to explain about heady issues such as death, euthanasia, and other ways pets become lost. We might also get away with lying to older children, who already acknowledge that they and adults don't necessarily agree on everything.

But remember that kids in the concrete phase are in the process of figuring out how adults see the world, and how adult reality is shaped. If we lie to them, how can they hope to accomplish this, and how can we blame them if they fail?

We know from many studies that American pet owners of all ages consider their pets family members. Consequently, it's likely that children will apply to themselves anything parents say to them about a pet's departure from the household. Put another way, whatever you do, *do not* blame the pet for its death, euthanasia, disappearance, or the fact that you chose to give it up.

NATURAL DEATH AND THE CONCRETE CHILD

We already agree that taxes probably carry more certainty than any definitions of death. Nonetheless, children facing the natural death of a beloved pet may summon a mind-boggling number and array of questions about it, most of which begin with "Why?"

- Why did Mahitable die?
- Why didn't you treat her for her injuries?
- Why didn't you let her die at home?
- Why did she die before I had time to say good-bye?

Parents trying to cope with their own feelings about the pet's death may find some of these questions and their answers so frightening that they go into the freeze, fight, or flee mode. Barry clams up when he can't answer ten-year-old Megan's questions. Older brother Jared becomes defensive—"She was only a cat, for Pete's sake! Stop asking so many questions!"—and her mother suddenly remembers an important meeting she must attend.

> *Many parents have told me that there children's open discussion of pet loss at school made it easier for the entire family to cope.*

However, every unanswered question leaves a void that these kids will try to fill some other way. If parents or other adults won't provide the necessary information or steer the child toward a reliable source, they can blame no one but themselves if the youngster assumes the worst rather than the best about the circumstances of the pet's death.

"But what if you don't know the answer?" Barry asks with more than a little exasperation.

The answer "I don't know, but why don't we find out together?" benefits everyone involved. It reminds the child that adults don't necessarily know everything; it acknowledges the validity of the child's question; and it provides the adult with an opportunity to show the child how to go about collecting meaningful information.

Funerals and other death-related rituals also take on a different meaning as kids grow older. While young Jessica uses her mock funerals primarily as connecting links between her multidimensional world and the adults' real one, Megan sees those same rituals as concrete proof that she comprehends the difference between a real animal and a toy, between a live animal and a dead one, and between just any dead animal and her beloved Mahitable. Consequently, whereas Jessica raids her toy box and combs the yard for worthy subjects to pray over and bury when she "plays funeral," Megan throws herself into the planning of the most perfect, *real* funeral service for Mahitable. The idea of children putting so much effort into the writing and reading of eulogies for their pets and arranging a myriad of details for a pet's funeral and burial may strike some adults as charming.

"Kids Megan's age are so cute," gushes Aunt Mary. "Imagine doing all that for a cat."

But remember that Megan takes all of her preparations and their implementation quite seriously as she seeks to discover the concrete facts about death, a process that becomes even more complex when a child in the concrete phase faces euthanasia.

EUTHANASIA AND THE CONCRETE CHILD

Like many owners, when Pete decided to euthanize Louie, he wrestled with the decision for days.

"The only thing worse was figuring out how much to involve Chip in the process," he admits later, a concern that plagues many adults.

I mentioned earlier that, regardless how much responsibility for the pet adults may wish to foist off on kids, we can't duck responsibility for making life and death decisions. On the other hand, parents should give children who want to become involved in the process every opportunity to ask questions, and they should answer those questions honestly, even if that means saying something the child doesn't want to hear.

"The day I told him about Louie's cancer, Chip must have asked me a hundred times, 'Why do we have to put Louie to sleep?'" Pete says. "Each time I explained all the factors that led me to that decision and answered all of his questions about them. When he ran out of questions, I asked him if he wanted to say goodbye to Louie before the vet put him down, whether he wanted to stay while we did it, and whether he wanted some time alone with Louie or with me and Louie after it was over. Finally, I asked him if he wanted to take charge of Louie's funeral and burial."

In this situation, Pete makes it quite clear to Chip that he's made the decision to euthanize the dog and feels comfortable with it, thus relieving his son of that burden. His willingness to answer Chip's questions honestly acknowledges the boy's right to know the details about this crucial event. By letting Chip take responsibility for Louie's funeral and burial if Chip wants to, Pete also respects Chip's need for involvement in the process.

Compare this to the horror scenarios in which parents involve the children in lengthy discussions about whether they should euthanize the pet even to the point that—shudder—some even decide the matter by family vote, or blame the children for the euthanasia. Which approach seeks to fulfill the *child's* needs?

THE GIVEN-UP PET AND THE CONCRETE CHILD

Because children going through this period of development may so strongly relate to themselves anything that befalls the pet, pets given up for "problems" naturally may raise troubling questions in some young minds. Megan already harbors an image of her rather stern Aunt Mary euthanizing her if she ever learns about her escapades with Ralphie, the cookie-snitching dog. Given the numbers of adult cats given up for not using the litter box, I can't help wonder how this awareness might affect the older child who still occasionally wets the bed.

Remember my first two commandments: *Don't lie*, and *Don't evade responsibility for the choice to give up the pet*. Moreover, when explaining why the pet must be given up, make sure you address any parallels you know or even suspect children might make with themselves.

"I know everyone snitches a cookie once in a while," Jeanne later tells Megan as they pick strawberries together. "And I'd never put a pet to sleep for doing that."

"But would you give the pet away?" Megan broaches the subject of her second greatest concern.

"I'd never give up you, Jessica, or Jared for *anything*, but if a pet had problems I knew I couldn't handle but I knew someone else who could, I might consider it," Jeanne admits truthfully. "But I'd do everything in my power to find the very best home for the animal. Better yet, I'd first learn everything I could about doing the right thing so that never happens to a pet of ours. You'd help me do that, wouldn't you?"

Many an adult has asked a child in this phase for help with something as a concerned but knee-jerk response rather than because they truly desired any such assistance. But as a result, many then discover that the child takes this request most seriously. In fact, given their often dogged consistency, some of these kids can be darned good pet trainers.

THE LOST PET AND THE CONCRETE CHILD

In chapter two, we discussed how long to continue searching for a lost pet. This issue especially plagues children in this age group. Jessica views helping Megan search for her best friend's lost puppy as more of a game. She begins the task somberly enough, but then the arrival of the letter carrier distracts her and she races off to greet him. Not so for Megan. She approaches finding the pup like a young woman on a sacred mission. Her best friend takes the job even more seriously.

"Come on, Mom!" urges the little girl. "The baby will be fine alone in the house. You have to help us find Twinkie."

When her mother refuses, the two little girls feel totally betrayed.

"I remember once when I got lost in a shopping mall and I was *so* scared," Megan says slowly. "But I just knew my parents would come and find me."

"I always felt the same way," admits her best friend. "But maybe I was wrong."

Adults who don't want to keep looking as long or as hard for a lost pet as the child does should explain exactly why they made this choice. On the other hand, those who allow children to spend an unreasonable amount of time on a fruitless search relinquish any right to blame the child for any hardships this may create.

More than anything else, kids in this age group need and depend upon quality communication from adults to help them make sense of what, to them, may seem like an overwhelming number of variables, some of which their parents and others consider more valid than others. But while these children may confound us with their loss-related questions as they seek to understand why it happened, their older counterparts in the breakaway phase want to know, "Why did this happen *to me*?"

LOSS AND THE BREAKAWAY GENERATION

After spending a great deal of time and effort trying to figure out the concrete rules governing the adult world, children become a bit more flexible. Fifteen-year-old Jared recognizes, more than Megan does, that there are many more shades of gray. Not only that, some of his shades of gray don't match his parents' grays at all. Once children think they understand how the adult world works, they begin striking out on their own. Admittedly, parents of teenagers often get the idea that they can't do anything right and that their offspring don't listen to them at all. But although peers and other external factors such as the media may wield tremendous influence over these youngsters, in times of crisis most of them automatically turn to their folks.

Ironically, when it comes to loss, a surprising number of adults focus all their attention on the very young, erroneously dismissing the older children as "old enough" to cope on their own. However, studies indicate that just the opposite holds true. And this makes sense, if you think about it. Imagine yourself in the process of staking out a whole new mental, emotional, and perhaps even physical territory for yourself: Wouldn't you want everyone and everything in your "old" life to remain stable so you could measure your own progress against it?

For many older kids, the pet often ranks as one of the most long-standing, intimate, stable, and reliable reference points in their lives. True, by the time they hit the teenage years and spend more time away from home, it may seem as if they barely acknowledge the pet at all. Nonetheless, a lot of pets still sleep with these kids every night. And even though the actual time spent with the pet may dwindle, the animal remains a repository of many hopes, fears, and dreams confided over the years.

Because of this, kids in this age group may take the loss of a pet under *any* circumstances particularly hard, and adults who scold them to "stop acting like a baby" rather than trying to understand the child's point of view do far more harm than good.

NATURAL DEATH AND THE BREAKAWAY CHILD

Although logic argues to the contrary, older kids want to believe that they and everyone they care for is immortal, and this includes the family pets. Consequently, kids in this stage may respond far more dramatically to the death of a pet than those who are much younger. Not surprisingly, these kids may also already display personalities that lean more strongly in the emotional or logical direction, perhaps because their lack of experience leads them to emulate gender stereotypes. Jared becomes a paragon of stoicism when Mahitable dies, defining his role as "being strong for Megan and Jessica." When his girlfriend's dog dies and she throws herself sobbing down on the animal's grave, he finds her outburst frightening while she considers it perfectly normal. I suspect almost every veterinary clinic sports at least one patched hole in a wall or dent in a door left by the fist of a young man who just learned of the death of his pet; and most veterinary staffs relate tales of young women whose emotional responses made Camille look like Pollyanna.

If the child grew up with the pet and then became involved in other pursuits as older kids inevitably do, guilt can rear its ugly head when the pet dies. Like working parents and adult pet owners, youngsters in this stage of development also easily succumb to the belief that, had they only been home, the life-threatening problem never would have arisen. Because of this, parents should do everything in their power to keep the child aware of any events that might threaten the animal's welfare.

"I learned that the hard way," Pete recalls with a grimace. "Chip's older sister was away at college when the vet diagnosed Louie's cancer. I didn't tell her because it was during finals, plus, to tell you the truth, she lives with her mom and I'd hoped her mother would tell her. When she found out, she was furious with all of us because we hadn't told her right away."

Nor can we blame children placed in this position. Here they are, making their first forays into the adult world and people they trust withhold information about an event that matters a great deal to them. How else could they feel under those circumstances?

EUTHANASIA AND THE BREAKAWAY CHILD

When you want to believe that you and all your loved ones are immortal, the idea of actually choosing to end a loved one's life may ignite passionate feelings. Parents facing this choice who avoid discussing the subject under less-threatening circumstances (such as when a friend or neighbor makes such a choice or an article on the topic appears in the local paper) find themselves broaching the subject under the worst possible conditions. When the Hearnes try to fit such a discussion into the period they allot to deal with all three of their children's needs, they fail miserably with Jared, who completely shuts them out.

Adults who have not worked through their own feelings about euthanasia and/or those who want to avoid taking responsibility for the choice may expect the older child to comfort *them*. By now I suspect you know exactly what I think of adults who try to dump this and other loss-related decisions on kids. You may add my memory of the mother who told her seventeen-year-old son, "You're the man of the house now, Kevin. Do you want to put Humphrey down?" to my list of least respected parents.

Admittedly some kids, and especially older ones in the breakaway phase, want and need to participate in the

> *Adults who have not worked through their own feelings about euthanasia and/or those who want to avoid taking responsibility for the choice may expect the older child to comfort them.*

decision-making process. However, no adult should ever leave the child with the impression that he or she must make such a decision alone. Even if the child insists on making the choice and appears to handle it well, adults should make it crystal clear that they totally agree with the choice. If they don't, they shouldn't euthanize the animal until they resolve this conflict.

Above all, give kids in this phase time to cope with the idea of euthanasia and say goodbye. Remember, the crucial role that believing that this choice constitutes the best alternative plays in the healing process. That is especially true for kids. One parent described feeling practically forced by her veterinarian to euthanize her well-loved dog immediately. To be fair, the veterinarian had detected a tumor that could have created horrendous problems any minute. On the other hand, the dog had shown no external signs except for a tiny mass by its anus. Consequently, the late-morning recommendation to euthanize the animal that day stunned the owner. When she and her husband called their sixteen-year-old son home from school, the boy asked for permission to take the dog on one final ride to all their favorite haunts, a farewell trip that barely allowed the owner time to make the four o'clock appointment to put the animal down.

In retrospect, the mother realized that she erred in allowing the veterinarian to scare the family into doing something that struck them as intuitively wrong, no matter how medically right. While she still lives with her guilty feelings about this episode three years later, I can't help admiring the love and courage that allowed her to forego saying her own final goodbyes so her son might have those few treasured hours for himself. The mere thought of how that young man would have felt had he come home to learn that all this had transpired in his absence makes me cringe.

Fortunately, although death and euthanasia can hit kids in this phase particularly hard, their maturity makes them less likely to make connections between themselves and the given up or disappearing pet.

THE GIVEN-UP OR LOST PET AND THE BREAKAWAY CHILD

By the time they reach this stage, most kids possess a pretty good idea about how the adults in their lives view animals, which the kids either accept or not. If everyone in the household respects and loves the animals, minimal conflict should arise regarding reasons for giving up a pet or how long to search for a lost one. If parents care more about the pet than the child does and willingly accept full responsibility for the pet, then the child essentially can remain outside the process.

Sometimes, however, a child will care more about the pet than the parents do, a situation that almost invariably arises when parents get pets for kids rather than because they wanted a pet themselves. Because the adults remain distanced from the animal, they may not provide proper training or guidance; this almost inevitably leads to problems.

When older kids don't want to give up a pet, most want to know what they must do to keep it. At that point, adults owe it to the child to clearly define what, if anything, the child can do to change their mind. Because older youngsters often have so many other obligations, many parents find that a contract system works best. For example, if the parents want to give up the pet because of destructive or other negative behavior, the child might sign a contract agreeing to assume the responsibility for training the pet.

At this stage, most children can assume such responsibility and the contract communicates the parents' sensitivity to this as well as an awareness of the animal's needs. The contract also clearly states what will happen if the child does not assume this responsibility.

"Isn't that the same as laying a guilt trip on the kid?" Pete wants to know.

In this situation, the parents have already acknowledged to the child that they personally can't give the animal the kind of care they believe it deserves, which has led them to decide to give it up. Of course, adults not prepared to monitor the fulfillment of the contract and remove the pet if the child reneges do nothing to help the pet and, instead, may make its problems much worse.

Older kids also can do a wonderful job mounting a search for a lost pet if parents lack the time for commitment to the animal. However, once again communication about the child's plans remains vital. One parent just about died when she learned her seventeen-year-old daughter had spent the whole night tacking up lost-pet announcements on utility poles in the most dangerous part of town.

When parents confront these and other dilemmas that crop up when kids of all ages lose a pet to any cause, the question "Should we replace the lost pet?" almost always arises.

SHOULD YOU REPLACE THE LOST PET?

The child–pet bond confers so many positive benefits that the idea of replacing a deceased or lost animal immediately comes to mind. However, remember two key points. First, you can't *replace* any lost pet, so don't even try. I'll even go so far as to recommend getting a pet as different from the lost animal as possible to avoid unfair comparisons. Second, recall the only valid reason to get a pet: Because you *want* a pet, that *particular* pet. Getting a pet to replace one you lost doesn't fulfill that criterion.

As far as when to replace a pet, a major change in our social structure makes this a more difficult question to answer now than in the past. Many latchkey kids like Chip Wyman spend at least a few hours alone while their parents work. Like Chip, many of these kids also belong to nontraditional families. Knowing what we do about the many positive effects of the human–animal bond, it's impossible to underestimate the role that a well-loved pet plays in these kids' lives. In fact, as I struggled to come up with an answer to how long latchkey kids' parents should wait before getting a new pet, I realized that the best solution meant having at least two pets in the household. That way if something should happen to one, the child still can rely on the companionship of the other. This, in turn, would eliminate any need to rush out and get another pet right away and avoid all the problems that often accompany that approach.

Allowing kids time to think about getting a new pet confers some distinct advantages:

- It gives them time to make peace with the loss of the other animal
- Learning about the breed or species of any prospective new pet enables family members to discuss any problems that may have led to the previous pet's loss and ways to avoid them
- It ensures that the family gets the new pet because they all want that particular animal

When selecting a new pet, latchkey kids once again present unique challenges. My youngest son, Dan, demonstrated this to me when I told him and his older brother that they could each pick the dog of their choice after I had to euthanize our old mongrel. Because both boys ranked as children in a non-traditional single-parent family as well as latchkey kids, I automatically began nudging Dan toward goldens and Labs. However, he gently but persistently reminded me that I said he could make the choice.

> Give kids time to cope with the idea of euthanasia and say goodbye.

His selection? Surely the sweetest little Chihuahua ever placed on this earth.

At first I was horrified, but once I got over my shock, I realized that my ten-year-old knew his needs and how to meet them far better than I. In spite of everything I knew about dogs and how they relate to kids, my maternal instincts automatically made me think in terms of the dog—forgive me for thinking this!—protecting Dan. However, at ten years of age, Dan no longer needed protection; he wanted to do some protecting himself. Thirteen years and a lot of boy–dog escapades later, Dan and that sweet little dog now face her inevitable death from an inoperable cancer we all know we can't cheat forever. Much as my maternal genes hate to admit it, that dog probably did far more to make my bungee-jumping, rough-and-tumble son a sensitive guy of the nineties than I ever did.

All the different ways the bond manifests in kids when they lose a pet could easily fill an entire book. To negotiate it all, just remember those two words: respect and balance. As long as we respect the child's and the animal's needs as well as our own, and as long as we balance those needs so we don't ask too much or too little at this critical time, we and our children may regret the loss, but never the way we handled it.

The idea of trying to orchestrate events to protect children when pet loss occurs seems so natural, it seems only right to respond in a similar fashion when dealing with people with special needs. As we'll see in the next chapter, however, sometimes we wind up caring unwisely rather than well.

CHAPTER NINE

DOUBLE JEOPARDY

Pet Loss and Those with Special Needs

It would be a great thing to understand pain in all its meanings.

—Peter Mere Latham
Collected Works

WHEN SEPTUAGENARIAN Noni Huntley realizes that something serious ails her terrier, Toivo, she immediately calls her daughter, Paige, to take him to the veterinary clinic for her.

"What am I going to do?" Paige asks her friend and coworker, Dianna Feldstein. "In dog years Toivo's even older than Mom and she'll just die if anything happens to him."

Dianna shakes her head sympathetically.

"I'm kind of going through the same thing with my brother. Jimmy has AIDS and his five cats are lifesavers because they take his mind off his illness. But he can't care for them the way he used to, plus his favorite, Millie, has multiple problems herself. I'm scared to death

Jimmy's going to catch something from her, but I can't imagine him getting rid of her, either."

"Must be something going around." Another co-worker, Gary Webber, smiles wanly. "The vet called this morning to tell me that the small lump I felt on the front leg of my daughter's service dog is highly malignant. How do you break that kind of news to someone who relies on the animal for her freedom?"

⌒⌒

IN THIS chapter we'll explore some of the factors that may delay or complicate the healing process for those with special needs. Discussions about people with special needs losing their pets often automatically elicit paternalistic responses. Take the case of senior citizens for instances.

"My mom *does* have special needs," Paige insists. "She's an old woman and she can't handle a crisis with her dog."

With that assumption Paige commits ageism, the tendency to assign physical, mental, and/or emotional limitations to people simply because of their age, not unlike discriminating against someone based on sex or race. Admittedly, Noni Huntley can't get around as well as she used to, but she remains mentally active, keeps in touch with her many friends, and relishes living alone. Paige's automatic assumption that age will make it impossible for her mother to cope with any bad news about Toivo amounts to little more than blatant paternalism. Quite frankly, if I faced a life-threatening condition in my beloved corgi, Violet, I'd feel as if I were going to die, too, and I'm only in my early fifties. I can think of people who are much younger who would feel the same way if they lost their pets.

Similarly, we often treat those of all ages who have various physical, mental, and emotional problems paternalistically. In reality, however, all of us go through periods during which we feel physically, mentally, and/or emotionally vulnerable. Not only that, the three states tend to work in tandem. When Noni's arthritis acts up and she can't meet her friends for lunch as planned, that awareness affects her mentally and emotionally, too.

"I'd never admit this to Paige because she worries so much," Noni confesses. "But every time this old body of mine doesn't do what I want it to, I can't help thinking about what will happen to me when I can't take care of myself any longer. And those kinds of thoughts make me depressed!"

In chapter eight I mentioned how readily kids apply adults' treatment of animals to themselves. Some adults may do the same thing when they don't feel up to snuff and must depend on others for care and support: "Sure, go ahead and kill Millie!" screams Jimmy when he learns Dianna wants to get rid of one of his cats. "You can do the same thing to me when I make a mess, too!" Luckily, in my experience, such exchanges occur far more frequently in our minds than in reality. More typically, Jimmy's family would avoid broaching the subject of his ailing cat because they fear it will remind him of his own terminal disease, while he wishes they'd help him make a difficult decision about his beloved pet.

Dealing with those with special needs, or facing these conditions ourselves, we can simplify matters if we apply similar principles to those discussed in chapter eight for dealing with pet loss and children:

- Whoever makes the choices should assume responsibility for their implementation.
- Don't lie
- Provide information that meets the person's special needs

In the field of bioethics the issue of personal autonomy, the right to make choices and accept responsibility for their consequences, comes up again and again. Many times we want to make our own choices, but then we expect someone else to assume the responsibility for any negative consequences. Paige withholds news of Toivo's deteriorating condition from her mother, then wants her mother to accept the news of Toivo's impending death calmly. Jimmy insists on keeping multiple cats, but he expects his sister, Dianna, to care for them when he can't. Gary believes his daughter, Vicki, can't handle any bad news about her service dog, Horatio, but he can't bear the idea of putting the dog down without her consent, either.

The very best of intentions may underlie our desire to make difficult choices for those we view as unable to make them for themselves. But we can save ourselves a lot of headaches and heartaches if we determine those people's willingness to make the decision *first*, and then willingly assume the responsibility for the choice and all consequences if they can't or won't.

We shouldn't lie to those in compromised physical, mental, or emotional states for the same reason we shouldn't lie to anyone else: Whatever benefits we might gain will be more than offset by the loss of that person's trust. If Dianna tells Jimmy that Millie ran away and he later discovers she had the cat euthanized, he'll doubt everything she tells him from then on.

Providing appropriate information may require some skill, and professional, nonpaternalistic caregivers can serve as valuable resources. In general, resist the urge to treat the physically and emotionally impaired as mentally impaired, too. Also, remember that a forty-year-old with the mind of a ten-year-old is *not* a ten-year-old. He or she has collected thirty more years of experience and thus may view events quite differently. Put another way, communicate with the person, not the stereotype.

> We shouldn't lie to those in compromised physical, mental, or emotional states for the same reason we shouldn't lie to anyone else: Whatever benefits we might gain will be more than offset by the loss of that person's trust.

If we accept that we all feel physically, mentally, and emotionally vulnerable at times, it stands to reason that the loss of a pet could coincide with one of these periods of vulnerability. When that occurs, then we must take the effect of this vulnerability on the healing process into account, too.

Let's examine how three different types of vulnerability may affect our responses to the different forms of pet loss.

PET LOSS AND PHYSICAL VULNERABILITY

Given what we know about the way our pets affect our physiology and vice versa, we can safely say that the loss of a pet *will* affect us physically to some degree, even if we don't specifically acknowledge the pet as the source of those changes. Two additional groups of people may feel particularly physically vulnerable when they lose a pet:

- Physically healthy folks who see their pets as a source of protection
- Physically impaired people who rely on their pets to perform functions the owner cannot

Many perfectly healthy pet owners view their pets as a source of protection, even though logic says that, with less fear and a little training, they could accomplish this task on their own. As we've seen, owners' definitions of "protective" behavior span the spectrum from the dog who mounts a full-blown attack every time someone knocks on the door to the cat who seeks out the owner and murmurs an inquisitive "Meow?" when a strange vehicle pulls into the driveway. Whether we openly encourage these displays or find them reassuring or maddening, the fact remains that when they suddenly disappear from our lives, we miss them. Toivo's daily barking at the letter carrier always caused Noni to yell at him to hush up. In the terrier's absence, though, she finds herself alert to countless sounds, which she used to ignore, around the time of day the mail arrives.

"It's not that the letter carrier threatened me," Noni clarifies that point immediately. "It's just that I feel like

I must pay attention to things going on outside the house more carefully now that Toivo's not here."

Noni's statement reflects yet another one of those fascinating paradoxes about our relationships with our pets: As little as most of us know about how our pets' extraordinary senses of hearing, motion-sensitive vision, and smell affect the animal, we intuitively recognize how these animal senses affect *us.* Thus when the pet disappears, we lose the equivalent of an ultrasensitive sound- and motion-detecting device, along with everything else. The more impaired our own senses, the more we come to rely on the pet, and the more physically vulnerable we feel without this furry or feathered sensory extension.

While adjusting to this particular aspect of the loss may not require much time and energy for someone like Noni who lives in a quiet neighborhood, those who live in more threatening spaces may find that the pet's loss generates considerable stress. One owner described how he gave up his long daily walks when he lost his spaniel because he didn't feel safe walking without his canine companion; another gave up her evening aerobics class because she didn't feel comfortable leaving her home unprotected after her Doberman died. In such cases, the loss of a pet may actually result in the physical deterioration of a once-healthy owner.

Additionally, we see owners with sufficient physical limitations, such as blindness, deafness, or limited mobility, who must depend on service animals to perform tasks they cannot. Gary's daughter, Vicki, lost the use of her legs following an accident and now uses a wheelchair to get around. Her black Lab, Horatio, retrieves various objects on command for her, carries her belongings in his backpack, and generally looks out for her welfare.

Thanks to the increasing number of studies of the human–animal bond, we also know that those who suffer from physical ailments such as high blood pressure and some forms of heart disease may benefit from animal companionship, too. Other studies indicate that people confined to nursing homes because of advanced age and/or other serious medical conditions also benefit from the presence of animals. Although the very nature of traditional science makes it unlikely that professionals in human medicine will readily embrace the notion that Jimmy's five cats *do* benefit his health, Jimmy and all of his family and friends know otherwise.

"I live for these cats," declares Jimmy. "It's as simple as that. If I didn't have them and their antics to occupy me, I know I'd feel a lot sicker than I do."

"I can appreciate that," Paige admits candidly. "On the other hand, can you blame those of us who dread what will happen if a pet belonging to one of these people dies?"

Not at all. However, responding to such a death out of knowledge rather than fear always proves the best course of action.

NATURAL PET DEATH AND
THE PHYSICALLY VULNERABLE

Those who feel physically vulnerable and depend on their pets for protection find themselves in the terrible position of facing one of life's worst challenges without the animal's support when it dies. As a group, people who live alone suffer the most. However, family and friends also *expect* those who live alone to suffer the most, too. I mention this because, even though pet owners in this position sometimes feel extremely tempted to immediately replace the lost animal themselves, family and friends are often more likely to give these folks pets as gifts shortly after the loss.

> Those who feel physically vulnerable and depend on their pets for protection find themselves in the terrible position of facing life's worst challenges without the animal's support when it dies. Those who live alone suffer the most.

"I know exactly what you mean!" Noni exclaims. "I barely had time to grasp that Toivo was dead before Paige showed up with a new puppy. I know her heart was in the right place, but it was the last thing I needed right then. I tried to make a go of it for a few days because I didn't want to hurt her feelings, but I finally got up the courage to ask her to take him away."

"In retrospect, I shouldn't have done it," Paige admits. "I had this dumb idea that Mom would make associations between Toivo's death and her own. She didn't, but *I* did."

Healthy people often believe that those they view as physically impaired see everything in terms of their vulnerability. Faced with the realization that her beloved mother has grown older, Paige can't imagine that her mom wouldn't view everything in life through the lens of that awareness. Because Toivo shared such an intimate relationship with her mom, Paige automatically assumed that Noni would view anything that happened to the old dog as handwriting on the wall: "Look! It happened to your old pet! It could happen to you, too, old woman!"

Admittedly, owners and pets succumb to similar or identical medical problems often enough that I can't deny the possibility that at least some of us use our pets to dry-run that final journey. On the other hand, a lot of owners of all ages with all kinds of physical ailments don't make that connection, and our believing that their tears reflect the fear of their own deaths rather than grief over the pet's demise does them a disservice.

"Stop fawning over me!" Noni shouts at Paige. "Don't you understand I need some time alone to deal with this?"

Because the possibility for miscommunication looms around every corner, communication before the fact can head off many problems. Whether Noni actually suffers from a physical condition that may get worse following Toivo's death or her loved ones merely *think* she does, they could have saved themselves a lot of agony by discussing the issues that surrounded Toivo's death before it happened.

"Oh, my God!" Dianna Feldstein exclaims. "I could never discuss pet death with Jimmy!"

"And I wouldn't dare bring it up with Vicki, either," Gary declares adamantly. "Not after all she's been through!"

In addition to their obvious paternalism, such reactions also ignore the value of a preventive discussion to the physically vulnerable person. Obviously, Dianna and

Gary's approach spares them from discussing a difficult subject. However, what do Jimmy and Vicki think about this? If these pet owners respond the same way that the majority of people with terminal diseases do, and nothing makes me doubt that they will, they'll say they want to know the truth, no matter how distressing, as soon as possible.

"I don't want to be treated like an idiot just because I'm sick," Jimmy states clearly. "My cats mean a lot to me, and if one of them becomes seriously ill or injured, I want to be the first to know."

"I depend on Horatio for my life, for Pete's sake!" Vicki sputters. "I can't afford not to know that he has problems!"

EUTHANASIA AND THE PHYSICALLY VULNERABLE

A case I've written about in the past deserves mention here because it not only sums up the exquisite range of the human–animal bond as it applies to euthanasia, but it also touches on the issue of human–animal physical codependency. Early in my medical practice, I diagnosed malignant lymphoma, a progressive, fatal disease in dogs, one week before a physician diagnosed the same condition in the owner. When I made my diagnosis, I frankly answered the owner's questions about various treatment options and what lay ahead for her pet.

"And if I don't treat him?" she asked.

Although, aside from his enlarged lymph nodes, the dog appeared perfectly normal at that time, I explained the different kinds of problems that could arise, such as the lymph nodes in the chest enlarging to the point that they interfered with the dog's ability to swallow. The owner opted to take the dog back home with the idea that we'd focus all treatment on keeping him comfortable for as long as possible. Six months later, the son brought the dog in for euthanasia. Until the previous week, the dog had continued eating and drinking normally and, even though he had slowed down some, he still greeted everyone cheerfully and gave no evidence of any discomfort. Given the dog's gracious temperament, it came as no surprise that he calmly slipped away from us in death.

"My mom died last week," the young man whispered as he stared down at the dog's body, an announcement that stunned me. Before I could respond, he continued. "From the time of her own diagnosis until she died, her life was filled with one treatment after another. She finally died in a hospital room filled with so much equipment it looked like the cockpit of a rocketship."

Stroking the inert dog's fur, he said many things about death and dying that have stuck in my mind over the years, but his last remark seems particularly appropriate for this discussion: "You know, I can't help wishing she'd made the same choice for herself that she made for her dog."

Whether we agree with the owner's choice or the young man's interpretation of the events, the fact remains that feelings we harbor about euthanasia may become greatly magnified when we feel physically vulnerable or perceive the pet's owner that way.

When Vicki must face the idea of euthanizing her service dog, that choice will affect almost every aspect of her and her parents' lives. In a Horatio-heartbeat, she'll go from being a relatively independent young woman to a dependent one. While we can appreciate why she might want to hang on to her canine companion for as long as possible, we also can understand why she might feel an equally strong desire to replace the dog, too.

The idea of euthanizing pets who don't specifically function as service animals doesn't provide much respite, either. When Dianna realizes that Millie, the very timid stray cat with multiple behavioral problems that Jimmy took in ten years ago, now urinates and defecates on his clothing and bedding as well as vomits throughout the house when stressed, she feels at her wit's end.

"I've tried to find a home for Millie, but no one wants an animal with all those long-standing problems," she explains. "I don't want to talk to Jimmy about euthanasia, but I don't want to risk him catching something from her, either."

Although good housekeeping and a pet's positive effects on the owner's well-being typically outweigh any risk posed by disease, we can't ignore the stress that such pet problems generate. Instead of talking to her brother and cheering him up, Dianna spends much of her time at his home doing laundry and cleaning up cat waste. This, in turn, undermines her relationship with all of his cats, something both he and the animals detect.

Consequently, when a pet's problems reach a level that compromises the health of the owner and no practical way of resolving the situation exists, euthanasia may become a sad but viable option. However, the sooner and more realistically the owner and any caregivers confront any pet problems, the less likely they will escalate to life-threatening proportions. Even if they do, the fact that the owner remained apprised of the situation from the beginning will make it easier for that person to cope with the loss.

What about giving up pets? Do owners with physical ailments experience any special problems?

"Oh, absolutely!" Dianna exclaims.

GIVEN-UP PETS AND THE
PHYSICALLY VULNERABLE

Giving up a pet poses the same good news/bad news scenario for the physically vulnerable owner as any other. The good news is that the given-up pet may go to a more suitable home and the former owner may still get to see it. By carefully placing a pet in the right home, owners who must give up an animal because they can no longer properly care for it can gain the best of both worlds: They keep in contact with their pets, but the pet also receives quality care. On the downside, though, the pet may not go to a good home or the new owner may not want to maintain contact with the previous one.

Additionally, another problem can come into play: prejudice.

"Everyone in our little town knows that Jimmy has AIDS. When I tell people I'm looking for a home for at least some of his cats, you can almost see them pulling away," Dianna remarks ruefully. "I couldn't believe it, but then a friend told me she had the same problem when she tried to find a good home for her dad's cat after he died of cancer."

Sadly, people will rush to adopt severely abused animals they lack the knowledge and skill to rehabilitate but shun perfectly healthy loving pets because they erroneously believe the animal may transmit the owner's condition, even conditions they know aren't contagious. Ironically, sometimes well-meaning family members or shelter personnel will naively share the details of the owner's medical history thinking this will increase the animal's chance of adoption. Although such sad tales may work in some situations, they may also work against the animal in other circumstances.

And even when sad tales seem to work in the pet's favor, they may backfire. I recall a case of a young blind woman who so spoiled her guide dog that he became unresponsive to her commands and thus unreliable as a service animal. A friend who lived in the same building felt sorry for both the dog and the woman and adopted the animal. Unfortunately, the second person lacked the skills and commitment needed to reverse the problems the first owner created. This put the dog in the untenable position of feeling responsible for his former owner who lived on the second floor as well as for his new owner who lived on the first. When the two women went out together and left the dog alone, he understandably chewed at himself or the window sills and furnishings in at attempt to relieve his frustration. In this situation, the new owner's desire to keep the dog near the former owner, as well as her willingness to mimic the previous owner's mistakes, made life much worse for the animal.

LOST PETS AND THE
PHYSICALLY VULNERABLE

Any physical limitation will affect the manner in which and how long we look for a lost pet. Conversations with physically vulnerable owners who have lost their pets lead me to conclude that the owner's relationship once again will determine the outcome: Owners who experienced what they considered quality relationships find it easier to accept the fact that they lacked the physical wherewithal to pursue a lost pet as vigorously as they would have liked than those who believed they failed the animal in some way do.

"I don't get it." Paige shakes her head in bewilderment. "If you had a really good relationship with your pet, wouldn't you want to do everything in your power to find it?"

> *Communicate. The more pet owners share with others regarding what they want done if and when these worst-case scenarios arise, the less horrifying the reality will be.*

Yes, you would. But if physical limitations made it impossible for you to do that, you'd trust that the animal would either find its way back or wind up with someone who would give it a good home.

"Sounds like a mind game to me," Paige remarks dubiously.

Indeed, it may well be. But once again we need to look at the alternative. We know our pets benefit our health. If we feel physically compromised, the loss of a pet can undermine our health even more. At that point, and because our own circumstances make it impossible for us to do anything for the lost pet, doesn't it make sense to adopt an attitude that will generate the most positive benefits?

"What if you can't do that?" Paige persists.

Then you should do whatever you can from your bed, hospital room, or wherever rather than wallow in guilt. Another paradox revealed by these owners seems so obvious, yet it came up again and again: If you don't ask anyone for help, you shouldn't complain if no one offers to help you. Ironically, sometimes we become so incredibly attached to our pets when we feel physically vulnerable that we feel embarrassed about asking others to help search for them. A particularly tragic variation on this theme occurs when folks who live alone get whisked away unconscious in ambulances, then lie fretfully in hospital beds far more concerned about whether the paramedics left the dog or cat out than for their own well-being. Unless some savvy friend or healthcare professional happens to broach the subject, these poor folks may hesitate to bring it up themselves.

Must I say it again? *Communicate.* The more pet owners share with others regarding what they want done if and when these worst-case scenarios arise, the less horrifying the reality will be.

PET LOSS AND MENTAL VULNERABILITY

If you consider the history of pet ownership in Western society in light of the human–animal bond, you can't escape the fact that we traditionally defined pet ownership as an elitist privilege we consistently denied to those who needed it the most: the physically, mentally, and emotionally compromised. Although research slowly chips away at this erroneous view, those with physical impairments won the right to keep pets, if only as service animals, long before those with mental or emotional problems. Those who prefer to perpetuate the pseudo-aristocracy defined by the old system cite the mentally and emotionally compromised person's inability to care for a pet properly as the reason for this discrepancy. However, we all know that, as a society, we still fear mental problems far more than physical ones.

Although many consider any problem to which science cannot attribute a specific physiological cause a "mental" problem, for this discussion I'm going to define mental impairment as a limited capacity for what others consider rational thought *in that person's particular circumstances*. In some individuals, such as those who have serious learning disabilities, this may be a continuous state. In others, such as those who display early symptoms of Alzheimer's disease, who take certain medications, or who are prone to substance abuse, periods of mental confusion may alternate with those of lucidity.

Using these definitions, and bearing in mind that any of us could fall into this category at any time, let's explore the role that mental competency plays when facing the loss of a pet.

NATURAL PET DEATH AND THE MENTALLY VULNERABLE

Many owners say they feel like they're going to lose their minds when their pets die. But does that mean we should

make an extra effort to protect those with limited or compromised mental faculties from this realization? That
question raises all kinds of ethical issues, as well as questions about the nature of the bond. Ethicists, far more
than scientists, worry a great deal about denying rights to
those we judge as having compromised mental faculties
for any reason—including the right to know about circumstances that might negatively affect their welfare—
because a "for their own good" mentality has fueled its
share of horrendous violations of human rights.

No one wants to bear bad news, let alone bear it to
someone who may lack the optimum mental wherewithal to process it. One crucial factor remains, however:
It's also wrong to lie to these people about their pet's
impending or actual death. Paige precipitated a cascade
of problems when she opted not to relay the veterinarian's concerns about Toivo's deteriorating condition to
her mother.

"But Mom was recovering from a mild heart attack at
the time and the medication made her spacey," Paige
protests. "I didn't want to upset her, plus she wouldn't
have remembered what I told her anyway."

If Paige considered Toivo her mother's dog, allowed
Noni to make all other choices about her pet, and willingly agreed to carry out those choices that Noni lacked
the wherewithal to carry out herself, then Paige had no
right to withhold information about Toivo's impending
death.

"Well, suppose Mom was drunk out of her mind?"
Paige retorts. "What good does it do to tell someone
their pet is dead then? That seems like a pretty darned
cowardly way out, too."

Earlier in the book, I mentioned that the human–animal bond most likely exists as a very primitive brain function on a par with the control of respiration and heartbeat, rather than as a lofty awareness we gain through serious, contemplative thought. It follows that on some level that we have yet to comprehend, people who are strongly attached to their pets *will* know when death severs that bond. Therefore, we have nothing to lose and possibly a great deal to gain by informing even those who appear "out of it" about the loss of their pets. Naturally, we should repeat this information when the owner becomes more lucid, providing more and more details as that person expresses a desire to know.

"OK, I can accept that," Paige presses on. "But how do you explain euthanasia to someone who's not completely with it?"

EUTHANASIA AND THE
MENTALLY VULNERABLE

Because euthanizing a pet requires that someone make a choice, this duty should rest with the person who assumes responsibility for the animal. We know that even a very young child may possess the mental capacity to care for a stable, healthy pet under most circumstances. So the idea of assigning the pet's ownership to an adult with limited mental capacity who adores the animal readily seduces family members and others, too. However, when the issue of euthanasia comes up, these people suddenly may want to assume full responsibility for what happens to the pet in order to spare the owner undue agony.

We can easily understand why people would want to do this; in fact, it may seem like the only caring thing to do. However, when Gary cuts Vicki out of the loop because he believes she can't "objectively" consider euthanizing Horatio (as if he could!), or Dianna actually considers putting down Jimmy's problem cat during a period she knows his medications will render him more forgetful, they don't spare their loved ones any agony at all. Remember: Anyone who forms a strong attachment to a pet, no matter how detached they may appear from everyone and everything else, *will* know when that pet disappears from their lives. People who experience periodic lapses almost universally condemn those who euthanize their pets without consulting them when their minds clear.

People who exist in a mental state where they are always separate from the mainstream may feel even more alienated if their pets suddenly disappear. In this situation, you may never successfully explain all the nuances of euthanasia or even gain the assurance that these people truly understand what you're trying to tell them. However, if you focus on speaking to them in their language rather than your own, and on taking them from their known world to the unknown aspect you wish to communicate, you'll fare much better. For example, Dianna's developmentally disabled nephew recognizes the difference between "here" and "gone." He also enjoys videos, especially those with animals, and he knows certain films from beginning to end. Using these as a foundation, she tells him about the death of his pet. She may need to repeat the story many times, and he may never get it all, but at least he knows his pet is gone and that his aunt cares.

Even when you don't think you can communicate at all, don't overlook the value of a long-standing relationship based on trust. A favorite client of mine, Bob, was a very childlike man who hardly spoke a coherent word during the years he brought his Newfoundland mix to me for care. The first time Bob arrived he came with a note requesting puppy shots written on the back of an old envelope. I vaccinated the pup and sent home a note describing what I'd done, as well as some additional treatment the dog required. I later learned that a friendly neighbor drove Bob to the clinic, wrote Bob's wishes for his dog down on scraps of paper for me, counted out the proper payment from Bob's earnings as a handyman, and interpreted my notes. However, the idea that we couldn't communicate never crossed my mind because it was so obvious from my client's expression and grunted replies that he personally took meticulous care of his pet and loved her very much. When the end came, well, what can I say? Because I'm not the sort of person who hides her feelings well, Bob read the dire prognosis on my face as clearly as a trained clinician. Being of old rural stock, he knew his options as well as any child raised on a farm in a harsh climate where life and death played tag with each other daily.

He gave me a questioning look: Hope?

I shook my head, no. No hope.

Tears filled his eyes and he nodded his head, yes. Yes, we must do it.

He cried. I cried. And we put the dog to sleep.

I have no idea whether Bob made his decision following what others would consider a logical, intelligent thought process. However, no doubt exists in my mind that he was not only capable of making such a decision, albeit in a way I still don't comprehend, but that he also deserved to make that decision himself.

Bob's case demonstrates the fallacy of blanket-labeling certain folks "mentally deficient" and using that as an excuse to deny them some of their rights, and it also points out the benefit of knowing the individual as well as that person's relationship with the pet. There is no reason for absentee family members, social workers, or anyone else to swoop down and make a decision to euthanize a mentally compromised owner's pet without the owner's knowledge or permission. Whether driven by fear or disinterest, such thoughtlessness may cause these owners avoidable pain as well as greatly undermine their trust of the very people who claim to have their best interests at heart.

LOST OR GIVEN-UP PETS
AND THE MENTALLY VULNERABLE

Healthcare professionals urge family and friends to speak to a comatose person as if he or she could hear and understand every word they say. When it comes to the loss of a pet, I believe the same holds true for communicating with the mentally vulnerable or developmentally disabled. They may not understand the same way we do, but they may understand on a level beyond our comprehension. Consequently, we lose nothing and may gain a lot by telling these folks why we gave up their pets or how the animal got lost or otherwise disappeared. Here again, if someone other than the owner makes the decision to give up the pet, that person should admit it.

Labeling a person mentally impaired and then laying the responsibility for the given-up or lost pet on him or her hardly ranks as a caring response.

Recall that the bond most likely lies within the deepest foundations of human awareness. That alone should show us that it can and will exist in those we view as mentally impaired. If so, at least some of these people will recognize when their pet disappears, even though they may not be able to articulate this clearly, a lesson I learned from another wonderful human–animal pair.

To say that Mr. Dimlar had a drinking problem was putting it mildly. At nine o'clock in the morning the man so reeked of alcohol that twenty minutes spent in a small examination room with him made me feel woozy. In spite of his problem, and the accompanying fear that he might light a match and blow us all to kingdom come, he loved his pets dearly. Nonetheless, the true nature of their relationship did not become clear to me until he lost his cat.

First came the phone call with the slurred announcement, and I duly affixed a notice to the clinic bulletin board describing his lost pet, a black-and-white, long-haired cat with green eyes. Later that day he weaved into the clinic bearing an orange, short-haired cat with yellow eyes.

"Thish my cat?" he asked very solemnly, staring at my receptionist intently as if to focus all his energy on her reply.

Somewhat taken aback, she managed to reply, "No, Mr. Dimlar. Your cat is black and white and has long hair."

Mr. Dimlar studied the cat in his arms for a very long time.

"Oh," he finally said. "I'll go back and try again. I really miss the little guy."

We then learned that he'd gone to the local shelter and inquired about cats who had arrived there in the days since his pet's disappearance, and that he fully intended to bring each and every one of them to us for verification. Fortunately, this story ended happily when his own cat returned. Otherwise, I'm convinced that this determined, if obviously impaired, owner would have made his erratic cycle from the shelter to the clinic and back with his furry candidates for as long as it took him to find his beloved pet.

> There is no reason for absentee family members, social workers, or anyone else to swoop down and make a decision to euthanize a mentally compromised owner's pet without the owner's knowledge.

The logical mind argues that my client wouldn't know his beloved pet if the animal showed him the family photo album and pointed to the cat's picture. On the other hand, Mr. Dimlar obviously was seeking to fill *some* very specific void that compelled him to take great pains to ensure that he made no mistakes. Admittedly, I can't begin to comprehend what standard he applied to his relationship with his pets. On the other hand, you'll never hear me say that some standard didn't exist.

Such tales remind us of the good news/bad news nature of the bond. The fact that the mentally compromised may garner so much support from their animal companions in a world that might otherwise reject them surely ranks as good news. On the other hand, what will happen to them when their pets become lost? How many people want to mount a search for an animal belonging to someone whose unusual behavior elicits distrust and fear? What kind of a search do you undertake, and how long should it continue? How many people want to adopt a pet knowing its previous "strange" owner may want to come visit it?

These questions raise such troubling images, it makes sense to take a preventive approach. That means that family, friends, or social workers and other professionals should provide the impaired owner with animal companionship under the best possible circumstances.

"What are the best possible circumstances?" Paige wants to know.

Regular visits from or access to a healthy, well-behaved pet cared for by a more capable person can provide the best of both worlds. The impaired person reaps all the benefits of animal companionship, but the pet also receives good care. Barring such cooperation, it is still absolutely necessary to tell these people the truth about the given-up or lost pet in an appropriate manner. Caregivers should also carefully observe that person to ascertain any negative effects the pet's loss may precipitate. If the given-up or lost animal suffered from avoidable problems, and someone close to the impaired owner willingly will accept the responsibility for helping the owner select, train, and care for a pet in a manner that will ensure the problem won't recur, then getting another pet represents a viable option.

PET LOSS AND EMOTIONAL VULNERABILITY

If we as a society find it difficult to interact with those we define as mentally impaired, people with emotional problems often trouble us even more. Even the idea of experiencing some negative emotion, such as sadness or depression, may so terrify us "normal" folk that we seek a quick fix to obliterate that symptom rather than deal with its underlying cause.

"Here, Mom, take one of these antidepressants your doctor prescribed," coaxes Paige. "I don't want you to get so upset about Toivo that you make yourself sick."

We can appreciate how Paige and others automatically would view their physically compromised loved ones as emotionally vulnerable and seek to spare them from anything that would generate negative emotions. However, we also know that acceptance only results from working through all our fears about the loss as well as any other difficult feelings they may evoke. Consequently, to deny anyone their emotions, regardless of their physical or mental state, is to deny them the chance to accept the loss.

The basic truths about pet loss and the mentally vulnerable apply to the emotionally vulnerable, too: Tell the truth, and do your best to tell it in a way that makes sense to the vulnerable person. As in the case of the mentally vulnerable, this may mean repeating the same message different ways on a trial-and-error basis until you discover the best way to communicate. Information also may sink in better at one time of day than at another time. When Jimmy starts taking antidepressants, Dianna discovers that these affect his ability to comprehend what she's telling him as well as his ability to react to it. She discovers that, if she tells him something shortly after he takes his medication but before it achieves its full mood-altering effect, he grasps complex issues better than if she waits until the medication reaches its peak or wears off completely. Unfortunately, different people respond to different medications, or even the same medication, differently, so it may take a coordinated effort on the part of family members and professional caregivers to determine the best time to discuss the pet's loss. One thing for sure, though, *never* is never the best time.

Also, bear in mind that denial and anger constitute natural first responses to the impending or actual loss of a pet, and this holds true for the emotionally vulnerable, too.

"I started to tell Jimmy we had to do something about Millie, but he got so angry, I dropped the subject because I didn't want him to flip out," Dianna says, describing her brother's reaction.

And how would Dianna feel if her spouse told her he planned to give away *her* beloved pet?

"I'd go crazy if he ever did that!" she sputters angrily.

Once again, we see how easily we may deny people we view as vulnerable or compromised in any way the same reactions to a loss that we so freely allow ourselves. Awareness of this should help us avoid treating people who are emotionally vulnerable in this counterproductive manner.

Although the same approaches described for helping the mentally impaired negotiate the healing process also apply to those with emotional problems, two particularly troubling emotional issues that may affect all owners deserve special mention:

- Emotional codependency
- Symbolic relationships

EMOTIONAL CODEPENDENCY

We all depend on our pets for emotional support at one time or another. In fact, I'd wager that this constitutes the most seductive aspect of pet ownership. However, as I noted in chapter six, such feelings can cross the line that separates a mutually rewarding relationship, which celebrates and respects both the owner's and the animal's unique needs, from those relationships in which such intimacy becomes problematic.

Recall my patient with malignant lymphoma whose owner succumbed to the same malady. In this and similar situations, sharing the same problem with the pet may enable the owner to gain valuable insights about that disease. On the other hand, when owners project their own negative emotions, such as fear or jealousy, onto a pet, that animal may experience avoidable life-threatening problems. Fearful owners often knowingly or unknowingly create fearful pets who eliminate in the house, chew on furniture, suffer from recurrent stress-related medical problems, or even attack people and other animals—an array of problems that ultimately could cause the animal's death or lead the owner to give it up.

"But why would people want to do that to their pets?" asks Vicki.

People tend to project their own negative emotions on pets because:

- It enables them to avoid dealing with the real problem
- They view the pet as a symbol of something else

Owners who define a pet's negative behavior as spiteful or mean (because that's how they perceive negative behavior aimed at themselves) impose a negative emotional state on the animal that blocks any resolution of the problem. Unlike destructive chewing or inappropriate elimination for which many solutions exist, no treatment exists for canine or feline "spite" and "meanness" aside from drugging the animal into a state that masks the actual cause of the problem.

Sadly, sometimes unknowledgeable family members and healthcare professionals will foster emotional codependence between pets and people they view as impaired for any reason, including those who are judged impaired simply because others consider them too young or too old to take care of themselves. While this could make good sense in terms of all the benefits of the human– animal bond, once again balance determines the outcome. No one can deny how much Horatio enhances the quality of Vicki's life. However, Horatio didn't *make* the young woman independent. Her own drive, courage, and willingness to work with her dog contributed a great deal to the process, too. Unfortunately, sometimes people overlook this critical fact.

I recall one blind woman who admitted that she gave up her dog because people paid more attention to the dog than they did to her, a confession that caused a wave of conflicting thoughts to wash over me.

"What an ungrateful and selfish woman!" my dog-loving self immediately thought.

But as we talked, I came to appreciate her view, too. She quickly had discovered that she used the dog as an excuse not to develop her social skills and independence.

"Can you imagine what would have happened to me when that dog died?" she asked.

At the time, I couldn't, but since then I've encountered enough healthy and impaired owners who did allow themselves to become emotionally dependent on a pet to the point that they truly believed that they'd die without the animal. Unfortunately, when the animal did die or disappear from their lives, these people suffered tremendously.

Needless to say, avoiding or facing up to the negative consequences of such relationships beforehand will do much to eliminate this kind of emotional stress. And the same holds true for those who form symbolic relationships with their pets.

PETS AS SYMBOLS

Pause here and recall the day you got your pet(s). For most pet owners, that day stands out clearly in the mind, as do all of the circumstances surrounding it. This brings me to another double-edged sword inherent in the human–animal bond: animal lovers' almost instinctual desire to link pets with specific individuals or periods in their lives. Physically, mentally, and emotionally healthy folks like Paige may link their first dog with their braces, acne, first date, and high school graduation, or with their first forays into adulthood, the birth of a child, or the collapse of a marriage. Those with various limitations naturally make symbolic connections, too. Noni received Toivo as a gift from her husband shortly before he died, and her spouse and the dog remained inextricably entwined in her heart ever since. Each one of Jimmy's cats reminds him of specific events in his life. Horatio embodies all the physical, mental, and emotional challenges Vicki had to surmount as she made the transition from a physically active young woman to one confined to a wheelchair.

As long as we keep the animal's own needs in mind, any symbolism we project does no harm. However, attaching such symbolism can create the following problems:

- It may cause us to make decisions that cause our pets to suffer needlessly

- We must deal with the symbolism before we can cope with the loss of the pet

Because Noni convinced herself that somehow her husband lived on in Toivo, this permitted her to avoid accepting her spouse's death. When Toivo became terminally ill, she faced two losses: that of her husband and that of her beloved dog. To buy time to cope with this double shock, she put the dog through countless treatments she would have shunned if her spouse were still alive.

Put another way, attaching strong symbolism to a pet creates a situation in which we must deal with two losses rather than one: the loss of the symbol and the loss of the animal itself. Given the emotional burden just coping with one loss may create, the addition of a second one may prove overwhelming.

At the risk of creating a major tempest in the behavioral teapot, I also propose that viewing pets as symbols of unconditional love with an eye toward only fulfilling our own human needs may complicate the healing process enormously.

"You don't view pets as the source of unconditional love?" Jimmy glares at me incredulously. "Do you have any idea how many people are afraid to be in the same room with me, let alone touch me or let me touch them, something my cats do every day?"

I totally agree that our pets' willingness to accept our frailties stands as their most appealing characteristic. However, accepting treatable pet problems as evidence of our unconditional love doesn't help the animal at all. Jimmy can't alter the fact that his declining health and certain medications may occasionally cause him to lose control of his elimination functions, a reality he, Dianna, and other family members accept. However, accepting Millie's inappropriate, fear-based elimination for years to prove his great love for her and her "little foibles" did nothing to help his pet.

In addition to using unconditional love as an avoidance tactic, some people see it as a one-way process. They can do whatever they want to the pet and expect the pet to forgive them, in the name of love. However, if the pet doesn't forgive them, or if it behaves in a manner contrary to how they believe a loving pet should act, then they often terminate the relationship. Thus, owners may regularly encourage fear-based behaviors in their dogs because they see it as evidence of the dog's willingness to die to protect them. The day the dog turns and bites them, an equally loving act if one truly understands the

> As long as we keep the animal's own needs in mind, any symbolism we project does no harm.

canine behavior, many owners feel so betrayed by this "hateful" behavior that they want the animal out of their lives immediately.

Even though taking either of these approaches won't cause most healthcare professionals to label us emotionally impaired, such symbolic emotion-based views that deny the animal its own needs can result in a great deal of emotional trauma when that animal dies, becomes lost, or must be given up. Whether owners project negative emotions or their beliefs about unconditional love onto the pet, when the loss occurs most find it difficult to evade the realization that they caused that loss. This, in turn, may precipitate a megadose of guilt and magnify all the fear-related stages of the healing process, sometimes to the point that the owner requires professional help.

This concludes our overview of the different ways owners respond to the loss of a pet. Before closing, however, let's look at what you can do now to ensure that love and knowledge rather than fear will guide your actions when your pet makes that final journey.

CHAPTER TEN

A FOND FAREWELL

Loss-Proofing Your Relationship with Your Pet

> *As many farewells as be stars in heaven.*
> —WILLIAM SHAKESPEARE
> *Troilus and Cressida*

THE SENSE of dread begins building the instant staff members at the Rocky Creek Veterinary Clinic becomes aware of the entry in the appointment book: *5 P.M.: Damiato, Buddy, euthanasia.*

"Oh, God, it's going to be terrible!" groans receptionist Cara Thorp, fighting back tears already. "The Damiatos all love that wonderful dog so much."

"I know," agrees the veterinarian, Dr. Miller. "I've dreaded this day for months. They've done such a great job caring for the old guy at home, I'd hoped he'd die there for their sake as much as my own."

At 4:59, the entire staff steels themselves for the ordeal ahead. At five o'clock the Damiato clan enters the clinic, all wearing their Sunday best. Cal Damiato holds Buddy in his arms, his son Tim carries a Buddy-size wooden box, and Alice Damiato and her daughter Sarah bring up the rear.

"We're going out to dinner," Cal Damiato announces as he hands Buddy to the veterinarian. "Just put him in the box when you're done. We'll pick him up on our way home."

Dr. Miller stares in stunned disbelief as the family disappears through the door.

"Those cowardly creeps!" explodes Cara.

"I can't believe it. I just can't believe it," Dr. Miller hisses through tightly clenched teeth. "Well, at least we can give the old guy a decent farewell."

The entire staff crowds into the tiny examination room and clusters around Buddy, stroking him and telling him how very much they love him, even if his owners don't. Dr. Miller carefully injects the euthanasia solution and the old dog dies as he'd lived, with gentle dignity and a final thump of his tail. Then everyone except for the tech who remains in the room to put Buddy's body in the box congregates in the hallway to vent their anger and frustration.

"Those awful people! How could they do such a rotten thing?"

"Who would've thought those people were so heartless?"

"They didn't even leave his collar on!"

"People like that shouldn't be allowed to own pets!"

Suddenly, the tech bursts out of the room, tears streaming down her face.

"The box!" she sobs. "Go look in the box!"

When the rest of the staff rush back into the room and look in the box, they see Buddy's handmade collar and leash, his favorite toys, and the old blanket that always accompanied him to the clinic. But more than that, they see that the entire box is lined with photos of Buddy with his owners, beginning with those obviously taken the first day they got him as a pup more than fifteen years before, and ending with a family portrait no more than a few weeks old. Taped to this collage of happy memories are four sealed envelopes bearing Buddy's name, surely filled with the final hopes, fears, dreams, prayers, and the very best good wishes with which each of the Damiatos want to surround Buddy on his final journey.

THE CONTENTS of Buddy's casket stunned the Rocky Creek veterinary staff, but conversations with owners who have lost pets indicate that similar fond farewells occur quite often. In fact, slipping notes and personal mementos into pet coffins and graves happens so often, I can't help wondering how many of us would do the same for human loved ones if convention didn't dictate otherwise. I know I never would have dared violate the pristine interior of my dad's coffin by slipping in his favorite garden spade—although I sometimes wish I had. To share something so personal seems so much more caring than a bouquet of flowers assembled by a stranger. I can't think of anything I'd rather have accompany me to the hereafter than one of my corgi's rubber bones, any more than I can imagine her taking her final journey without the oldest and most used bone in her collection.

"Don't you think it's kind of, well, *morbid*, to talk about what you want to bury with your pet?" asks Dr. Miller's receptionist, Cara Thorp.

As a new graduate stuffed with a medical education intent on saving lives, I might have agreed with Cara's view. However, with age as well as personal and shared experience with countless owners and animals, I see things quite differently now. I undoubtedly will mourn the loss of any of my pets, even the goldfish in my aquarium, but I also realize that fear rather than love most commonly keeps us from thinking about such losses before the fact. But not thinking about it does neither owner nor pet any good for two reasons.

> Finding out as much as we can about those aspects of pet loss we fear the most before they occur will empower us and give us strength.

First, we know how much fear of the unknown can cripple us. Consequently, finding out as much as we can about those aspects of pet loss we fear the most before they occur will empower us and give us strength.

Second, fear keeps us from enjoying our time with our pets to the fullest. Every fear-free day we share with them is like emotional life insurance: When the time comes to say goodbye, we can rely on all those good memories to ease us over the rough spots.

Throughout this book, we've considered many loss-related fears and ways to prevent or to cope with them. Nonetheless, as much as many owners can grasp the logic underlying that approach, some, like Cara Thorp, still can't bring themselves to think the unthinkable. Because of this, let's conclude our discussion with a look at three techniques commonly used in the human arena that can also help you confront any lingering fears about losing your pet:

- Hospice care
- Advance directives
- Visualizing

Hospice care focuses on the quality and comfort of a patient's final days rather than on the specific treatment of any diseases. Advanced directives (also called "living wills") describe a person's end-of-life preferences, which permit them to die on their own terms and spare their loved ones from making these painful decisions. The use of visualizing still lags behind the other two techniques in human medicine, but it's steadily gaining recognition as a valuable method for altering both physical and mental states. All three techniques also can benefit pet owners facing life-threatening pet conditions as well as pet loss.

Let's consider each one of these in more detail to see how you might use them to prepare for the loss of your pet.

SAFE PASSAGE

In the late seventies when the first home-care hospice opened its doors to dying patients, some people viewed it with the same fear and skepticism some now view homeless shelters. At that time, many people still believed that we must vigorously treat all medical conditions up to the last minute, no matter how painful or dehumanizing the process might be for the patient. The idea of promoting palliative care that focused on the patient's comfort and quality of life rather than on the treatment of a specific disease—even if this approach ultimately shortened the patient's life—shocked some people. But pet owners have taken this path with their pets for years. However, whereas many owners and veterinarians pursued this course somewhat arbitrarily in the past, advances in the human hospice movement have made it a much more thoughtful option for pets as well.

Like other owners who opt for this approach, the Damiatos chose it for themselves as much as for their pet.

"We knew Buddy was failing and all the trips to Dr. Miller's plus Buddy's stays there for tests or treatment bothered us as much as they bothered him," Alice Damiato explains. "We didn't want to spend our remaining time with him like that, so we asked Dr. Miller what we could do at home instead."

In addition to pets with age-related decline, those that are diagnosed with other problems may benefit from hospice care, too. These include pets that:

- are terminally ill with six or fewer months to live
- are incapable of walking, urinating and/or defecating, feeding, or otherwise caring for themselves
- suffer from chronic problems, such as anemia, fluid retention, or dehydration
- suffer from pain or breathing problems

As far as what the Damiatos and other owners can do for their pets at home, palliative treatment focuses on five primary areas:

1. Pain control.

2. Symptomatic treatment.

3. Wound care.

4. Sustaining bodily functions.

5. Maintaining a healthy mental state.

In addition to giving Buddy medications to relieve his pain, the Damiatos also administered intravenous fluids daily when his kidneys began to fail. Cal or Tim carried the old dog outdoors and held him while he relieved himself. Alice and Sarah gently cleansed the area around Buddy's anus and penis when he could no longer clean these areas himself. They also routinely groomed him and kept his bedding spotlessly clean. Even though Buddy could no longer chase his ball, the family would roll it to him or encourage him just to mouth it or other favorite toys to keep his spirits up.

How much owners who opt for hospice care can accomplish, however, depends on both the animal and the owner. The Damiatos could do a lot for Buddy because he possessed a wonderfully gentle temperament.

"I never knew that dog to growl or even curl his lip," Alice remarks. "And I know he never would have bitten anyone."

But pets who don't share Buddy's good nature may make it extremely difficult for their owners to help them.

"I agree," Cara pipes up. "My cat, Lucy, barely lets me touch her under the best of circumstances and when something bothers her, she goes ballistic."

The hospice option is not for every owner, either. The Damiatos, sustained by Alice's nursing background, wanted to do everything they could to make Buddy comfortable. However, other owners may feel hesitant about certain aspects of caring for a terminally ill or injured pet, such as treating oozing sores, expressing (emptying) the pet's bladder, or injecting medication. They may opt for daily visits from a veterinary technician or even a more skilled friend to accomplish these tasks for them. Remember, though, that if the mere idea of the treatment bothers you, your pet will pick up on your apprehension.

"My mom got so upset when she saw me injecting Buddy, I had to ask her to leave the room," Alice recalls later. "He sensed her fear right away and I could see him getting all tensed up, the last thing the old guy needed."

While owners who opt for home care of the dying pet need an almost sixth sense regarding their pet's physical and mental needs, they also must guard against projecting their own inappropriate beliefs onto the animal. Skilled veterinarians realize that treating the owner often takes precedence over treating the animal, and nowhere does this come into play more than in the handling of pain. Obviously, because pain control plays such a critical role in palliative care, how the pet expresses pain will determine how and when the owner medicates it. As simple as that sounds, however, many times owners project their own beliefs about pain onto their pets, leading them to medicate the animals far more than necessary.

"Alice and I had some pretty heated discussions about that," Cal confesses sheepishly. "I wanted to go for the maximum dose right off, but she said we should medicate him according to his needs rather than our own."

Once they made that choice, the Damiatos quickly learned how to use Buddy's appetite, his response to their presence, and even a certain look in his eyes as evidence of his discomfort. However, some owners don't trust their ability to read their pets, or they let their own fear of pain preclude such an approach. In that case, regular doses of pain medication that relieve the owners' apprehension as well as the animal's discomfort will work better for all concerned.

These variables bring up another critical component in pet hospice care: solid rapport with the veterinarian. Admittedly, many owners have opted to let their pets die at home with little or no input from their veterinarians. However, for those who want to do more than just hope that their pet will go quickly and quietly in its sleep, veterinary assistance plays a vital role in the following key areas:

- Educating the owner about how to anticipate and respond to critical symptoms

- Providing medications for palliative care and information about their proper use

- Emotionally supporting the owner during the hospice period

Dr. Miller not only told the Damiatos exactly what they could expect as Buddy's condition deteriorated, but he also described symptoms that would require immediate action to prevent Buddy from suffering needlessly. He also helped Alice assemble a kit that contained all the medications the family might need in an emergency, and he offered his support and encouragement when they or Buddy experienced a bad day.

Some individuals may balk at keeping certain medications, and particularly injectable ones, in their homes; they may also hesitate to administer them to their pets. However, for those who are willing to work closely with their veterinarians and take a proactive approach to their pets' final days, such procedures can do a great deal to ensure the animal's comfort.

Finally, although some owners who opt for hospice care do so because they want their pets to die at home, others take this approach because they want their pets to spend their final days in a soothing environment. I mention this because some owners mistakenly believe that hospice care rules out euthanasia. It doesn't. Some owners may begin hospice care because they can't even consider euthanasia. However, once they actually care for the pet on a daily basis and see its deteriorating quality of life, they come to view this option more objectively. Others, like the Damiatos, want to keep their pets with them as long as possible, but they don't want the animal to suffer, either.

"As a family, we defined what we felt Buddy considered a quality life," Alice explains. "When his life no longer fulfilled that definition, we would say goodbye."

Although that may seem like a heartbreaking, impossible task to accomplish, any loving owner can do it.

ADVANCE DIRECTIVES FOR PETS

The idea of writing advance directives for pets occurred to me when a colleague called me in a panic about an invitation he'd received to speak to residents of a retirement community about pet death. It seemed that although the medical and mental health professionals fully appreciated how much these animals enriched their older owners' lives, they dreaded what would become of these folks if something happened to their pets. Because I knew how much comfort people could derive from preparing advance directives for themselves, I suggested doing the same thing for pets. Aside from benefiting the pets, preparing the advance directives for the pet would give the folks who shied away from creating such a document for themselves an opportunity to consider the subject obliquely through their animals. Unlike the legally binding human document, the pet version serves primarily as a learning tool for owners and a source of guidelines for others who may need to care for the animal in the owner's absence.

"But how do you write advance directives for a pet?" asks Cara, her fear giving way to curiosity and concern for her own beloved pets, LucyCat and DesiDog.

Writing an advance directive is a four-step process:

1. Consider your personal values as these apply to your pet's care.

2. Apply your values to possible pet life-threatening scenarios.

3. Write the advance directives.

4. Discuss your wishes with your veterinarian and others who might need to make choices regarding your pet in your absence.

"But what if I change my mind?" Cara says, voicing a common concern. "I don't want to get locked into something I later regret."

As we and our pets grow older, our ideas about what constitutes a quality life may change. Age and experience may cause owners who initially thought they'd do anything to keep their pets alive to reconsider that option. Other owners who initially couldn't imagine supplying a pet with anything beyond the most rudimentary care later may become so attached to the animal that they want it to receive the most sophisticated state-of-the-art treatment. However, changing your mind poses no problem: Just rewrite the document and distribute new copies. Advance directives don't force you to do something you don't want to do, but rather help you avoid making a decision in haste that you may later regret.

To that end, you first need to know how your own values may affect your decisions about your pet's care.

PERSONAL VALUES AND
PET-CARE DECISIONS

Of all the techniques proposed for working out personal values, the question-and-answer approach works best. By answering the following ten questions adapted from the human advance directives guidelines Alice Damiato loaned her, Cara gains a sense of her own beliefs about loss and how these relate to her pets.

1. *What do you believe your pet values the most about its life?*
Cara links Lucy's and Desi's quality of life to their ability to enjoy their food and go for walks with her. Other owners consider a positive response to the owner's presence sufficient proof of a quality life.

2. *How do you feel about death and dying?*
When Cara considers this question, she realizes that she holds two quite different views.

"At the veterinary clinic, it makes me sad when a pet dies from some serious illness or injury or when the owners opt to euthanize it, but I consider it a normal part of pet ownership," she explains. "But when I think of Lucy or Desi dying, that reminds me of how I felt when my mom died."

Other owners, particularly those who have never experienced the loss of a loved one, find the prospect of their pet's death too frightening to consider. If you're among them, just becoming aware of this fear will help you prepare for it.

3. *Do you believe you should do everything in your power to preserve your pet's life as long as possible?*

"Sometimes I do and sometimes I don't," Cara confesses. "When I think about how I'd feel if I lost my pets, I want to do everything. But if I think of the kind of life they might have to live under those circumstances, I don't."

Most of us face similar dilemmas, and working them through also will help us avoid making pet healthcare decisions in the heat of the moment.

4. *If you don't believe in prolonging your pet's life as long as possible, what physical, behavioral, or bond conditions would cause you either not to initiate or to terminate treatment?*

Like many owners, Cara puts pain that doesn't respond to treatment at the top of her list. After further consideration, she adds to her list conditions such as her pets becoming unaware of their surroundings, losing their ability to control urination and/or defecation, and behaving in a manner that threatens human welfare.

5. *What conditions might cause you to at least temporarily treat the conditions listed in question 4?*

"At first I thought it was a dirty trick to ask me to consider changing my mind about conditions I'd already decided not to treat, but then I realized that this could happen," Cara admits after some thought. "My dad's grown terribly attached to my pets since Mom died and I know that, no matter what the problem, I'd treat it if it occurred during one of his visits."

Like Cara, other owners who ponder this question also discover situations that would cause them to change their minds. This, in turn, allows them to broaden their views to encompass a wider range of probabilities. The more scenarios we consider, the less likely we'll be unprepared.

6. *How much pain and risk would you be willing to put yourself, your pet, and others through if recovery seemed likely?*

"Another tough one!" Cara exclaims. "I'm pretty good at coping with pain myself and admire that quality in both of my pets. On the other hand, if they had some problem, like a disease or behavioral problem that could harm people, then I wouldn't risk treating them unless there was some way I could isolate them from others during that time."

If you share Cara's view, but want to keep your pets under these conditions, asking this question allows you the opportunity to consider ways you could keep the animal safe and secure if such problems arose.

7. *What if the chance of your pet's recovery were poor?*

"If Lucy or Desi had a poor chance of recovery, I wouldn't put them through any treatment that would cause them pain or pose a risk to others," Cara declares with certainty.

Some owners may agree while others would disagree. What about you?

8. *Would your pet's age affect your choice to treat or not treat it?*

Here again, most owners maintain relatively strong views. Cara's maternal instincts lead her to want to do *anything* to save a young animal, whereas she takes a more conservative view toward older animals that she views as having lived a full life. Her father, on the other hand, sees pouring a lot of effort into a young animal that may never be healthy as less advisable than treating one you already consider a fine pet. I recall one client who seemed fully determined to treat her fourteen-year-old cat for its chronic territorial marking until I mentioned that it naturally would take longer to treat such a long-standing behavioral problem in an older animal.

"You think she's old?" my client asked in surprise. "I thought cats lived twenty to twenty-five years on the average."

When I told her that, while some cats did reach those ripe old ages, most succumbed earlier, she stunned me with her reply.

"Oh, in that case maybe I'll just put her down rather than treat her," she said. "I was only going to treat her because I felt guilty about euthanizing what I thought was a young animal."

9. *Would any religious or personal views affect your treatment of your pet if it developed serious problems?*
Although I haven't found any directive in Western religious doctrine about how we should treat life-threatening problems in animals, I do know that we tend to apply our beliefs about ourselves to our pets. Thus, owners whose religious or moral beliefs negate

euthanasia for humans often won't consider it for their pets, either. Similarly, owners who have lost other loved ones, both humans and animals, to cancer or other diseases following drug or therapy with negative side effects may vow never to put another pet through that. Other owners eschew traditional (allopathic) medical treatments in favor of alternatives such as homeopathy or acupuncture. If such views may affect your pet's treatment in a life-threatening situation, how will you react when and if these challenges arise?

10. *Will financial considerations affect if and how you treat your pet?*

If your answer is yes, pause to consider how much you could comfortably spend. If you don't want financial considerations to play a role in your response to your pet's physical, behavioral, or bond problems, then plan for it now. If your budget allows, consider pet health insurance. If it doesn't, ask your veterinarian about payment options as soon as a problem arises, if not sooner.

"Good point," Cara agrees. "I've known owners to put a pet down because they just assumed they had to pay for treatment all at once. But Dr. Miller's really good about working out payment plans for people."

Again, if you don't ask, you won't know. If you do ask but you don't like the answer, you can consider your other options unhampered by the awareness that your pet is suffering from some life-threatening condition while you agonize over this dilemma.

Once you nail down your values regarding your pet's care, then you can test them on some worst-case scenarios.

TESTING YOUR VALUES

When our pets succumb to life-threatening problems, we face four options:

1. Do everything possible to treat the problem.
2. Do everything possible up to a certain limit, then terminate treatment if the response doesn't meet our needs or expectations.
3. Focus any care on making the animal comfortable or ensuring its safety (and others' safety too, if necessary) rather than treating the problem.
4. Euthanize the animal.

Consider these options, then apply them to the following situations:

Your pet suffers from a terminal condition and could die at any time, with or without treatment.

or

An accident leaves your pet paralyzed with little hope of recovering the use of its limbs. However, modern technology could keep your pet alive in this state for years.

or

Because of disease or advancing age, your pet doesn't recognize you, becomes easily confused, and needs constant supervision. Medical treatment could allow the animal to continue in this state for some time, although nothing could reverse its condition.

or

Your pet suffers from a nonfatal physical, behavioral, or bond problem (such as a chronic skin condition, barking, or dependency), but then develops an illness that could prove fatal.

Owners who perform this exercise often discover that they maintain some pretty strong ideas about how to resolve some crisis situations, but not others.

"If Lucy or Desi ever fell into one of the first two categories, I know I'd put them to sleep." Cara easily dismisses the idea of treating her pets under those circumstances. "But I'd need a lot more information before I could make up my mind about the other two."

If investigating hypothetical death or illness scenarios for your pets strikes you as akin to opening a Pandora's box you would rather keep tightly closed, remember that nothing dissipates fear like knowledge. The idea that one of her pets might require constant supervision causes Cara for the first time to view her own lifestyle in terms of how it affects her pets' welfare. The realization that what seems like a minor problem now might cause her not to treat a more serious one later causes her to rethink her decision to ignore rather than treat treatable problems.

Using these and any other scenarios you consider relevant to test your views will allow you to see what does and doesn't work for you and your pet. Once you feel comfortable with the results, then you can write them down.

WRITING AN ADVANCE DIRECTIVE FOR YOUR PET

"Why do I need to put all this in writing?" Cara wants to know. "Isn't it enough that I know what I want for my pets?"

Committing your pet's advance directive to paper provides three benefits. First, putting ideas in writing often enables us to evaluate them much more thoroughly than when we rework them in our heads. When Cara puts her views about her pets' final moments down on paper, her words compel her to consider other related issues that she hadn't thought of before, like how her lifestyle or her pets' temperaments could affect her choices.

Second, writing gives us the opportunity to articulate our thoughts.

"But I'm a terrible writer!" Cara wails.

Unfortunately, many people who don't like to write also get tongue-tied under pressure. Because we're often called upon to make life-and-death decisions about our pets under stressful conditions, written directives that remind us of the values we hold dear for ourselves and our pets can help even the most flustered owners get their points across to others.

Third, if you must leave your pet in the care of others, written advance directives will enable them to make your desired life-and-death decisions in your absence. No one likes to think of their pet succumbing to some rare virus while kenneled, or of it getting hit by a car and taken to the veterinary clinic while the owner runs errands in the next county. However, such situations do arise, and providing others with copies of your wishes will spare them the burden of making these choices for you, in addition to sparing you from living with the consequences of others' choices that run counter to your will.

Obviously, just handing a copy of your pet's advance directives to those who might need to care for the animal won't suffice. You need to discuss your wishes with these folks, too.

DISCUSSING YOUR PET'S
ADVANCE DIRECTIVES

A sad reality about advance directives of any kind is that others don't always heed them.

"I thought you said that advance directives for people were legally binding," Cara reminds me.

If properly prepared, they are. However, when the moment of crisis occurs, physicians may decide to ignore the patient's or family's wishes anyhow. Almost invariably these problems occur because the patients, their families, or their representatives didn't clearly discuss any advance directives *first*.

"But what if the doctor disagrees with the directives?" Cara asks.

Good question. Then the patient can switch to a physician who does share his or her views. The same holds true for veterinarians and others to whom we may entrust the implementation of our wishes for the handling of any life-and-death situations that may befall our pets in our absence. Just as some people maintain the same anti-euthanasia views for animals that they do for themselves, some animal caregivers maintain what they call a "no-kill" policy. If you would consider euthanasia and, indeed, would request it for your pet under certain circumstances, then a practitioner who maintains no-kill views most likely wouldn't carry out your wishes. By discussing this in advance before a crisis, you can discover and resolve such issues.

Similarly, think of all the negative feelings Dr. Miller and his staff expressed simply because they didn't know how the Damiatos intended to handle Buddy's euthanasia. Some might argue it was none of the veterinarian's business how the family responded, but I totally disagree. To me, euthanasia remains *the* most difficult task in the veterinary repertoire. Trying to guess the owner's wishes regarding any aspect of this only makes a difficult situation harder for everyone involved.

Discussing your pet's advance directive also allows you to get input from others regarding your choices. For example, when Cara discusses the financial limits she would place on any treatment for Lucy and Desi with her father, he surprises her by offering to help her pay for any treatments where cost might become a limiting factor.

"I had no idea he'd be willing to do that," she marvels later.

Discussions with family members may reveal different values that could precipitate disaster if not confronted until the time of crisis. I recall one tragic situation in which the wife's control of the purse strings negated treatment of the animal's problems while the husband's anti-euthanasia stance negated putting the poor creature to sleep. Bizarre as this sounds, I have seen how pet crises expose deep cracks lying just below the surface of seemingly solid relationships. Consequently, I can't stress enough the importance of discussing your wishes for your pet beforehand—for the animal's sake.

Given all the mental anguish often required to put together advance directives for a pet, it comes as no surprise that many owners never find the time to do it. On the other hand, owners who do make the effort often credit the process with two quite opposite results. Not only does nailing down our thoughts decrease the probability that our pets will die under regrettable conditions, but it also may enable us to save our pets' lives.

"That's all well and good if you can stand the idea of losing your pet to death or any other cause," Cara points out. "But what if the very idea so freaks you out, you can't think at all?"

When fear garbles our thoughts to the point that we can't even think about anything bad happening to our pets in advance, we can turn to visualiziation for help.

THE MIND TO THE RESCUE

Once scientists realized how much our thoughts can influence our actions, the idea of using our minds to train our bodies to respond in a particular way began to catch on. While we westerners traditionally scoffed at the eastern mystics who walked on hot coals or slept on beds of nails, few could deny the results of experiments demonstrating how biofeedback could enable people to alter heart rate and pulse and even abort migraine headaches and asthma attacks. A spinoff of biofeedback, visualizing involves mentally picturing a specific event and then manipulating that image to achieve the desired result. For example, athletes use it to envision themselves sharpening particular skills. Perhaps surprisingly to some, those who use this technique improve almost as much as those who actually practice every day. Within medicine, cancer patients who envision their bodies rejecting cancer cells can create measurable improvement in their conditions.

I first began using visualization to help clients who feared their pets, particularly dogs who had bitten or attempted to bite someone. I knew that the only guarantee that an animal won't bite demands that we first believe that the animal won't bite. Fear alters our physiology (spanning the spectrum from the way we move to the way we sound and how we smell), which animals can readily detect. Once they sense our fear, which they interpret as submission, they're more likely to respond aggressively. Because of this, I began looking for some way owners could deal with their fears in nonthreatening conditions. Initially, I asked clients to wear whatever clothing or outer protection was necessary to make them feel safe interacting with the animal. However, this quickly proved impractical: Some owners felt foolish in the full battle gear sufficient to do the job, and others simply couldn't wear it every time they interacted with the pet.

The search for a viable alternative led me to suggest visualizing—with a twist. Whereas those who use this technique in sports and medicine recommend focusing on the best results, I ask my clients to focus on the worst.

"Sounds kind of sadistic to me," Cara notes warily.

Perhaps it does. It certainly runs counter to my usual upbeat nature. However, my clients quickly taught me that focusing on the best rarely poses a problem when dealing with fear. It's thinking about the worst that ties us up in knots. Unfortunately, as long as we deny the possibility that the feared situation may occur, we can't formulate any viable plans for dealing with it.

Much as I like to get to the root of behavioral problems, I also know that certain methods, such as drugs and shock collars, can at least temporarily mask the negative behavior, and thus may satisfy owners who don't want to endure the mental discomfort of worst-case visualizing. However, no pill or device can bring a dead pet back to life. Nor does it seem likely that a pet given up because of problems will miraculously show up problem-free on the owner's doorstep months later, or that an owner paralyzed by fear will mount an effective search for the pet when it becomes lost. Because of this, visualizing a pet-loss scenario before the fact to prevent nightmares of regret afterward makes a lot of sense.

"So, how do I start?" Cara asks.

Throughout this book, we have discussed a wide variety of crises that could befall our pets as well as the various human responses to these different forms of loss. Some of these may have hit home harder than others. If so, did you zip through that material as quickly as possible in an effort to escape your negative feelings?

If you did, I'd like you to consider rereading those sections, then envisioning yourself in exactly that kind of situation with your pet. To get you started, let's apply visualizing to the various forms of pet loss and see what we can learn from it.

PET LOSS AND NATURAL DEATH

When Cara considers using visualization to prepare for the death of one of her pets, she shakes her head vigorously.

"No, I can't do it," she insists. "It makes my stomach churn just to think about it."

One good thing about fear is that no matter how hard we may strive to deny it, it tends to make its presence known. The stomach churns, pulse and heartbeat quicken, hands tremble and become sweaty or icy cold, and the mind screams, "Freeze!" "Fight!" "Run!" Once Cara realizes this, though, and particularly if she experiences it in her cheerful bedroom with Lucy and Desi snuggled beside her, she can deal with the fear rather than let it overwhelm her. She breathes slowly and evenly until she calms herself, and then she tries again. It takes her almost a week of visualizing just to get past the fear, but eventually she does.

Some people do their visualizing right after they turn in for the night; others prefer doing it first thing in the morning. Although I typically recommend that owners do visualizing exercises in quiet settings, that approach doesn't work for everyone. One woman's considerable fears sprang from her vivid imagination, which served up such horribly realistic images as she lay in her bed that she couldn't sleep afterward. Instead, she found the technique worked much better for her if she practiced it in her brightly lit, noisy office during her coffee breaks. Owners who have experienced previous pet losses that they don't want to repeat but find painful to recall in their entirety, visualize the event a bit at a time; once they master the fear related to one piece, they move on to the next. Still others find that alternating positive images of their interactions with their pets with the frightening ones makes it easier for them to think the unthinkable.

Regardless what approach you use, the goal remains to become aware of your feelings first, and how you react to them second. When Cara first visualizes Lucy getting hit by a car, she also sees herself paralyzed with fright at the sight of her pet's lifeless body lying in the street. But once she does this, she then programs herself to move beyond that fear and envision herself coming to her pet's aid. At this point, even though she works in a veterinary hospital, Cara realizes that she doesn't have a clue what to do next, so she vows to find out. She then discusses the scenario with Dr. Miller, who explains the basics of pet first aid, recommends a good book on the subject, and suggests that Cara assemble a first aid kit for her pets. Now when Cara imagines her worst-case scenario, a completely different picture unfolds.

"Instead of going completely to pieces, I can see myself checking Lucy's pulse and other vital signs, and even performing first aid procedures that could save her life," she reports happily. "If I hadn't visualized her getting hit, though, I never would have gotten that information and developed those skills."

And how does Cara feel about one of her pets getting hit by a car now?

"While the idea of them dying still horrifies me, at least now I don't need to live with the fear that they'll die because I didn't know enough to save them," she admits. "Plus, the visualizing also convinced me that I *could* find the time to teach my pets not to bolt out the door."

But what happens if her pets in her visualizing sessions don't respond to her first aid and die anyway?

"Once I worked through what I could do to try to prevent the problem or save it if it occurred, I could visualize losing them," she says, describing the process. "But what if an owner can't do that? What then?"

In my experience, owners who can't face the idea of losing a pet by any means usually consciously or subconsciously view the animal as a symbol of something else. Under those circumstances, professional counseling to identify that symbolism and the real source of the fear may help alleviate it. While the nature of the human–animal bond guarantees that the idea of losing any well-loved pet will cause us to fear for our own well-being, allowing those fears to block the formulation of a plan that will help us respond well under the worst of circumstances just ends up hurting us or our pets.

How did Cara deal with her fears about her pets dying?

"I worked through a lot of negative feelings about it when I began writing advance directives for them," she confides. "After that, it was just a matter of deciding about burial or cremation. This may sound kind of weird, but I found that part comforting."

No, it doesn't sound weird at all. People who confront their worst fears about losing their pets to death by any means often find that visualizing the event right up to and including disposition of the body, as well as any rituals they may want to engage in to mark that event, brings a certain peace.

"Now I realize how the Damiatos could act so serene when they dropped Buddy off," Cara admits. "Once I visualized Lucy or Desi dying and how and where I wanted to bury them, I felt I could handle it. I'm not saying that I won't still be sad. I will be. But I won't be afraid."

But did the Damiatos feel the same way when they euthanized their beloved pet?

VISUALIZING AND EUTHANASIA

Because of his advanced years, Buddy gave his owners plenty of time to think the unthinkable. However, where other owners denied the inevitable, the Damiatos faced it head-on.

"But we didn't think of it as visualizing," Cal Damiato admits. "We'd made the decision that we wouldn't let him suffer when he started to fail, so my wife and I talked to the kids about what we wanted to do when the time came. But I know we each ran that last-day scenario in our minds time and time again, too."

Did it work?

"At first I tried to block the image out because it made me so sad," Alice volunteers. "But then I could tell from the questions the kids were asking about euthanasia that what they were imagining was far worse than any reality, and that forced me to dry-run the event. In retrospect, doing that to answer their questions helped me alleviate a lot of my own fears."

"I know Dr. Miller and his staff were flabbergasted when we just dropped Buddy off," adds her husband. "But that was my daughter's idea. We'd asked the kids what they wanted to do to remember Buddy, and Tim said he wanted to make the coffin and arrange all our mementos in it. I could understand that, but then Sarah said she'd like to get dressed up and go out to dinner like we always did when special things happened. At first it floored me that she saw euthanizing Buddy as one of those special times. After I thought about it, though, I realized she was right. In a way, it *was* an honor to be able to let such a great dog go like that."

In this situation, the parents wisely chose not to disregard their children's images of what they considered a meaningful farewell for their pet. When a lack of knowledge led the children to visualize euthanasia as a painful process, the parents alleviated those fears. When all family members agreed that they couldn't imagine watching Buddy die—"Gee, Mom, he didn't even like us to watch him go to the bathroom!"—they all adopted the youngest Damiato's celebratory image instead.

Scientists have recognized the power of the so-called "self-fulfilling prophecy" for years. We *do* consciously or subconsciously tend to create those situations we think about the most, and this includes any emotions with which we imbue those events. Thus, for those who envision euthanizing a pet as the absolute worst event that ever could befall them, it often does turn into the worst day of their lives. On the other hand pet owners like the Damiatos who make a conscious choice to picture the event beforehand and mentally rework it until it fits their needs as well as their pet's see the actual event quite differently.

"I can't say I ever want to go through something like that again," concedes Cal. "But it *was* one of the most special times we ever shared as a family."

VISUALIZING AND GIVING UP A PET

Pause here and imagine the different circumstances that could cause you to give up your pet.

"You gotta be kidding!" exclaims Cara. "*Nothing* could cause me to give up my pets!"

What if Cara herself became seriously ill?

"Oh, I never thought about that," she replies meekly, then ponders that possibility for a moment before speaking again. "I'd definitely want them to go to a good home, preferably to someone I knew would let me visit them or bring them to me if I couldn't travel. In fact, I have a good friend who feels the same way about her pets. If she wouldn't, I know my dad would take care of my pets, just like I'd take care of his, too."

In this situation, Cara initially wants to believe that nothing but death could separate her from her pets—or at least nothing that she wants to think about. However, when pressed, she looks at the problem more objectively. Visualizing helps her realize that she does know people who would care for her pets; she also realizes she could offer them the assurance that she would take care of their pets, too.

As we've seen, behavioral and bond problems more likely lead people to give up their pets than medical ones. Interestingly, sometimes owners will hesitate to visualize with these problems because they feel guilty or embarrassed about them. But when they do visualize them, the mere fact that they do so before they give up the pet gives them an opportunity to solve the problem. When Cara takes what she considers Desi's "lovable clinginess" and magnifies this behavior to problem proportions in her mind, she decides to focus on building the dog's confidence rather than encouraging his fears. Had she not consciously envisioned this worst-case scenario, such treatment may have never crossed her mind.

Unlike losing a pet to death, giving up a pet rarely involves circumstances beyond our control. By using visualizing to confront this form of pet loss, we can increase the probability that our pets will go to the very best homes if we must give them up or, better yet, we can use it to detect and respond to problems early enough that we never need to make this choice at all.

"I suppose you want me to visualize one of my pets disappearing, too." Cara sighs and closes her eyes again.

VISUALIZING AND THE LOST PET

As helpless as owners feel when their pets disappear, visualizing this form of pet loss often yields some surprisingly concrete results.

"At first I drew a complete blank," Cara admits. "But then I remembered that little hole under the fence where I've caught Desi several times. There's something happening on the other side of that fence that really interests him and I'm going to find out what it is!"

When she goes on her fact-finding mission, Cara discovers that her neighbor has gotten a pet rabbit, which he keeps in a hutch next to the fence.

"Well, I guess I know where to look for Desi first!" she laughs.

When other owners try to visualize where their pets might go, they come up empty. This holds particularly true for owners of strictly housebound cats. They simply can't picture the animals doing anything other than huddling on the doorstep waiting for someone to let them back into the house. However, with so many free-roaming cats in almost every urban, suburban, and rural neighborhood, one of these could conceivably sense the resident cat's presence within the house and mark and claim the owner's yard as its own. The housecat who accidentally (or foolishly) finds itself outdoors may feel extremely vulnerable in these surroundings. Rather than hiding in its own rose bushes, it may disappear under the porch of a neighbor who owns no cats and doesn't tolerate any on her property. Such images lead some owners to make changes that will eliminate any chance the pet could deliberately or accidentally escape, or to survey their neighborhoods critically through their pets' eyes to determine where the animals might go.

Other owners who draw a blank when trying to visualize their pets' daily activities put a leash on their own free-roaming pets or follow the animals on their jaunts to see where they go. Again, in the case of cats, veterinarians who practice in populated areas often harbor suspicions that more than one owner unknowingly claims the same cat. One owner lets the cat out for the night, assuming it goes off to hunt. Instead, the animal goes through the woods to a nearby housing development where it meows on another doorstep to be let in. The cat then eats and sleeps with these folks who then let it out before they go to work in the morning.

While such stories of feline ingenuity might enchant us, the fact remains that one of those owners could move and take the cat with them without the other's knowledge. That owner could even hunt for the animal in the very neighborhood where the second owners lived and no one there would mention it. Someone might say, "Gee, your cat looks a lot like the Billings' cat. They just moved a few days ago, but they've had that cat for years," but the chances are slim that the searching owners would link those remarks to their own pet. Even if they did, what could they do?

"I *don't* want to visualize what I'd do if I discovered my pets had another owner, but I can make sure they both wear collars with my name on them, in addition to their microchips," Cara announces. "Plus, even though I always keep an eye on them, I'm going to start paying more attention to what they pay attention to during our walks and rides."

Like visualizing the given-up pet, visualizing the lost one often provides us with as many ways to prevent the problem as to cope with it after it happens.

And, finally, no matter how bad it seems, we can't forget the role humor plays when we face all these worst-case scenarios and our fears of losing our pets.

A FOND FAREWELL

In addition to allowing us to work through our options and discover ways we can prevent problems that might cause us to lose our pets, taking a before-the-fact approach to pet loss also allows us the luxury of joy.

"You're kidding!" Cara can't suppress her surprise.

No, I'm not. Without a doubt, some of the greatest, most enduring lessons I've learned about life I've learned from animals. Back in the old days of science, the dour Victorian gurus of animal behavior insisted that only young animals played, and they only played in order to learn how to hunt and mate. However, as any observant pet owner knows, and as more enlightened scientists later proved, animals of all ages play. While animals do, indeed, use play to learn (because doing so constitutes the most efficient way to learn), they also communicate an entirely different message with their play. Through their playful spirits, animals make it known that, no matter how bad circumstances may appear to others, they not only can cope, but they possess enough energy to enjoy themselves, too.

> *Without a doubt, some of the greatest, most enduring lessons I've learned about life I've learned from animals.*

This realization can create a paradox for us humans, however. Logic tells us that the more we need to learn and the more difficult the situation, the more we also need playfulness and humor to help us, too. Unfortunately, many in our society still apply that same dour Victorian view to humans, saying we can't express joy or playfulness during a time of mourning or sadness.

"It's at least disrespectful," they warn us ominously. "If not downright crazy."

So what to do?

I say express it anyhow.

I dedicated this book to an animal-loving friend and veterinary technician of more than twenty years with whom I've loved and lost a mind-boggling number of patients and personal pets under the best and worst of circumstances. I suspect you could build a pyramid sufficient to hold both of our bodies out of the empty boxes once filled with the Kleenex we and our clients used to wipe our tears during that time. On the other hand, I can't remember a single instance when one or the other of us didn't muster the wherewithal to say or do something that made us both smile.

Maybe in our line of work you do that to keep your sanity. Still, I know of many owners who somehow managed to do the same thing, and I know it sprang from their confidence in their ability to cope and, above all, their confidence in the quality of their relationship with the animal. I think one of my clients summed up this particular magic best when he made a comment that caused us both to laugh through our tears after we put his pet to sleep.

"She was such a great friend," he said. "I just had to say goodbye to her with a smile."

Surely no one could ask for a final tribute greater than that.

INDEX

Also from Prima

True Stories of Animal Courage and Kindness

A dog swallows a lit firecracker to protect a child in strife-torn Belfast. A pet pig steers his human family to safety before a propane gas explosion. A horse keeps vigil over an old woman until help arrives.

With dozens of touching, true-life stories like these, this heartwarming book gathers compelling proof of the intense love that animals feel for humans.

"Nobody writes about animals better than Kristin von Kreisler."

— Chris Willcox, editor-in-chief, *Reader's Digest*

"These wonderful stories show once again how close we are to our evolutionary cousins."

— From the foreword by Jeffrey Mousaieff Masson, coauthor of *When Elephants Weep*

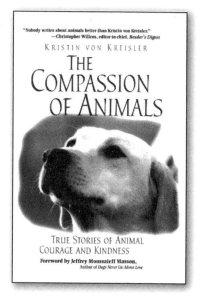

"Nobody writes about animals better than Kristin von Kreisler."
—Christopher Willcox, editor-in-chief, *Reader's Digest*

KRISTIN VON KREISLER

THE COMPASSION OF ANIMALS

TRUE STORIES OF ANIMAL COURAGE AND KINDNESS

Foreword by Jeffrey Moussaieff Masson, Author of *Dogs Never Lie About Love*

ISBN 0-7615-0990-9
hardcover / 272 pages
U.S. $22.95 / Can. $29.95

PRIMA

To order, call (800) 632-8676 or visit us online at www.primapublishing.com

Also from Prima

The Amazing Truth About Your Dog's Health!

Most people know that good nutrition and proper supplementation together with a healthy dose of exercise are the foundation for good human health. But did you know that the very same is true for your dog? Dr. Earl Mindell and Elizabeth Renaghan have compiled years of studies and observations to bring you the most up-to-date reference guide ever on how best to care for your dog. Inside you'll find out:

- **How to supplement your dog's diet with the proper amounts of vitamins and minerals**
- **How to rid your house and your pet of fleas—naturally**
- **How to treat and protect your dog from common ailments and diseases**
- **And much, much more!**

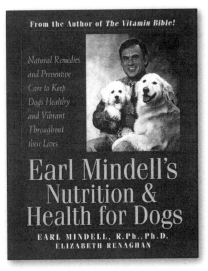

From the Author of *The Vitamin Bible!*

Natural Remedies and Preventive Care to Keep Dogs Healthy and Vibrant Throughout their Lives

Earl Mindell's Nutrition & Health for Dogs

EARL MINDELL, R.Ph., Ph.D.
ELIZABETH RENAGHAN

ISBN 0-7615-1158-X
paperback / 336 pages
U.S. $16.00 / Can. $23.50

PRIMA

To order, call (800) 632-8676 or visit us online at www.primapublishing.com

To Order Books

Please send me the following items:

Quantity	Title	Unit Price	Total
_____	_____	$ _____	$ _____
_____	_____	$ _____	$ _____
_____	_____	$ _____	$ _____
_____	_____	$ _____	$ _____
_____	_____	$ _____	$ _____

Subtotal	$ _____
Deduct 10% when ordering 3–5 books	$ _____
7.25% Sales Tax (CA only)	$ _____
8.25% Sales Tax (TN only)	$ _____
5% Sales Tax (MD and IN only)	$ _____
7% G.S.T. Tax (Canada only)	$ _____
Shipping and Handling*	$ _____
Total Order	$ _____

*Shipping and Handling depend on Subtotal.

Subtotal	Shipping/Handling
$0.00–$14.99	$3.00
$15.00–$29.99	$4.00
$30.00–$49.99	$6.00
$50.00–$99.99	$10.00
$100.00–$199.99	$13.50
$200.00+	Call for Quote

Foreign and all Priority Request orders:
Call Order Entry department
for price quote at 916-632-4400

This chart represents the total retail price of books only (before applicable discounts are taken).

By Telephone: With American Express, MC or Visa, call 800-632-8676 or 916-632-4400. Mon–Fri, 8:30–4:30.

WWW: http://www.primapublishing.com

By Internet E-mail: sales@primapub.com

By Mail: Just fill out the information below and send with your remittance to:

Prima Publishing
P.O. Box 1260BK
Rocklin, CA 95677

Name _____

Address_____

City _____ State _____ ZIP_____

American Express/MC/Visa# _____ Exp. _____

Check/money order enclosed for $_____ Payable to Prima Publishing

Daytime telephone _____

Signature _____